CAMBRIDGE TEXTS IN THE
HISTORY OF PHILOSOPHY

——

FRIEDRICH NIETZSCHE
Beyond Good and Evil

CAMBRIDGE TEXTS IN THE HISTORY OF PHILOSOPHY

Series editors

KARL AMERIKS
Professor of Philosophy at the University of Notre Dame

DESMOND M. CLARKE
Professor of Philosophy at University College Cork

The main objective of Cambridge Texts in the History of Philosophy is to expand the range, variety, and quality of texts in the history of philosophy which are available in English. The series includes texts by familiar names (such as Descartes and Kant) and also by less well-known authors. Wherever possible, texts are published in complete and unabridged form, and translations are specially commissioned for the series. Each volume contains a critical introduction together with a guide to further reading and any necessary glossaries and textual apparatus. The volumes are designed for student use at undergraduate and postgraduate level and will be of interest not only to students of philosophy, but also to a wider audience of readers in the history of science, the history of theology and the history of ideas.

For a list of titles published in the series, please see end of book.

FRIEDRICH NIETZSCHE

Beyond Good and Evil

Prelude to a Philosophy of the Future

EDITED BY

ROLF-PETER HORSTMANN
Humboldt-Universität, Berlin

JUDITH NORMAN
Trinity University, Texas

TRANSLATED BY

JUDITH NORMAN

CAMBRIDGE
UNIVERSITY PRESS

PUBLISHED BY THE PRESS SYNDICATE OF THE UNIVERSITY OF CAMBRIDGE
The Pitt Building, Trumpington Street, Cambridge, United Kingdom

CAMBRIDGE UNIVERSITY PRESS
The Edinburgh Building, Cambridge CB2 2RU, UK
32 Avenue of the Americas, New York, NY 10013-2473, USA
477 Williamstown Road, Port Melbourne, VIC 3207, Australia
Ruiz de Alarcón 13, 28014 Madrid, Spain
Dock House, The Waterfront, Cape Town 8001, South Africa

http://www.cambridge.org
Information on this title: www.cambridge.org/9780521770781

First published 2002
Fourth printing 2006

Printed in the United Kingdom at the University Press, Cambridge

Typeface Ehrhardt 11/13 pt.   *System* LaTeX 2$_\varepsilon$ [TB]

A catalogue record for this book is available from the British Library.

Library of Congress Cataloguing in Publication data

Nietzsche, Friedrich Wilhelm, 1844–1900.
[Jenseits von Gut und Böse. English]
Beyond good and evil: prelude to a philosophy of the future / Friedrich Nietzsche;
edited by Rolf-Peter Horstmann; [translated by] Judith Norman.
p.   cm. – (Cambridge texts in the history of philosophy)
Includes bibliographical references and index.
ISBN 0 521 77078 5 (hardback) – ISBN 0 521 77913 8 (paperback)
1. Philosophy.   I. Horstmann, Rolf-Peter, 1940–   II. Norman, Judith, 1965–
III. Title.   IV. Series.

B3313.J43 E5   2001
193 – dc21   2001035672

ISBN-13   978-0-521-77078-1 hardback
ISBN-10   0-521-77078-5 hardback
ISBN-13   978-0-521-77973-5 paperback
ISBN-10   0-521-77913-8 paperback

Contents

v

Introduction

I

Beyond Good and Evil (*BGE*) is often considered to be one of Friedrich Nietzsche's greatest books.[1] Though it is by no means clear what criteria this assessment is based on, it is easy to understand how it comes about. It seems to be an expression of the feeling that in this book Nietzsche gives the most comprehensible and detached account of the major themes that concerned him throughout his life. Nietzsche was suspicious of almost everything addressed in this book – whether it be knowledge, truth, philosophy, or morality and religion. He regarded them as the source, or at least the effect, of a misguided tendency in the development of human nature: one that has led to disastrous cultural, social, and psychological consequences. At the same time he lets us share his more constructive views as well, mainly his views on how he wants us to perceive the world and to change our lives in order to live up to this new perception. He speaks of perspectivism, the will to power, of human nobility (*Vornehmheit*) and of the conditions of a life liberated from the constraints of oppressive tradition. In the middle of the book, he even adds a number of short

I thank Dartmouth College and especially Sally Sedgwick and Margaret Robinson, whose generous hospitality gave me the opportunity to write this text. Special thanks to Karl Ameriks and Gary Hatfield for transforming my "English" into English and to Andreas Kemmerling for helpful suggestions. Very special thanks to Dina Emundts for all sorts of comments. The version printed here owes much to careful editing by Hilary Gaskin.

[1] See, for example, the Introductions to *BGE* by Walter Kaufmann (Vintage: New York, 1966) and Michael Tanner (Penguin: Harmondsworth, 1999; translation R. Hollingdale), and also Kaufmann, *Nietzsche: Philosopher, Psychologist, Antichrist* (Meridian Books: New York, 1956), and Tanner, *Nietzsche* (Oxford University Press: Oxford/New York, 1994). References for all quotations from *BGE* are to section numbers.

aphorisms, and he ends the book with a poem that hints at the artistic background to his concern with decadence and the means for overcoming it. Thus it would seem that the whole range of Nietzsche's interests, his prejudices and his preferences, his loathings and his hopes, and above all his deep insights into our situation in the modern world, are united in an exemplary way in *BGE*, and for this reason it is a great book.

Although there is something to be said for this view, it is not the only view that is possible. There are quite a number of thinkers who would insist that it makes no sense at all to attribute greatness to any of Nietzsche's works. For these readers, all of Nietzsche's writings are flawed by serious shortcomings that justify fundamental complaints, ranging from accusations that they are utterly irrational, or devoid of informative content, to the conviction that they contain nothing but silly proclamations based on unwarranted generalizations – or a mixture of both. According to proponents of this view, the best way to think of Nietzsche's works is as the disturbing documents of the creative process of someone who was on the verge of madness. To call any of his works great would therefore amount to a categorical mistake. Interestingly enough, this bleak evaluation is not based on any disagreement with what the work's admirers tell us we will find in it, or even any disagreement with the claim that it gives us the quintessential Nietzsche.

It is a perplexing fact that it is by no means easy to decide which of these two conflicting attitudes towards *BGE* should prevail, and in the end it may be a rather personal matter. Nevertheless it is possible to identify some conditions that will influence how we are likely to think about the merits of this work. Three main factors should be taken into consideration. First, much depends on how we interpret the aims pursued by Nietzsche's work in general and *BGE* in particular. Second, our evaluation will depend on the amount of tolerance and sympathy that we are prepared to mobilize towards Nietzsche the person, and also towards certain tendencies in bourgeois culture in Germany in the second half of the nineteenth century. The third and most important factor, however, is the way that we feel about the very framework in which all our dealings with what we take to be reality are embedded: if we are confident that our normal outlook on whatever concerns us has been proven to be ultimately right, or at least on the right track, then chances are high that we will end up thinking of Nietzsche and *BGE* as a nuisance. If we are not convinced of the soundness of our normal views, then we might have second thoughts about things, and in that case a book like *BGE* might be considered illuminating and even helpful.

II

Let us start with Nietzsche the person. In the history of art, science, philosophy, and even literature one very often finds that in order to appreciate or to evaluate a work it is not much of an advantage to be familiar with its author and his life: an intellectual or artistic product is better judged on its own merits than on the basis of uncertain knowledge about the idiosyncratic features and muddled purposes of its author. Moreover, in some cases authors intentionally withdraw from their products in an attempt to become invisible and to let the work speak for itself, and thus leave us very few personal clues in their works. Rousseau could serve as an example of the first kind of case and Kant of the second; Kant goes so far as to use the phrase *de nobis ipsis silemus* ("of our own person we will say nothing") as a motto for his main work. We therefore tend to believe that a distinction can be drawn between the private views of the author and the meaning of the work which the author produces.

Yet there are some works with respect to which such a consideration does not so easily apply. These are works whose very meaning is tied intrinsically to the person of their author, as is the case with diaries, letters, personal notes, or autobiographies. Here our knowledge about the author, or perhaps an understanding of the situation the author is in, are necessary ingredients for an appreciation of the text. There are many reasons to presume that Nietzsche thought of many of his texts as being like diaries or personal notes that tell us something about himself and about his perspective on the matters they address, rather than as products that aim at objective, non-personal results. Hence, his biography may be of interest in any attempt to assess his work.

Nietzsche's life is surely not a success story; on the contrary, it is a rather sad story of misery and failure. It is the story of a man who from the beginning of his adult life, until the sudden and catastrophic end of his productive period, was confronted with embarrassing and humiliating experiences. This is true of his private life as well as of his relations with the intellectual community of his time. He was plagued by ill health, a psychosomatic wreck, suffering from all sorts of diseases ranging from chronic nervous ailments and severe eye problems, which left him almost blind, to extremely exhausting states of prolonged migraine. These conditions made life tolerable for him only in a few places in northern Italy (in the winter) and the Swiss Engadine (in the summer), and it is in these places that he spent most of his time in the 1880s. His social relations were always, to put it mildly, somewhat complicated. Those who apparently cared most about him, his mother and his sister, he found oppressive and distasteful because they represented a type of personality he deeply despised.[2] Though he prided himself on being comfortable with women, he does not seem to have been very successful in establishing emotionally satisfying relationships with them, which is hardly surprising given his views on women and on femininity (*Weiblichkeit*) in general.[3] Things did not go much better with his friends. The people whom he called "friends" he quite often spoke of with great resentment: he charged all of them with a lack of sensitivity toward him, he complained that none of them ever bothered to study his works, and he accused them of failing to defend him against public neglect.[4] In short, he suffered deeply from a sense of solitude and isolation, from not being appropriately acknowledged because of the supposed imperfections of the people around him.

To make things even worse, Nietzsche was not given the opportunity to compensate for the shortcomings of his private life by enjoying institutional and public success in his roles as a university teacher and author. Although he made a very promising start – he was appointed professor of classics at Basle university at the early age of twenty-four – his academic career disintegrated rapidly, in part because of his poor health and in part because he became annoyed with his teaching duties. As for his fortunes as an author, not much can be said that is positive. His first book, the now highly acclaimed treatise *The Birth of Tragedy*, did at least attract the attention of classicists (though their reaction to it was for the most

---

[2] See the annihilating remark aimed at both of them in *Ecce Homo* which culminates in Nietzsche's pronouncement: "I confess that the deepest objection to the Eternal Recurrence, my real idea from the abyss, is always my mother and my sister" (*KSA* VI, § 267, translation from Tanner, *Nietzsche*, p. 68). *KSA* refers to *Sämtliche Werke: Kritische Studienausgabe*, ed. G. Colli and M. Montinari, 15 vols. (de Gruyter: Berlin, 1980); this edition is based on the critical edition of Nietzsche's works, *Werke: Kritische Gesamtausgabe*, ed. G. Colli and M. Montinari, 28 vols. to date (de Gruyter: Berlin, 1967–).

[3] Though Nietzsche addresses this topic in *BGE* as well (§ 232 *et seq.*), the general tendency of his outlook on women is documented most succinctly in the relevant passage of *Ecce Homo* ("Why I write such good books," § 5).

[4] A good example of this assessment of his friends is again to be found in *Ecce Homo* ("The case of Wagner," § 4).

part emphatically negative) and of members of the Wagnerian community (including Wagner himself).[5] But soon he had to realize that there was only a marginal interest among the public in his way of dealing with issues, whether they were philosophical topics such as truth and the metaphysical foundations of knowledge, topics concerning the history and value of religion and morality, or topics such as the critical assessment of modern culture and ideas about how to overcome what he considered to be the fundamental problems of modernity. This lack of interest showed in the dismal number of copies sold of his books.[6]

The most discouraging experience for Nietzsche, however, may not have been this failure to gain a wider recognition. If he could have believed that his few readers represented some sort of elite, perhaps a group of distinguished intellectuals, then their taking notice of his writings would have been of importance to him and this might have counterbalanced his lack of public success. Unfortunately he could not entertain even that belief. From the very few reactions he became aware of – mostly reviews of his books in more or less obscure journals – he had to conclude that he was read by only a few readers – and the wrong ones. In his view, his readership consisted of people either unable or unwilling (or both) to understand him adequately. He blamed his readers for not being in the least prepared to give credit to his intentions and for being attentive only to those points which conveniently confirmed them in their own negative preconceptions. What he was missing on a fundamental level was a readiness on the part of readers to explore things his way, a feeling of intellectual kinship between author and audience, or, to put it another way, he deeply craved recognition from an audience that he thought fitting. This is touchingly expressed in two short remarks from *Ecce Homo*. The first relates explicitly only to his *Zarathustra*, though it is quite likely that Nietzsche thought it true of his other writings as well: "In order to

---

[5] See the Introduction by Raymond Geuss to the edition of *The Birth of Tragedy* in this series (Cambridge University Press, 1999).

[6] Of the book Nietzsche valued most, *Zarathustra*, whose first three parts were published separately in 1883 and 1884, only about sixty to seventy copies each were sold within the first three years after their appearance (see letter to Franz Overbeck, summer 1886: *KSB* VII, pp. 206–9). The fourth part of the *Zarathustra* was published in 1885 in a private edition of only forty copies and was not accessible to a wider public before 1892. *BGE* did not fare much better: 114 copies were sold within a year (see letter to Peter Gast, 8 June 1887: *KSB* VIII, pp. 86–8). Nietzsche comments (in the same letter to Gast): "Instructive! Namely, they simply don't want my literature." It seems that most of his other books had the same fate – they too were utterly neglected during the period in his life when he would still have cared about their success.

understand anything at all from my *Zarathustra*, you might need to be conditioned as I am – with one foot *beyond* life."[7] The second remark delineates what he takes to be his ideal reader, and there is no doubt that he meant what he says: "When I call up the image of a perfect reader, what emerges is a monster of courage and curiosity, who is also supple, clever, cautious, a born adventurer and discoverer."[8]

What emerges is a picture of a totally isolated, highly neurotic man who had to try hard to avoid thinking of himself as a complete failure. His way of dealing with this situation seems to have been simply not to accept the idea that all these annoying circumstances might have been brought about partly by particularities or deficiencies that could be traced back to his own person, so he managed to combine a perfectly clear and even realistic assessment of what was happening to him with an unshakeable conviction that all this had nothing to do with him and revealed nothing about him. It is this ability which, in my view, accounts for two dominant traits that appear in his published works. The first is that he never even came close to considering the possibility that – given the general intellectual climate of his time – his lack of success as an author might have something to do with his pursuing the "wrong" topics in a "wrong" way. It never crossed his mind that what he thought to be an interesting, novel, and valuable insight might indeed have been exactly what it seemed to be to almost all of his contemporaries – an overstated triviality, an extremely one-sided exaggeration or an embarrassing piece of bad reasoning. He simply stuck to the points he felt he had to make, deeply convinced of being on the right track, and fending off all signs of criticism or neglect with the maxim "so much the worse for the critic."[9]

---

[7] *Ecce Homo* ("Why I am so wise," end of § 3).

[8] *Ibid.* ("Why I write such good books," end of § 3). In the same text he mentions explicitly the reactions to *BGE* as an example of how severely it was misunderstood or, to use his terminology, how gravely this book was sinned against because its readers were not up to its challenge ("Why I write such good books," end of § 1).

[9] In *Ecce Homo* Nietzsche even presents an explanation as to why he believes this stance to be perfectly reasonable: "Ultimately, nobody can get more out of things, including books, than he already knows. For what one lacks access to from experience one will have no ear. Now let us imagine an extreme case: that a book speaks of nothing but events that lie altogether beyond the possibility of any frequent or even rare experience – that it is the first language for a new series of experiences. In that case, simply nothing will be heard, but there will be the acoustic illusion that where nothing is heard, nothing is there ... Whoever thought he had understood something of me, had made up something out of me after his own image ... and whoever had understood nothing of me, denied that I need to be considered at all." "Why I write such good books," § 1,

This attitude becomes increasingly visible in his writings after *Zarathustra* and culminates in his late texts of 1888, especially in *Ecce Homo*. Here we find brilliant and witty remarks which rightly became notorious (though Nietzsche himself might not have found them very amusing, because they can also be read as documents of despair). I quote two of them: "We all know, several of us even know from experience, what it is to have long ears. Well then, I will dare to claim that I have the smallest ears. This is of no little interest to women – it seems they think I understand them better? . . . I am the *anti-ass par excellence* and this makes me a world-historical monster – I am, in Greek, but not only in Greek, the *Antichrist*."[10] The other is: "I know my fate. One day, my name will be associated with the memory of something tremendous – a crisis the like of which the world has never seen, the most profound collision of conscience, of a decision brought about *against* everything that has ever been believed, demanded, or held holy so far. I am not a man. I am dynamite."[11]

The second trait which we find in Nietzsche's writings is closely connected to his inability to assess himself in the light of others' reactions. It consists in his total unconcern about the tenability of his views when judged according to standards that he thinks are alien to his approach. Starting from the conviction that there is no common ground between him and his reader, that what he has to say is most likely incomprehensible to almost everybody else, he does not feel obliged to enter the social game of competitive discourse. He refuses to try to convince people by somehow connecting to their way of thinking; he does not refute possible arguments against the points he wants to make by giving reasons in their favor. Instead, he makes abundantly clear his contempt for "normal" thinking and his impatience with the evaluations of others. It is this stance which gives so many readers the impression of an overwhelming polemical element in Nietzsche's literary presentation of his views. He reinforces it by insisting over and over again that what he has to tell us are above all *his* truths. The claim to exclusivity is meant to imply both that his main concern is not whether we find these truths convincing, and

translation from W. Kaufmann, *On the Genealogy of Morals and Ecce Homo* (Vintage: New York, 1967), p. 261.

[10] *Ecce Homo*, "Why I write such good books," end of § 2, translation Kaufmann, p. 263.

[11] *Ibid.*, "Why I am a destiny," beginning of § 1, translation Kaufmann, p. 326.

that he does not pretend to have found *the* Truth, for he thinks this is a metaphysical illusion anyway.

Thus we find embedded in Nietzsche's basic view of himself the recommendation not that we read his texts as aiming at "objectively valid" judgments, at judgments that are (metaphysically) true irrespective of the cultural and psychological context in which they are made (whatever that may be), but that we think of them as narratives that he invites us to listen to, without really obliging us to believe them if we are not the right kind of person. This does not mean that the stories he has to tell us about, say, truth, morality, the will to power, or culture are, in his view, on a par with fictions, pleasant or otherwise. On the contrary, he believed his stories to be the ultimate stories, the stories that are destined to become the standard versions of our assessment of these phenomena. This is not because his narratives are objectively, or in a context-free sense, the most fitting; rather, they will succeed because eventually people will change to a condition where they appreciate the fact that these narratives are best suited to capture their sense of the right perspective on phenomena if they are considered against the background of what for them is the real meaning of life.

Before looking more closely at some aspects of *BGE* itself, let me summarize what I take to be the lessons for approaching Nietzsche's writings that can be learned from his personal situation and his way of dealing with it. They take the form of three warnings: (1) do not expect these writings to express impartial views on whatever subject they address – they express, in an emphatic sense, Nietzsche's own views; (2) do not be annoyed by his obsession with apodictic statements whose immense generality very often contradicts both normal expectations of modesty and the most obvious requirements of common sense – these stylistic eccentricities reflect his resolute disdain for what most people cherish, especially people who he suspects are not willing to listen to him; (3) never forget that the author does not want to get mixed up with "us," his normal insensitive "academic" readers. He does not want to be "one of us" – instead he insists on what he calls "distance," in order to uphold his view of himself and to remind us of his uniqueness. A last quotation from *Ecce Homo* may highlight these points: "*Listen to me* [the emphasis is on the 'me']. *For I am thus and thus. Do not, above all, confound me.*"[12]

---

[12] *Ibid.*, Preface, § 1.

III

BGE is the first book Nietzsche published after *Thus Spoke Zarathustra*. He never gave up on the notion that all he really wanted to say is contained in *Zarathustra*, and this led him to claim that the works he wrote after *Zarathustra* are essentially nothing but elaborations and explications of ideas already present in his *opus magnum*. This claim has been disputed by quite a number of his commentators, firstly because many of the most central ideas in *Zarathustra* cease to play an important role in his later writings, and secondly because the literary form of the later writings connects them much more closely to his books prior to *Zarathustra* than to *Zarathustra* itself.[13] However that may be, Nietzsche himself was of the opinion that *Zarathustra* set the stage for everything he had to do subsequently. He writes: "The task for the years that followed [i.e. the years after *Zarathustra*] was mapped out as clearly as possible. Once the yes-saying part of my task had been solved [by means of *Zarathustra*], it was time for the no-saying, no-doing part."[14] This seems to imply that he regarded his post-*Zarathustra* writings as consisting of predominantly critical essays.

BGE is best known to a wider public for its proverbs. Indeed, some of Nietzsche's best-known maxims are assembled in this text, ranging from perspicuous insights to highly controversial statements. Starting with the Preface, where we find his much used and misused saying, "Christianity is Platonism for the 'people,'" almost every one of the nine parts of the book contains lines that have entered the repertoire of educated or polemical discourse: "life as such is will to power" (§ 13); "humans are *the still undetermined* [*nicht festgestellte*] *animals*" (§ 62); "When a woman has scholarly inclinations, there is usually something wrong with her sexuality" (§ 144); "*Morality in Europe these days is the morality of herd animals*" (§ 202); and (slightly paraphrased here): "saintliness – the highest spiritualization of the instinct of cleanliness" (§ 271).

These proverbs are in a way the least of what *BGE* has to offer. Its primary fascination lies on a deeper level: this book introduces us into a world of remarkable conjectures, suspicions, and implications. Though one might say this is true of most of Nietzsche's other published works as well, with the exception of *Zarathustra*, there is nevertheless a difference

---

[13] See, e.g., M. Tanner, Introduction to *BGE* and *Nietzsche*, p. 59.

[14] *Ecce Homo*, '*Beyond Good and Evil*', § 1, translation Kaufmann, p. 310.

in emphasis between *BGE* and the other writings. Whereas the other texts pursue their subjects from many different angles, *BGE* (like *The Genealogy of Morals*, which Nietzsche announced on the back of its title page as "a sequel to my last book, *Beyond Good and Evil*, which it is meant to supplement and clarify") is highly focused on the psychological aspects of its topics. In *BGE* Nietzsche confronts us primarily (though not exclusively) with a dimension of his thought that he was particularly proud of – his psychological stance. This integration of what he calls a psychological point of view into his general practice of casting doubts on received convictions by tracing their origins, of throwing into question our most fundamental beliefs by pointing out their shakiness, and of scrutinizing available alternatives in the light of a new vision of the value of life – this I take to be the most distinctive feature of *BGE*.

Nietzsche himself gives the following account of what he is doing in *BGE*: "This book (1886) is in every essential a *critique of modernity*; modern sciences, modern arts, even modern politics are not excluded. Besides this, it is an indication of an opposing type, which is as un-modern as possible, a noble, yes-saying type."[15] Though this characterization is accurate and confirms the view that Nietzsche considers his task to be mainly a critical one, it is by no means complete. Interestingly enough, it does not mention two topics which some readers take to be the subject of the most disturbing reflections in the book: morality and religion. This is surprising because these are the topics which seem to emerge most strongly in any consideration of its main message.

In order to appreciate the distinctive approach which Nietzsche favors in *BGE* in his dealings with what he calls "modernity," it might be worthwhile to say a few words about his more general outlook. The starting point for almost everything Nietzsche is interested in throughout his entire intellectual career can be nicely summarized in the form of the question "how are we to live?" or, more poignantly, "how are we to endure life?" He considered this question to be of the utmost importance, because of three interconnected convictions that he treated virtually as facts. His first conviction was that life is best conceived of as a chaotic dynamic process without any stability or direction. The second is articulated in the claim that we have no reason whatsoever to believe in any such thing as the "sense" or the "value" of life, insofar as these terms imply the idea

---

[15] *Ibid.*

of an "objective" or "natural" purpose of life. The third is that human life is value-oriented in its very essence – that is, without adherence to some set of values or other, human life would be virtually impossible. Whereas the first conviction is supposed to state an ontological fact, the second is meant to be an application of the ontological point to the normative aspects of human life in particular. The third conviction, though somewhat at odds with the other two, is taken by Nietzsche to reveal a psychological necessity. (How Nietzsche came to hold these convictions, and whether they can be supported, there is not space to examine here, although a closer look would no doubt lead back to his use of some of Schopenhauer's ideas and to his picture of what constituted the cultural life of pre-Socratic ancient Greece.)

Against the background of these convictions, Nietzsche became interested in the question of the origin of values, a question that eventually led him to a whole array of unorthodox and original answers. All his answers ultimately follow from a pattern of reasoning which in its most basic structure is quite simple and straightforward: if there are no values "out there," in the sense in which we believe stars and other physical objects to be "out there" and if, at the same time, we cannot do without values, then there must be some value-creating capacity within ourselves which is responsible for the values we cherish and which organizes our lives. Though presumably we are all endowed with this capacity,[16] there are very few of us who manage to create values powerful enough to force people into acceptance and to constitute cultural and social profiles. To create such constitutive values seems to be, according to Nietzsche, the prerogative of real philosophers (not philosophy professors), of unique artists (if there are any), of even rarer founders of religions, and, above all, of institutions that develop out of the teaching of creative individuals, i.e., of science, philosophy, and theology. Thus, anyone interested in the function and the origin of values should scrutinize the processes which enabled these persons and institutions to create values.

At this point Nietzsche's more detailed investigations tend to start spreading out in a remarkable number of different directions. It is here, too, that in one sense we should take *BGE* to have its point of departure. That the detailed analysis of all the phenomena connected with the

---

[16] For, after all, there seems to be no reason to think that Nietzsche would not allow in principle that each of us could be transformed into a "free spirit," i.e., a person who has the capacity and strength to create and stick to the "right" values.

concept of value is a very tricky task methodologically is documented not only in *BGE* but also in almost all of Nietzsche's other writings. Acknowledging the fact that the different features of the value-creating processes are much too complex to be accessible by means of a single explanatory scheme, Nietzsche tentatively pursues several different approaches. He merges psychological hypotheses with causal explanations, and combines them with historical observations and linguistic considerations into a multi-perspectival technique that he fondly refers to as his "genealogical method." In *BGE*, where he is occupied mainly with the psychological dimension of the process of value formation, he applies this method primarily in an attempt to come to an understanding of those aspects of the value problem that pertain to its normative elements, that is, to the question of good and bad.

At the risk of oversimplification one can say the bulk of this work addresses three topics, each one of which can be expressed best in terms of a question. The first is this: why is it impossible for us to live without values, why do we need values at all, or, more in line with Nietzsche's terminology, what is the value of values? The second is this: how does it happen that the values we and the overwhelming majority of the members of our culture subscribe to have either been bad from the beginning or have degenerated into bad values? The third topic is this: what is the right perspective on values; what should we expect values to be? Though these three questions are in a certain sense perennial, Nietzsche relates them directly to what he saw as the manifest historical situation of his age and the prevailing conditions of the cultural tradition he lived in, so much of what he has to say is deeply rooted in his response to late nineteenth-century central European conceptions. This is something we should never forget when we confront his texts. Nietzsche speaks to us from the past, and this fact alone might account for some features of his writing that we would now consider idiosyncratic – for example, his way of talking about women and about national characteristics.

IV

At this point we face a problem that I take to be crucial for any adequate assessment of Nietzsche's project. It concerns the manner in which we are to comprehend his approach to the topics under examination. Now that we have identified a number of central questions that he discusses in

BGE, it is tempting to proceed in the way normally used in dealing with philosophical texts: stating the questions addressed, and then trying to line up the arguments that the advocate of a position puts forward in favor of the answers he comes up with. However, in the case of Nietzsche and *BGE* it is by no means evident that such a procedure would capture what Nietzsche is doing and what *BGE* is all about. There are few arguments to be found in *BGE*, and those which can be extracted are seldom of the most convincing kind. Following the normal procedure would also encourage the illusion that Nietzsche designed *BGE* to be understood simply in terms of arguments, whether good or bad, and I cannot find anything in *BGE* which would encourage such an illusion.[17]

There is considerable evidence that we should try a different approach, and the clue lies in Nietzsche's numerous allusions to the practices of what he calls the "new philosophers." To be the type of philosopher Nietzsche values is to follow hunches, to think at a "presto" pace (§ 213), to embark on experiments both intellectual and existential (§§ 205, 210),[18] to transform and to create values (§§ 203, 211), to put forward hypotheses that are risky: in short, to be interested in what he calls "dangerous perhapses" (§ 2). One would not expect a person with this conception of philosophy to hold the idea that what counts most in the endeavor to reach highly unorthodox and sometimes even shocking insights is to be in possession of a "good argument," and that one could or should present one's views in compliance with this idea. Rather, one would expect such a person to pursue a very different path in expressing his views, which would involve starting with a bold claim or striking observation and then using it in a variety of different ways. It might form the basis for an analysis of something in terms of that claim or observation, or it might point to a symptom, presupposition, or consequence of a very general or a very particular state of affairs. It even might be related tentatively to topics which at first sight have nothing

---

[17] There are passages that make it very hard to believe in this illusion. See, e.g., remarks in § 5 that the activity of reason-giving is a *post hoc* affair intended to justify "some fervent wish that they have sifted through and made properly abstract," or (in the same section) his making fun of Spinoza's *mos geometricus* as a masquerade. In my eyes, the most striking passage for discouraging this illusion is to be found in § 213, where Nietzsche talks about what he calls philosophical states or moods. Here he compares the "right" way of doing philosophy with the "normal" attitude and writes concerning the latter: "You ['normal' philosophers] imagine every necessity is a need, a painful having to follow and being compelled." This "having to follow" and "being compelled" I read as a reference to the procedure of establishing results via sound arguments.

[18] Nietzsche uses the German word *Versuch* (attempt, experiment) in a broad way which makes that term cover the connotations of *Versuchung* (temptation) and *Versucher* (tempter) as well. Cf. § 42.

xix

to do with what the original claim or the first observation was about. In short, one could envision a philosopher under the spell of Nietzschean "new philosophy" as someone whose methodology is deeply entangled in and in thrall to what could be called "what if" scenarios.[19]

If this is how a "new philosopher" approaches problems, it seems beside the point to treat Nietzsche's proclaimed insights as based on arguments. The concept of a "result" or a "solution" also becomes obsolete, since this type of philosophy is obviously not oriented towards results and solutions understood in the sense of statements which can be defended against thorough critical resistance. Its aim consists instead in the uncovering of surprising possibilities and the playful presentation of innovative perspectives that do not aspire to the status of rock-hard "truths" but are meant to be offerings or propositions for a like-minded spirit.[20]

Nietzsche obviously intended *BGE* to exemplify as clearly as possible all the characteristics he attributes to the style, the method, and the intentions of the "new philosophers" – and yet it is remarkable how often this fact is not sufficiently acknowledged by his interpreters. This oversight is remarkable not only because it seems to be in part responsible for awkward attempts to integrate Nietzsche's intellectual products into traditional academic philosophy,[21] but above all because it tends to miss what might be called, for want of a better term, the "socio-hermeneutical" dimension of what has become known as his doctrine of "perspectivism." This doctrine

[19] It should go without saying that this imagined scenario does not exclude "good arguments." Rather, the scenario is meant to show that if one deals with topics in the way outlined above, the guiding intention is not to give or to find "good arguments." In Nietzsche's terminology, this amounts to the claim that a "good argument" is not an overriding methodological "value." Invoking his polemical inventory, one could say, in his spirit: to be obsessed by "the will to a good argument" indicates bad taste.

[20] Again, this characterization is not meant to suggest that what these "new philosophers" are proclaiming is something they are not serious about or do not want us to take seriously. It is only meant to emphasize that what they put forward is connected very intimately with their personal point of view, and hence it is nothing that they can force on someone if there is no shared basis of experience, of resentment (*ressentiment*), or suffering. See *BGE* § 43, where Nietzsche expresses this point in an especially belligerent fashion.

[21] These attempts do not necessarily result in uninformative or misleading accounts of aspects of Nietzsche's thought. On the contrary, many of them shed considerable light on the historical background of his ideas and on the impact they could have on various discussions that happen to take place within the framework of academic philosophy. They are, however, operating under the unavoidable (and, perhaps, reasonable) restrictions of that framework. This puts them in the position of having to abstract from the personal or "perspectival" features essential to Nietzsche's conceptions. That there is a price to be paid for this "academization" is obvious. It is revealed in the difference between the excitement and fun that one can have in reading Nietzsche and the boredom that one sometimes experiences when reading the literature on him.

in its most trivial reading amounts to the claim that our view of the world and, consequently, the statements we take to be true, depend on our situation, on our "perspective" on the world. Perspectivism thus understood gives rise to the epistemological thesis that our knowledge claims can never be true in an absolute or an objective sense, partly because of the necessary spatial and temporal differences between the viewpoints that each knower is bound to occupy when relating to an object, and also because of the fact that we can never be certain that what appears to us to be the case really is the case. Though it is true that in some of his more conventional moods Nietzsche seems to have thought about perspectivism along these lines, this reading gives no hint whatsoever of why he should have been attracted to such a doctrine in his more inspired moments. In this epistemological version the doctrine is neither original nor interesting, but merely a version of skeptical or idealist claims that used to be connected in popular writings with names like Berkeley and Kant.[22]

However, perspectivism takes on a much more promising dimension if it is put into the broader context of the problem of justifying or at least of making plausible an insistence on integrating a personal or subjective element into the expression of one's views as a condition of their making sense at all. By looking at this doctrine in this context, we can appreciate it as stating conditions for understanding an expression that purports to express something true, be it a text, a statement, or a confession. These conditions can be summarized in terms of two essential convictions. (1) In order to understand a claim for truth embodied in an expression, one has to have an understanding of the situation from which that claim originates, and this presupposes being acquainted with and involved in the personal attitudes, subjective experiences, and private evaluations which form the basis of the view expressed. (2) In order

---

[22] Here I have to confess that this sketch of the epistemological interpretation of Nietzsche's perspectivism may not be the most sympathetic one, and no doubt one can find in the literature much more sophisticated versions of this doctrine. However, this does not affect the main point I want to make, which consists in the claim that the epistemological reading misses the central feature of Nietzsche's doctrine. There are some other misgivings concerning the reading that deserve mention. The first consists in the fact that Nietzsche – especially in *BGE* – is not in sympathy with skepticism (see § 208). Hence, why should he be interested in putting forward a doctrine containing skeptical implications? A further reservation about the feasibility of the epistemological reading can be seen in the annoying consequence of having to credit Nietzsche with all sorts of paradoxical and self-refuting claims such as "If perspectivism is true we cannot know it to be true." It should be noted that the "German form of skepticism" discussed approvingly in § 209 has nothing to do with epistemological skepticism.

to judge the correctness, or perhaps merely the plausibility, of such a claim, one has to have an experiential or existential background similar to that of the person who made the claim. It is because of this insistence on integrating subjective aspects into the process of understanding, and because of the idea that judging the truth of a view presupposes shared experiences, that I call this the "socio-hermeneutical" reading of perspectivism.

If perspectivism is understood in these terms, then much of what is going on in *BGE* and other texts by Nietzsche begins to look considerably less arbitrary and idiosyncratic than has been claimed. For example, his so-called "theory of truth" which he alludes to quite often in the first two books of *BGE*, seems less absurd than many commentators have taken it to be. According to these critics Nietzsche's perspectival conception of truth endorses the following three statements: (1) there is no absolute or objective truth; (2) what is taken to be truth is nothing but a fiction, that is, a perspectival counterfeit or forgery (*Fälschung*) of what really is the case; and (3) claims (1) and (2) are true. These three statements together seem to imply the paradoxical claim that it is true that there is no truth. So the critic argues.[23] However, when read in the light of the preceding remarks a much less extravagant interpretation of Nietzsche's theory of truth suggests itself which is completely independent of the issue of whether he really subscribes to these three statements. On this interpretation, Nietzsche's theory claims only (1) that there are no context-free truths, where a context is to be defined as the set of subjective conditions that the utterer of a truth is governed by and that anyone who wishes correctly to judge it is able to apprehend.[24] It also claims (2) that as an utterer or judger of a truth we are never in a position to be familiar with a context in its entirety, that is, with all the conditions that define it, and therefore we have to settle for an incomplete version of a context where the degree of incompleteness depends on differences between our capacities to understand ourselves and others. From this it follows (3) that, given our situation, every truth is defined by this necessarily

[23] That there are many epistemological and logical problems connected with holding such a paradoxical claim is not difficult to point out. The most comprehensive discussion of these problems with reference to Nietzsche that I know of is by M. Clark, *Nietzsche on Truth and Philosophy* (Cambridge University Press: Cambridge, 1990).

[24] Put a bit more bluntly, this claim amounts to the assertion that the concept "objective or absolute truth" is an empty concept when understood in contraposition to "perspectival truth."

incomplete context. Thus every truth is a partial truth or a perspectival fiction.[25]

This "socio-hermeneutical" reading of perspectivism points to a more commonsensical understanding of Nietzsche's claims regarding truth. It also suggests that some of the stylistic peculiarities of *BGE* and other texts had a methodological function. *BGE*, like most of Nietzsche's other texts, has an aphoristic form.[26] It looks like a collection of impromptu remarks, each of which explores to a different degree of depth some aspect or other of a particular observation, specific claim, or surprising phenomenon. These remarks are numbered and loosely organized into topic-related groups, each one of which carries a short descriptive phrase that functions as its title. The impression is of an apparently arbitrary compilation of notes which are actually presented in an artful, though idiosyncratic way. Thus it has been maintained that we should approach *BGE* as we would a work of literature rather than strictly in terms of philosophical text. Though this impression is by no means misleading, it fails to be sensitive to the intentions guiding the architectonic of this text. If a claim is fully comprehensible only when placed in its appropriate subjective and existential context, then it is incumbent on an author to convey as much information about this context as possible. One way of doing this consists in presenting a whole array of thoughts which are designed primarily to inform us about the various subjective stances characteristic of the individual making the claim. The resulting collection may seem random because it can include almost any conceivable digression under the pretense of being informative about the subjective context. However, if the socio-hermeneutical interpretation is correct, the seeming randomness of Nietzsche's aphorisms can equally well be taken as a calculated and methodologically appropriate consequence of his perspectivism. In Nietzsche's writings, as in life, randomness can turn out to be an applied method in disguise.

---

[25] It should be noticed that this reading is compatible with some of the most disturbing features of Nietzsche's talk about truth. It allows us to make sense of his insistence that there are degrees of truth, which is exhibited most clearly in *BGE* in his reflection on how much "truth" one can take (§ 39). It also makes understandable the idea, very important to him, that truth is just a special case of error. And it allows for the use of personal pronouns in connection with truth, a habit Nietzsche is very fond of (cf. §§ 5, 43, 231).

[26] Though there is some question as to the applicability of terms such as "aphorism" or "aphoristic form" to Nietzsche's texts, he himself does not seem to have problems with such a characterization. His own use of these terms in reference to his writings is documented in *On the Genealogy of Morals*, Preface § 2 (*KSA* V, p. 248) and § 8 (*KSA* V, p. 255) and in *Twilight of Idols*, §§ 9, 51 (*KSA* VI, p. 153).

V

BGE deals with questions of how values arise psychologically and how we should evaluate them. It discusses the origin and the meaning of philosophical values such as truth, the religious practice of establishing and enforcing specific values such as faith, piety, and love of man, and the motives and mechanisms involved in our cultivation of moral values such as pity, fairness, and willingness to help each other. It also treats such political and social values as democracy, equality, and progress, seeing them as means of oppression and as indicators of decay and degeneration. Most of this is done with the aim of finding out what brought about the modern way of life, and what made modern culture such a doomed enterprise. The general tendency of the book is to claim that at the base of the most deeply habitualized normative evaluations that modern people take for granted, their most fundamental judgments about what has to be considered "good" or "bad" in almost every sphere of human activity, there ultimately lies a mixture of appalling character traits, ranging from weakness and fear to wishful thinking and self-betrayal, and all these find their symptomatic expression in the modern condition.

Neither this critical message nor the material Nietzsche relies upon in order to substantiate his assessment of modernity is peculiar to *BGE*. In almost all his other writings,[27] he discusses the shortcomings of philosophy, the dangers of religion, the built-in biases of science, and the damaging consequences of institutionalized moral and cultural values, and he arrives at similar bleak conclusions. Thus, the message of *BGE* is just another version of Nietzsche's general project. However, *BGE* is distinctive not only in its emphasis on a psychological explanation of the rise to dominance of specific values, but also in two further respects. The first relates to the doctrine of the "will to power," the second to his views on what might be called "good" or "adequate" ways of confronting reality. Both topics belong to his relatively rare excursions into the world of "positive" thinking.

---

[27] Obviously this overlap is intended by Nietzsche. It seems to be an architectonic device, for he frequently quotes from and alludes to his other texts. The best example of this practice is to be found right at the beginning (§ 2) of *BGE* where he cites almost verbatim from the beginning of *Human, All Too Human*. This quotation refers to his diagnosis of the most fundamental mistake of traditional metaphysicians, i.e., their conception of the origin of oppositions. Cf. B. Glatzeder: *'Perspektiven der Wünschbarkeit'. Nietzsches Metaphysikkritik in Menschliches Allzumenschliches* (Philo Verlag: Berlin, 2000). In quoting this appraisal, which forms the basis of his far reaching criticism of metaphysics and its notion of "objective" truth, he can treat it like a result whose justification is already given elsewhere.

The "will to power" makes its first public appearance in *Thus Spoke Zarathustra*. There it is introduced as one of the three major teachings Zarathustra has to offer, the other two being his advocacy of the overman (*Übermensch*) and the conception of the Eternal Recurrence. It is somewhat surprising that in *Zarathustra* Nietzsche has little to say about what the "will to power" means. Fortunately he is a bit more explicit in *BGE*, although here too the doctrine receives what is by no means an exhaustive treatment.[28] There is, however, some evidence that he wants us to think of this doctrine as advancing or at least implying an ontological hypothesis. Focusing on the hints he gives in *BGE*, the following picture emerges: if we look at the phenomenon of organic life as an integral part of reality, we find that it consists not in a static condition but in a dynamic and chaotic process of creation and decay, of overpowering and becoming overpowered, of suppressing and being suppressed. This suggests that what governs these processes is some sort of power struggle where every single form of life has a tendency to overpower every other form. However, to think of life in this way we have to assume that each living particle is endowed with a certain amount of power that it has a will to realize. This amount is supposed to define its "will to power" and thus is ultimately decisive for its ability to develop itself and to survive, or, to use a famous Nietzschean phrase, for its potential to become what it is. It is this line of thought which led Nietzsche to the assertion that life is "will to power" (§§ 13, 259).

But this is merely one part of the story. In *BGE* Nietzsche tentatively tries to pursue the conception of a "will to power" in a further direction. He aims at a broader application of the conception by transforming it from a principle of organic life into a much broader axiom pertaining to the essence of nature in general. It is here that it acquires an ontological meaning. The main motive for his attempt to conceive of the "will to power" as a general ontological principle seems to be that there is no

---

[28] It is because of the relatively superficial and vague treatment of this doctrine in his published writings that many interpretations of the meaning and function of "will to power" rely heavily on Nietzsche's *Nachlass*, the voluminous collection of his unpublished notes. However, though the *Nachlass* indeed contains a considerable amount of material pertaining to that conception, it has the disadvantage of giving support to widely divergent, if not contradictory, interpretations. This is due to the fact that Nietzsche seems to have been experimenting with different meanings of this concept without reaching a definite position. To appreciate the whole range of readings possible see, for example, G. Abel, *Nietzsche: Die Dynamik der Willen zur Macht und die ewige Wiederkehr* (de Gruyter: Berlin, 1998, 2nd edn), and V. Gerhardt, *Vom Willen zur Macht: Anthropologie und Metaphysik der Macht am exemplarischen Fall Friedrich Nietzsches* (de Gruyter: Berlin, 1996).

reason to restrict the explanatory force of that concept to organic life. Why not think of inorganic matter, of the material world, in terms of "will to power" as well? Matter would then have to be conceived as "will to power" paralyzed, as "will to power" in a state of potentiality. According to Nietzsche this view would allow for a unified account of the world in its totality: "The world seen from inside, the world determined and described with respect to its 'intelligible character' – would be just this will to power and nothing else" (§ 36). This view would also have the advantage of overcoming the basic bias of traditional metaphysics that there is a difference in kind between being and becoming, because it implies that being static and stable is in the end nothing but a degenerative form of becoming, or nothing but an unactualized power process. It goes without saying that Nietzsche is very much in favor of this claim.

Even if it is conceded that Nietzsche never really elaborated his concept of the "will to power" sufficiently, it does not appear to be one of his more attractive ideas. The reason for this is that it purports to give us insight into the essence of nature, what nature is "in itself," but this does not square well with his emphatic criticism, put forward in *BGE* and elsewhere, of the very notion of an "in itself." According to Nietzsche there is no "in itself," no essence, no fixed nature of things, and all beliefs to the contrary are founded on deep and far-reaching metaphysical illusions. It seems therefore that one cannot avoid the unsettling conclusion that the doctrine of a "will to power" shares all the vices which Nietzsche attributes to metaphysical thinking in general.

There are no such untoward consequences of the second piece of "positive" thinking in *BGE*, but this is because it scarcely qualifies as thinking at all, consisting instead of fantasies about what the ideal conditions would be for a person to be able to participate in productive thinking. Here productive thinking seems to mean the capacity to live up to the task of enduring an unbiased assessment of reality. Nietzsche summarizes these fantasies in the picture he gives of the "new philosophers" and in remarks on what it means to be noble. Nobility, for him, has to do with putting oneself at a distance from people and things. It is rooted in and is the product of the "pathos of distance," to use his influential formula (§ 257). This pathos has to be conceived as the socially inherited ability (1) to have a sense for differences in rank between persons, (2) to accept these differences as pointing to differences in distinction (defined as a positive quality of worthiness), and (3) to strive for higher distinction. A person possessing this ability is able to strive for unique states of awareness: "Without the *pathos of distance* . . . that *other* more mysterious pathos could not have grown at all, that demand for new expansions of distance within the soul itself, the development of states that are increasingly high, rare, distant, tautly drawn and comprehensive, and, in short, the enhancement of the type 'man,' the constant 'self-overcoming of man' (to use a moral formula in a supra-moral sense)" (§ 257). The ability to achieve such states seems to function as a condition of gaining important insights and having the psychological resources needed to live with them, and it indicates a certain stance towards reality superior to "normal" or "common" attitudes (cf. § 268).

With this plea for nobility Nietzsche states again his conviction that what ultimately counts in our epistemic dealings with reality is not knowledge *per se*, that is, knowledge detached from the knower. What deserves the title of knowledge has to be intimately connected with the special and unique situation a knowing subject is in. This is so not only because according to Nietzsche knowledge is not an "objective" or impersonal affair, something one can have like a detached thing that one possesses, but above all because the knowing subject has to *live* his knowledge. The extent to which a subject can do this depends on personal constitution, character traits, and intellectual robustness. Knowledge thus becomes associated with the question of how much truth one can endure (cf. § 39). It is in this context that the concept of nobility reveals itself to be part of a "positive" teaching: nobility that is the product of the social pathos of distance increases the potential of a subject for enduring "uncommon" knowledge because it promotes more comprehensive states, and these in turn indicate a growing strength in the subject's character that enables it to cope with more of "the truth." This at least seems to be Nietzsche's message.

What is it that makes reading *BGE* and other writings of Nietzsche such an attractive and stimulating experience? The main reason, I believe, has little to do with the plausibility, let alone the correctness, of his views. On the contrary, we like many of his ideas precisely because of their pointed one-sidedness, their extravagance, and their eccentricity. Nor, I suspect, are we now especially preoccupied with the topics which he obviously took to be decisive for an evaluation of our way of living under modern conditions. Many of his themes we now consider rather obsolete, and to some of them we no longer have any immediate access because they are deeply rooted in their nineteenth-century contexts. The fascination his works still have must therefore originate from somewhere else. If one wants to account for the appeal of his writings, it is perhaps advisable not to look too closely at his actual teachings, but to think of his texts as a kind of mental tonic designed to encourage his readers to continue to confront their doubts and suspicions about the well-foundedness of many of their most fundamental ideas about themselves and their world. This would suggest that Nietzsche's works may still be captivating because they confront a concern that is not restricted to modern times. They address our uncomfortable feeling that our awareness of ourselves and of the world depends on conceptions that we ultimately do not understand. We conceive of ourselves as subjects trying to live a decent life, guided in our doings by aims that fit the normal expectations of our social and cultural environment; we believe certain things to be true beyond any doubt, and we hold others and ourselves to many moral obligations. Although all this is constitutive of a normal way of life, we have only a vague idea of why we have to deal with things in this way; we do not really know what in the end justifies these practices. In questioning not the normality but the objectivity or truth of such a normal world view, Nietzsche's writings can have the effect of making us feel less worried about our inability to account for some of our central convictions in an "absolute" way. It is up to each of us to decide whether to be grateful for this reminder or to loathe it.

Rolf-Peter Horstmann

Chronology

1844	Born in Röcken, a small village in the Prussian province of Saxony, on 15 October.
1846	Birth of his sister Elisabeth.
1848	Birth of his brother Joseph.
1849	His father, a Lutheran minister, dies at age thirty-six of "softening of the brain."
1850	Brother dies; family moves to Naumburg to live with father's mother and her sisters.
1858	Begins studies at Pforta, Germany's most famous school for education in the classics.
1864	Graduates from Pforta with a thesis in Latin on the Greek poet Theogonis; enters the University of Bonn as a theology student.
1865	Transfers from Bonn, following the classical philologist Friedrich Ritschl to Leipzig where he registers as a philology student; reads Schopenhauer's *The World as Will and Representation*.
1866	Reads Friedrich Lange's *History of Materialism*.
1868	Meets Richard Wagner.
1869	On Ritschl's recommendation is appointed professor of classical philology at Basle at the age of twenty-four before completing his doctorate (which is then conferred without a dissertation); begins frequent visits to the Wagner residence at Tribschen.
1870	Serves as a medical orderly in the Franco-Prussian war; contracts a serious illness and so serves only two months. Writes "The Dionysiac World View."

1872   Publishes his first book, *The Birth of Tragedy*; its dedicatory preface to Richard Wagner claims for art the role of "the highest task and truly metaphysical activity of this life"; devastating reviews follow.

1873   Publishes "David Strauss, the Confessor and the Writer," the first of his *Untimely Meditations*; begins taking books on natural science out of the Basle library, whereas he had previously confined himself largely to books on philological matters. Writes "On Truth and Lying in a Non-Moral Sense."

1874   Publishes two more *Meditations*, "The Uses and Disadvantages of History for Life" and "Schopenhauer as Educator."

1876   Publishes the fourth *Meditation*, "Richard Wagner in Bayreuth," which already bears subtle signs of his movement away from Wagner.

1878   Publishes *Human, All Too Human* (dedicated to the memory of Voltaire); it praises science over art as the mark of high culture and thus marks a decisive turn away from Wagner.

1879   Terrible health problems force him to resign his chair at Basle (with a small pension); publishes "Assorted Opinions and Maxims," the first part of vol. II of *Human, All Too Human*; begins living alone in Swiss and Italian boarding-houses.

1880   Publishes "The Wanderer and His Shadow," which becomes the second part of vol. II of *Human, All Too Human*.

1881   Publishes *Daybreak*.

1882   Publishes *Idylls of Messina* (eight poems) in a monthly magazine; publishes *The Gay Science*; friendship with Paul Ree and Lou Andreas-Salomé ends badly, leaving Nietzsche devastated.

1883   Publishes the first two parts of *Thus Spoke Zarathustra*; learns of Wagner's death just after mailing part one to the publisher.

1884   Publishes the third part of *Thus Spoke Zarathustra*.

1885   Publishes the fourth part of *Zarathustra* for private circulation only.

1886   Publishes *Beyond Good and Evil*; writes prefaces for new releases of: *The Birth of Tragedy, Human, All Too Human*, vols. I and II, and *Daybreak*.

1887   Publishes expanded edition of *The Gay Science* with a new
        preface, a fifth part, and an appendix of poems; publishes *Hymn
        to Life*, a musical work for chorus and orchestra; publishes *On
        the Genealogy of Morality*.

1888   Publishes *The Case of Wagner*, composes a collection of poems,
        Dionysian Dithyrambs, and four short books: *Twilight of Idols*,
        The Antichrist, *Ecce Homo*, and *Nietzsche contra Wagner*.

1889   Collapses physically and mentally in Turin on 3 January; writes
        a few lucid notes but never recovers sanity; is briefly
        institutionalized; spends remainder of his life as an invalid,
        living with his mother and then his sister, who also gains control
        of his literary estate.

1900   Dies in Weimar on 25 August.

Further reading

There is a good deal of material in Nietzsche's unpublished notes that makes interesting supplementary reading for the study of *BGE*. It can be found in vols. VII/2 and VII/3 of *Werke: Kritische Gesamtausgabe*, ed. G. Colli and M. Montinari (de Gruyter: Berlin, 1974). Also very useful is vol. XIV of *Sämtliche Werke: Kritische Studienausgabe*, ed. G. Colli and M. Montinari (de Gruyter: Berlin and Deutscher Taschenbuch Verlag: Munich, 1980), pp. 345–76, which contains earlier and often much more extensive versions of many of the aphorisms collected in *BGE*. This material is not yet available in the *Kritische Gesamtausgabe*. Nietzsche's own assessment of the aims and merits of *BGE* can be found in his late autobiographical work *Ecce Homo*, written in 1888 and published in 1908.

The literature on Nietzsche is immense, though there are almost no books and very few articles dealing directly and exclusively with *BGE*. Titles worth mentioning would be: A. Nehemas, "Will to Knowledge, Will to Ignorance, and Will to Power in 'Beyond Good and Evil,'" in Y. Yovel, ed., *Nietzsche as Affirmative Thinker* (Reidel Publishing Company: Dordrecht, Boston, and Lancaster, 1986), pp. 90–108; P. J. van Tongeren, *Die Moral von Nietzsche's Moralkritik. Beitrag zu einem Kommentar von Nietzsches "Jenseits von Gut und Böse"* (Bouvier Verlag: Bonn, 1987); and D. B. Allison, "A Diet of Worms: Aposiopetic Rhetoric in 'Beyond Good and Evil,'" *Nietzsche Studien* 19 (1990), pp. 43–58.

Some people might find it rewarding to approach Nietzsche's thought before reading about its biographical background. There are quite a number of interesting and well-researched (German) biographies, of which the best known are C. P. Janz, *Friedrich Nietzsche. Biographie*, 3 vols. (Hanser Verlag: Munich, 1978–9), W. Ross, *Der ängstliche Adler*

(Deutsche Verlags-Anstalt: Stuttgart, 1980), and R. Safranski, *Nietzsche. Biographie seines Denkens* (Hanser Verlag: Munich, 2000). All of these works discuss aspects of *BGE* as well.

Nietzsche, his themes, and his topics have been subject to some very different interpretations, depending on the philosophical tradition in which the interpreter is located. This has led to quite interesting "regional" schools of interpretation, especially with respect to the will-to-power doctrine and to Nietzsche's epistemological views, topics which surface prominently in *BGE*. These schools are best characterized in geographical terms as "German," "French," and "Anglo-American." The best-known and most influential representative of the "German," metaphysically oriented school is Martin Heidegger, whose two-volume study *Nietzsche* (Neske: Pfullingen, 1961; English translation: Harper and Row: New York, 1979) had an enormous impact on the discussion about Nietzsche and his role in the history of metaphysics, at least in parts of Europe. The "French" school, which tends to be more interested in the destructive or "deconstructive" motives in Nietzsche's thought, is impressively represented in the works of Gilles Deleuze, *Nietzsche et la philosophie* (Presses Universitaires de France: Paris, 1962), and *Nietzsche* (Presses Universitaires de France: Paris, 1965), P. Klossovski, *Nietzsche et le cercle vicieux* (Mercure de France: Paris, 1969), and S. Kofman, *Nietzsche et la metaphore* (Editions Payot: Paris, 1972). Their books have led to lively controversies not only about specific Nietzschean views but also about how to read Nietzsche at all. The "Anglo-American" school seems to be mainly interested in integrating Nietzsche into the gallery of "serious" thinkers, committed to what their emissaries take to be the normal standards of rationality. Convincing examples of this approach are A. Nehemas, *Nietzsche: Life as Literature* (Harvard University Press: Cambridge, 1985), and M. Clark, *Nietzsche on Truth and Philosophy* (Cambridge University Press: Cambridge, 1990). All of these schools and all the books mentioned have interesting things to say on many aspects of Nietzsche's views that are expressed in *BGE*.

Note on the text

The translation follows the German text as printed in the critical edition of Nietzsche's works edited by G. Colli and M. Montinari (de Gruyter: Berlin, 1967–). The footnotes are not meant to provide a commentary to Nietzsche's text. They are restricted to (1) translations of phrases and terms from foreign languages, (2) explanations of peculiarities of Nietzsche's German terminology, and (3) some comments on material used or alluded to by Nietzsche. The glossary of names on pp. 181–5 contains short descriptions of all persons mentioned in the text. The notes and the glossary make use of information supplied by vols. XIV and XV of *Sämtliche Werke: Kritische Studienausgabe*, ed. G. Colli and M. Montinari, 15 vols. (de Gruyter: Berlin and Deutscher Taschenbuch Verlag: Munich, 1980). They are the joint product of Dina Emundts, Rolf-Peter Horstmann, and Judith Norman.

The translator would like to thank all the people whose advice and suggestions have helped with the project. In particular, Alistair Welchman, Thomas Sebastian, Rolf-Peter Horstmann, and Karl Ameriks have provided considerable assistance with the translation, and Richard, Caroline, and Sara Norman, and Alistair Welchman have given invaluable encouragement and support. Their contribution to the project is gratefully acknowledged.

Beyond Good and Evil
Prelude to a Philosophy of the Future

Preface

Suppose that truth is a woman – and why not? Aren't there reasons for suspecting that all philosophers, to the extent that they have been dogmatists, have not really understood women? That the grotesque seriousness of their approach towards the truth and the clumsy advances they have made so far are unsuitable ways of pressing their suit with a woman? What is certain is that she has spurned them – leaving dogmatism of all types standing sad and discouraged. *If* it is even left standing! Because there are those who make fun of dogmatism, claiming that it has fallen over, that it is lying flat on its face, or more, that dogmatism is in its last gasps. But seriously, there are good reasons for hoping that all dogmatizing in philosophy was just noble (though childish) ambling and preambling, however solemn, settled and decisive it might have seemed. And perhaps the time is very near when we will realize again and again just *what* actually served as the cornerstone of those sublime and unconditional philosophical edifices that the dogmatists used to build – some piece of folk superstition from time immemorial (like the soul-superstition that still causes trouble as the superstition of the subject or I), some word-play perhaps, a seduction of grammar or an over-eager generalization from facts that are really very local, very personal, very human-all-too-human. Let us hope that the dogmatists' philosophy was only a promise over the millennia, as was the case even earlier with astrology, in whose service perhaps more labor, money, ingenuity, and patience was expended than for any real science so far. We owe the great style of architecture in Asia and Egypt to astrology and its "supernatural" claims. It seems that all great things, in order to inscribe eternal demands in the heart of humanity, must first wander the earth under monstrous and terrifying masks; dogmatic philosophy

3

was this sort of a mask: the Vedanta doctrine in Asia, for example, or Platonism in Europe. We should not be ungrateful towards dogmatism, but it must nonetheless be said that the worst, most prolonged, and most dangerous of all errors to this day was a dogmatist's error, namely Plato's invention of pure spirit and the Good in itself. But now that it has been overcome, and Europe breathes a sigh of relief after this nightmare, and at least can enjoy a healthier – well – sleep, we, *whose task is wakefulness itself*, are the heirs to all the force cultivated through the struggle against this error. Of course: talking about spirit and the Good like Plato did meant standing truth on its head and disowning even *perspectivism*, which is the fundamental condition of all life. In fact, as physicians we could ask: "How could such a disease infect Plato, the most beautiful outgrowth of antiquity? Did the evil Socrates corrupt him after all? was Socrates in fact the corrupter of youth? did he deserve his hemlock?" – But the struggle against Plato, or, to use a clear and "popular" idiom, the struggle against the Christian–ecclesiastical pressure of millennia – since Christianity is Platonism for the "people" – has created a magnificent tension of spirit in Europe, the likes of which the earth has never known: with such a tension in our bow we can now shoot at the furthest goals. Granted, the European experiences this tension as a crisis or state of need; and twice already there have been attempts, in a grand fashion, to unbend the bow, once through Jesuitism, and the second time through the democratic Enlightenment: – which, with the help of freedom of the press and circulation of newspapers, might really insure that spirit does not experience itself so readily as "need"! (Germans invented gunpowder – all honors due! But they made up for it – they invented the press.) But we, who are neither Jesuits nor democrats, nor even German enough, we *good Europeans* and free, *very* free spirits – we still have it, the whole need of spirit and the whole tension of its bow! And perhaps the arrow too, the task, and – who knows? the *goal* . . .

Sils-Maria, Upper Engadine,
June, 1885

Part 1 On the prejudices of philosophers

1

The will to truth that still seduces us into taking so many risks, this famous truthfulness that all philosophers so far have talked about with veneration: what questions this will to truth has already laid before us! What strange, terrible, questionable questions! That is already a long story – and yet it seems to have hardly begun? Is it any wonder if we finally become suspicious, lose patience, turn impatiently away? That *we ourselves* are also learning from this Sphinx to pose questions? *Who* is it really that questions us here? *What* in us really wills the truth? In fact, we paused for a long time before the question of the cause of this will – until we finally came to a complete standstill in front of an even more fundamental question. We asked about the *value* of this will. Granted, we will truth: *why not untruth instead?* And uncertainty? Even ignorance? The problem of the value of truth came before us, – or was it we who came before the problem? Which of us is Oedipus? Which one is the Sphinx? It seems we have a rendezvous of questions and question-marks. – And, believe it or not, it ultimately looks to us as if the problem has never been raised until now, – as if we were the first to ever see it, fix our gaze on it, *risk it*. Because this involves risk and perhaps no risk has ever been greater.

2

"How *could* anything originate out of its opposite? Truth from error, for instance? Or the will to truth from the will to deception? Or selfless action from self-interest? Or the pure, sun-bright gaze of wisdom from a covetous leer? Such origins are impossible, and people who dream about

5

What's the origin?

such things are fools – at best. Things of the highest value must have another, separate origin *of their own*, – they cannot be derived from this ephemeral, seductive, deceptive, lowly world, from this mad chaos of confusion and desire. Look instead to the lap of being, the everlasting, the hidden God, the 'thing-in-itself' – *this* is where their ground must be, and nowhere else!"[1] – This way of judging typifies the prejudices by which metaphysicians of all ages can be recognized: this type of valuation lies behind all their logical procedures. From these "beliefs" they try to acquire their "knowledge," to acquire something that will end up being solemnly christened as "the truth." The fundamental belief of metaphysicians is the *belief in oppositions of values*. It has not occurred to even the most cautious of them to start doubting right here at the threshold, where it is actually needed the most – even though they had vowed to themselves "*de omnibus dubitandum*."[2] But we can doubt, first, whether opposites even exist and, second, whether the popular valuations and value oppositions that have earned the metaphysicians' seal of approval might not only be foreground appraisals. Perhaps they are merely provisional perspectives, perhaps they are not even viewed head-on; perhaps they are even viewed from below, like a frog-perspective, to borrow an expression that painters will recognize. Whatever value might be attributed to truth, truthfulness, and selflessness, it could be possible that appearance, the will to deception, and craven self-interest should be accorded a higher and more fundamental value for all life. It could even be possible that whatever gives value to those good and honorable things has an incriminating link, bond, or tie to the very things that look like their evil opposites; perhaps they are even essentially the same. Perhaps! – But who is willing to take charge of such a dangerous Perhaps! For this we must await the arrival of a new breed of philosophers, ones whose taste and inclination are somehow the reverse of those we have seen so far – philosophers of the dangerous Perhaps in every sense. – And in all seriousness: I see these new philosophers approaching.

does self-interest skew our view of truth?

3

I have kept a close eye on the philosophers and read between their lines for long enough to say to myself: the greatest part of conscious thought

[1] Cf. *Human, All too Human*, I, §1.

[2] Everything is to be doubted.

must still be attributed to instinctive activity, and this is even the case for philosophical thought. This issue needs re-examination in the same way that heredity and "innate characteristics" have been re-examined. Just as the act of birth makes no difference to the overall course of heredity, neither is "consciousness" *opposed* to instinct in any decisive sense – most of a philosopher's conscious thought is secretly directed and forced into determinate channels by the instincts. Even behind all logic and its autocratic posturings stand valuations or, stated more clearly, physiological requirements for the preservation of a particular type of life. For example, that the determinate is worth more than the indeterminate, appearance worth less than the "truth": despite all their regulative importance for *us*, these sorts of appraisals could still be just foreground appraisals, a particular type of *niaiserie*,[3] precisely what is needed for the preservation of beings like us. But this assumes that it is not man who is the "measure of things" ...] Then what is?

4

We do not consider the falsity of a judgment as itself an objection to a judgment; this is perhaps where our new language will sound most foreign. The question is how far the judgment promotes and preserves life, how well it preserves, and perhaps even cultivates, the type. And we are fundamentally inclined to claim that the falsest judgments (which include synthetic judgments *a priori*) are the most indispensable to us, and that without accepting the fictions of logic, without measuring reality against the wholly invented world of the unconditioned and self-identical, without a constant falsification of the world through numbers, people could not live – that a renunciation of false judgments would be a renunciation of life, a negation of life. To acknowledge untruth as a condition of life: this clearly means resisting the usual value feelings in a dangerous manner; and a philosophy that risks such a thing would by that gesture alone place itself beyond good and evil.

5

What goads us into regarding all philosophers with an equal measure of mistrust and mockery is not that we are struck repeatedly by how innocent

---

[3] Silliness.

they are – how often and easily they err and stray, in short, their childish childlikeness – but rather that there is not enough genuine honesty about them: even though they all make a huge, virtuous racket as soon as the problem of truthfulness is even remotely touched upon. They all act as if they had discovered and arrived at their genuine convictions through the self-development of a cold, pure, divinely insouciant dialectic (in contrast to the mystics of every rank, who are more honest than the philosophers and also sillier – they talk about "inspiration" –): while what essentially happens is that they take a conjecture, a whim, an "inspiration" or, more typically, they take some fervent wish that they have sifted through and made properly abstract – and they defend it with rationalizations after the fact. They are all advocates who do not want to be seen as such; for the most part, in fact, they are sly spokesmen for prejudices that they christen as "truths" – and *very* far indeed from the courage of conscience that confesses to this fact, this very fact; and very far from having the good taste of courage that also lets this be known, perhaps to warn a friend or foe, or out of a high-spirited attempt at self-satire. The stiff yet demure tartuffery used by the old Kant to lure us along the clandestine, dialectical path that leads the way (or rather: astray) to his "categorical imperative" – this spectacle provides no small amusement for discriminating spectators like us, who keep a close eye on the cunning tricks of the old moralists and preachers of morals. Or even that hocus pocus of a mathematical form used by Spinoza to arm and outfit his philosophy (a term which, when all is said and done, really means "*his* love of wisdom") and thus, from the very start, to strike terror into the heart of the attacker who would dare to cast a glance at the unconquerable maiden and Pallas Athena: – how much personal timidity and vulnerability this sick hermit's masquerade reveals!

6

I have gradually come to realize what every great philosophy so far has been: a confession of faith on the part of its author, and a type of involuntary and unself-conscious memoir; in short, that the moral (or immoral) intentions in every philosophy constitute the true living seed from which the whole plant has always grown. Actually, to explain how the strangest metaphysical claims of a philosopher really come about, it is always good (and wise) to begin by asking: what morality is it (is *he* –) getting at? Consequently, I do not believe that a "drive for knowledge" is the father of

8

philosophy, but rather that another drive, here as elsewhere, used knowledge (and mis-knowledge!) merely as a tool. But anyone who looks at people's basic drives, to see how far they may have played their little game right here as *inspiring* geniuses (or daemons or sprites –), will find that they all practiced philosophy at some point, – and that every single one of them would be only too pleased to present *itself* as the ultimate purpose of existence and as rightful *master* of all the other drives. Because every drive craves mastery, and *this* leads it to try philosophizing. – Of course: with scholars, the truly scientific people, things might be different – "better" if you will –, with them, there might really be something like a drive for knowledge, some independent little clockwork mechanism that, once well wound, ticks bravely away *without* essentially involving the rest of the scholar's drives. For this reason, the scholar's real "interests" usually lie somewhere else entirely, with the family, or earning money, or in politics; in fact, it is almost a matter of indifference whether his little engine is put to work in this or that field of research, and whether the "promising" young worker turns himself into a good philologist or fungus expert or chemist: – it doesn't *signify* anything about him that he becomes one thing or the other. In contrast, there is absolutely nothing impersonal about the philosopher; and in particular his morals bear decided and decisive witness to *who he is* – which means, in what order of rank the innermost drives of his nature stand with respect to each other.

[handwritten margin note: philo = Power (game)]

[handwritten margin note: Something deeper inside of us]

[handwritten note: Philo - self morals posed onto others · persuasive aspect of drives ~ some drives have higher rank]

[handwritten note: new criticism]

7

How malicious philosophers can be! I do not know anything more venomous than the joke Epicurus allowed himself against Plato and the Platonists: he called them Dionysiokolakes.[4] Literally, the foreground meaning of this term is "sycophants of Dionysus" and therefore accessories of the tyrant and brown-nosers; but it also wants to say "they're all *actors*, there's nothing genuine about them" (since Dionysokolax was a popular term for an actor). And this second meaning is really the malice that Epicurus hurled against Plato: he was annoyed by the magnificent style, the *mise-en-scène* that Plato and his students were so good at, – that Epicurus was not so good at! He, the old schoolmaster from Samos, who sat hidden in his little garden in Athens and wrote three hundred books,

---

[4] Epicurus, Fragment 93.

who knows? perhaps out of anger and ambition against Plato? – It took a hundred years for Greece to find out who this garden god Epicurus had been. – Did it find out?

8

In every philosophy there is a point where the philosopher's "conviction" steps onto the stage: or, to use the language of an ancient Mystery:

> adventavit asinus
> pulcher et fortissimus.[5]

9

So you want to *live* "according to nature?" Oh, you noble Stoics, what a fraud is in this phrase! Imagine something like nature, profligate without measure, indifferent without measure, without purpose and regard, without mercy and justice, fertile and barren and uncertain at the same time, think of indifference itself as power – how *could* you live according to this indifference? Living – isn't that wanting specifically to be something other than this nature? Isn't living assessing, preferring, being unfair, being limited, wanting to be different? And assuming your imperative to "live according to nature" basically amounts to "living according to life" – well how could you *not?* Why make a principle out of what you yourselves are and must be? – But in fact, something quite different is going on: while pretending with delight to read the canon of your law in nature, you want the opposite, you strange actors and self-deceivers! Your pride wants to dictate and annex your morals and ideals onto nature – yes, nature itself –, you demand that it be nature "according to Stoa" and you want to make all existence exist in your own image alone – as a huge eternal glorification and universalization of Stoicism! For all your love of truth, you have forced yourselves so long, so persistently, and with such hypnotic rigidity to have a *false*, namely Stoic, view of nature, that you can no longer see it any other way, – and some abysmal piece of arrogance finally gives you the madhouse hope that *because* you know how to tyrannize yourselves – Stoicism is self-tyranny –, nature lets itself be

---

[5] "In came the ass / beautiful and very strong." According to *KSA* these lines could be taken from G. C. Lichtenberg's *Vermischte Schriften* (*Miscellaneous Writings*) (1867), V, p. 327.

tyrannized as well: because isn't the Stoic a *piece* of nature? ... But this is an old, eternal story: what happened back then with the Stoics still happens today, just as soon as a philosophy begins believing in itself. It always creates the world in its own image, it cannot do otherwise; philosophy is this tyrannical drive itself, the most spiritual will to power, to the "creation of the world," to the *causa prima*.[6]

10

All over Europe these days, the problem "of the real and the apparent world" gets taken up so eagerly and with such acuity – I would even say: shrewdness – that you really start to think and listen; and anyone who hears only a "will to truth" in the background here certainly does not have the sharpest of ears. In rare and unusual cases, some sort of will to truth might actually be at issue, some wild and adventurous streak of courage, a metaphysician's ambition to hold on to a lost cause, that, in the end, will still prefer a handful of "certainty" to an entire wagonload of pretty possibilities. There might even be puritanical fanatics of conscience who would rather lie dying on an assured nothing than an uncertain something. But this is nihilism, and symptomatic of a desperate soul in a state of deadly exhaustion, however brave such virtuous posturing may appear. With stronger, livelier thinkers, however, thinkers who still have a thirst for life, things look different. By taking sides *against* appearance and speaking about "perspective" in a newly arrogant tone, by granting their own bodies about as little credibility as they grant the visual evidence that says "the earth stands still," and so, with seemingly good spirits, relinquishing their most secure possession (since what do people believe in more securely these days than their bodies?), who knows whether they are not basically trying to re-appropriate something that was once possessed even *more securely*, something from the old estate of a bygone faith, perhaps "the immortal soul" or perhaps "the old God," in short, ideas that helped make life a bit better, which is to say stronger and more cheerful than "modern ideas" can do? There is a *mistrust* of these modern ideas here, there is a disbelief in everything built yesterday and today; perhaps it is mixed with a bit of antipathy and contempt that can no longer stand the bric-a-brac of concepts from the most heterogeneous sources, which is

---

[6] First cause.

how so-called positivism puts itself on the market these days, a disgust felt by the more discriminating taste at the fun-fair colors and flimsy scraps of all these reality-philosophasters who have nothing new and genuine about them except these colors. Here, I think, we should give these skeptical anti-realists and epistemo-microscopists their just due: the instinct that drives them away from *modern* reality is unassailable, – what do we care for their retrograde shortcut! The essential thing about them is not that they want to go "back": but rather, that they want to get – *away*. A bit *more* strength, flight, courage, artistry: and they would want to get *up and out*, – and not go back! –

11

It seems to me that people everywhere these days are at pains to divert attention away from the real influence Kant exerted over German philosophy, and, in particular, wisely to overlook the value he attributed to himself. First and foremost, Kant was proud of his table of categories,[7] and he said with this table in his hands: "This is the hardest thing that ever could have been undertaken on behalf of metaphysics." – But let us be clear about this "could have been"! He was proud of having *discovered* a new faculty in humans, the faculty of synthetic judgments *a priori*. Of course he was deceiving himself here, but the development and rapid blossoming of German philosophy depended on this pride, and on the competitive zeal of the younger generation who wanted, if possible, to discover something even prouder – and in any event "new faculties"! – But the time has come for us to think this over. How are synthetic judgments *a priori possible*? Kant asked himself, – and what really was his answer? *By virtue of a faculty*, which is to say: *enabled by an ability*:[8] unfortunately, though, not in these few words, but rather so laboriously, reverentially, and with such an extravagance of German frills and profundity that people failed to hear the comical *niaiserie allemande*[9] in such an answer. In fact, people were beside themselves with joy over this new faculty, and the jubilation reached its peak when Kant discovered yet another faculty, a moral faculty: – because the Germans were still moral back then, and

---

[7] The reference in this section is to Kant's *Kritik der reinen Vernunft* (*Critique of Pure Reason*) (1781, 1787).

[8] In German: *Vermöge eines Vermögens*.

[9] German silliness.

very remote from *Realpolitik.* – The honeymoon of German philosophy had arrived; all the young theologians of the Tübingen seminary[10] ran off into the bushes – they were all looking for "faculties." And what didn't they find – in that innocent, abundant, still youthful age of the German spirit, when Romanticism, that malicious fairy, whispered, whistled, and sang, when people did not know how to tell the difference between "discovering" and "inventing"![11] Above all, a faculty of the "supersensible": Schelling christened it intellectual intuition, and thus gratified the heart's desire of his basically piety-craving Germans. We can do no greater injustice to this whole high-spirited and enthusiastic movement (which was just youthfulness, however boldly it might have clothed itself in gray and hoary concepts) than to take it seriously or especially to treat it with moral indignation. Enough, we grew up, – the dream faded away. There came a time when people scratched their heads: some still scratch them today. There had been dreamers: first and foremost – the old Kant. "By virtue of a faculty" – he had said, or at least meant. But is that really – an answer? An explanation? Or instead just a repetition of the question? So how does opium cause sleep? "By virtue of a faculty," namely the *virtus dormitiva* – replies the doctor in Molière,

> *quia est in eo virtus dormitiva,*
> *cujus est natura sensus assoupire.*[12]

But answers like this belong in comedy, and the time has finally come to replace the Kantian question "How are synthetic judgments *a priori* possible?" with another question, "Why is the belief in such judgments *necessary*?" – to realize, in other words, that such judgments must be *believed* true for the purpose of preserving beings of our type; which is why these judgments could of course still be *false*! Or, to be blunt, basic and clearer still: synthetic judgments *a priori* do not have "to be possible" at all: we have no right to them, and in our mouths they are nothing but false judgments. It is only the belief in their truth that is necessary as a foreground belief and piece of visual evidence, belonging to the perspectival optics of life. – And, finally, to recall the enormous effect that "the German philosophy" – its right to these quotation marks

---

[10] A reference to Hegel, Hölderlin, and Schelling.

[11] In German: "'*finden*' und '*erfinden*.'"

[12] "Because there is a dormative virtue in it / whose nature is to put the senses to sleep." From Molière's *Le Malade imaginaire* (*The Hypochondriac*) (1673).

is, I hope, understood? – has had all over Europe, a certain *virtus dormitiva* has undoubtedly had a role: the noble idlers, the virtuous, the mystics, artists, three-quarter-Christians, and political obscurantists of all nations were all delighted to have, thanks to German philosophy, an antidote to the still overpowering sensualism that was spilling over into this century from the previous one, in short – *"sensus assoupire"* . . .

12

As far as materialistic atomism goes: this is one of the most well-refuted things in existence. In Europe these days, nobody in the scholarly community is likely to be so unscholarly as to attach any real significance to it, except as a handy household tool (that is, as an abbreviated figure of speech). For this, we can thank that Pole, Boscovich, who, together with the Pole, Copernicus, was the greatest, most successful opponent of the visual evidence. While Copernicus convinced us to believe, contrary to all our senses, that the earth does *not* stand still, Boscovich taught us to renounce belief in the last bit of earth that *did* "stand still," the belief in "matter," in the "material," in the residual piece of earth and clump of an atom: it was the greatest triumph over the senses that the world had ever known. – But we must go further still and declare war – a ruthless fight to the finish – on the "atomistic need" that, like the more famous "metaphysical need," still leads a dangerous afterlife in regions where nobody would think to look. First of all, we must also put an end to that other and more disastrous atomism, the one Christianity has taught best and longest, the *atomism of the soul.* Let this expression signify the belief that the soul is something indestructible, eternal, indivisible, that it is a monad, an *atomon*: this belief must be thrown out of science! Between you and me, there is absolutely no need to give up "the soul" itself, and relinquish one of the oldest and most venerable hypotheses – as often happens with naturalists: given their clumsiness, they barely need to touch "the soul" to lose it. But the path lies open for new versions and sophistications of the soul hypothesis – and concepts like the "mortal soul" and the "soul as subject-multiplicity" and the "soul as a society constructed out of drives and affects" want henceforth to have civil rights in the realm of science. By putting an end to the superstition that until now has grown around the idea of the soul with an almost tropical luxuriance, the *new* psychologist clearly thrusts himself into a new wasteland and a new suspicion. The

Does he believe in soul? Yes ~ wants us to approach soul in a new way old psychologists might have found things easier and more enjoyable –: but, in the end, the new psychologist knows by this very token that he is condemned to *invention* – and, who knows? perhaps to *discovery*.[13] –

13

" Biologists"

Physiologists should think twice before positioning the drive for self-preservation as the cardinal drive of an organic being. Above all, a living thing wants to *discharge* its strength – life itself is will to power –: self-preservation is only one of the indirect and most frequent *consequences* of this. – In short, here as elsewhere, watch out for *superfluous* teleological principles! – such as the drive for preservation (which we owe to Spinoza's inconsistency –). This is demanded by method, which must essentially be the economy of principles.

14 *Difference between interpretation vs explanation?*

Now it is beginning to dawn on maybe five or six brains that physics too is only an interpretation and arrangement of the world (according to ourselves! if I may say so) and *not* an explanation of the world. But to the extent that physics rests on belief in the senses, it passes for more, and will continue to pass for more, namely for an explanation, for a long time to come. It has our eyes and our fingers as its allies, it has visual evidence and tangibility as its allies. This helped it to enchant, persuade, *convince* an age with a basically plebeian taste – indeed, it instinctively follows the canon of truth of the eternally popular sensualism. What is plain, what "explains"? Only what can be seen and felt, – this is as far as any problem has to be pursued. Conversely: the strong attraction of the Platonic way of thinking consisted in its *opposition* to precisely this empiricism. It was a *noble* way of thinking, suitable perhaps for people who enjoyed even stronger and more discriminating senses than our contemporaries, but who knew how to find a higher triumph in staying master over these senses. And they did this by throwing drab, cold, gray nets of concepts over the brightly colored whirlwind of the senses – the rabble of the senses, as Plato said.[14] There was a type of *enjoyment* in overpowering

---

[13] Nietzsche is again making a pun by contrasting the terms *Erfinden* (invention) and *Finden* (discovery).

[14] Cf. *Nomoi (Laws)* 689a–b.

and interpreting the world in the manner of Plato, different from the enjoyment offered by today's physicists, or by the Darwinians and anti-teleologists who work in physiology, with their principle of the "smallest possible force" and greatest possible stupidity. "Where man has nothing more to see and grasp, he has nothing more to do" – this imperative is certainly different from the Platonic one, but for a sturdy, industrious race of machinists and bridge-builders of the future, people with *tough* work to do, it just might be the right imperative for the job.

15

To study physiology with a good conscience, we must insist that the sense organs are *not* appearances in the way idealist philosophy uses that term: as such, they certainly could not be causes! Sensualism, therefore, at least as a regulative principle, if not as a heuristic principle. – What? and other people even say that the external world is the product of our organs? But then our body, as a piece of this external world, would really be the product of our organs! But then our organs themselves would really be – the product of our organs! This looks to me like a thorough *reductio ad absurdum*:[15] given that the concept of a *causa sui*[16] is something thoroughly absurd. So does it follow that the external world is *not* the product of our organs –?

16

There are still harmless self-observers who believe in the existence of "immediate certainties," such as "I think," or the "I will" that was Schopenhauer's superstition: just as if knowledge had been given an object here to seize, stark naked, as a "thing-in-itself," and no falsification took place from either the side of the subject or the side of the object. But I will say this a hundred times: "immediate certainty," like "absolute knowledge" and the "thing in itself" contains a *contradictio in adjecto*.[17] For once and for all, we should free ourselves from the seduction of words! Let the people believe that knowing means knowing to the very end; the philosopher has to say: "When I dissect the process expressed in the proposition

---

[15] Reduction to an absurdity (contradiction).

[16] Cause of itself.

[17] Contradiction in terms.

'I think,' I get a whole set of bold claims that are difficult, perhaps impossible, to establish, – for instance, that *I* am the one who is thinking, that there must be something that is thinking in the first place, that thinking is an activity and the effect of a being who is considered the cause, that there is an 'I,' and finally, that it has already been determined what is meant by thinking, – that I *know* what thinking is. Because if I had not already made up my mind what thinking is, how could I tell whether what had just happened was not perhaps 'willing' or 'feeling'? Enough: this 'I think' presupposes that I *compare* my present state with other states that I have seen in myself, in order to determine what it is: and because of this retrospective comparison with other types of 'knowing,' this present state has absolutely no 'immediate certainty' for me." – In place of that "immediate certainty" which may, in this case, win the faith of the people, the philosopher gets handed a whole assortment of metaphysical questions, genuinely probing intellectual questions of conscience, such as: "Where do I get the concept of thinking from? Why do I believe in causes and effects? What gives me the right to speak about an I, and, for that matter, about an I as cause, and, finally, about an I as the cause of thoughts?" Whoever dares to answer these metaphysical questions right away with an appeal to a sort of *intuitive* knowledge, like the person who says: "I think and know that at least this is true, real, certain" – he will find the philosopher of today ready with a smile and two question-marks. "My dear sir," the philosopher will perhaps give him to understand, "it is improbable that you are not mistaken: but why insist on the truth?" –

So theres no answer?

17

As far as the superstitions of the logicians are concerned: I will not stop emphasizing a tiny little fact that these superstitious men are loath to admit: that a thought comes when "it" wants, and not when "I" want. It is, therefore, a *falsification* of the facts to say that the subject "I" is the condition of the predicate "think." It thinks: but to say the "it" is just that famous old "I" – well that is just an assumption or opinion, to put it mildly, and by no means an "immediate certainty." In fact, there is already too much packed into the "it thinks": even the "it" contains an *interpretation* of the process, and does not belong to the process itself. People are following grammatical habits here in drawing conclusions, reasoning that "thinking is an activity, behind every activity something is

So is I or it in control?

active, therefore –." Following the same basic scheme, the older atomism looked behind every "force" that produces effects for that little lump of matter in which the force resides, and out of which the effects are produced, which is to say: the atom. More rigorous minds finally learned how to make do without that bit of "residual earth," and perhaps one day even logicians will get used to making do without this little "it" (into which the honest old I has disappeared).

18

That a theory is refutable is, frankly, not the least of its charms: this is precisely how it attracts the more refined intellects. The theory of "free will," which has been refuted a hundred times, appears to owe its endurance to this charm alone –: somebody will always come along and feel strong enough to refute it.

19

Philosophers tend to talk about the will as if it were the most familiar thing in the world. In fact, Schopenhauer would have us believe that the will is the only thing that is really familiar, familiar through and through, familiar without pluses or minuses. But I have always thought that, here too, Schopenhauer was only doing what philosophers always tend to do: adopting and exaggerating a *popular prejudice*. Willing strikes me as, above all, something *complicated*, something unified only in a word – and this single word contains the popular prejudice that has overruled whatever minimal precautions philosophers might take. So let us be more cautious, for once – let us be "unphilosophical." Let us say: in every act of willing there is, to begin with, a plurality of feelings, namely: the feeling of the state *away from which*, the feeling of the state *towards which*, and the feeling of this "away from" and "towards" themselves. But this is accompanied by a feeling of the muscles that comes into play through a sort of habit as soon as we "will," even without our putting "arms and legs" into motion. Just as feeling – and indeed many feelings – must be recognized as ingredients of the will, thought must be as well. In every act of will there is a commandeering thought, – and we really should not believe this thought can be divorced from the "willing," as if some will would then be left over! Third, the will is not just a complex of feeling and thinking; rather, it is fundamentally an *affect*: and specifically the affect of the command. What is called "freedom of the will" is essentially the affect of superiority with respect to something that must obey: "I am free, 'it' must obey" – this consciousness lies in every will, along with a certain straining of attention, a straight look that fixes on one thing and one thing only, an unconditional evaluation "now this is necessary and nothing else," an inner certainty that it will be obeyed, and whatever else comes with the position of the commander. A person who *wills* –, commands something inside himself that obeys, or that he believes to obey. But now we notice the strangest thing about the will – about this multifarious thing that people have only one word for. On the one hand, we are, under the circumstances, both the one who commands *and* the one who obeys, and as the obedient one we are familiar with the feelings of compulsion, force, pressure, resistance, and motion that generally start right after the act of willing. On the other hand, however, we are in the habit of ignoring and deceiving ourselves about this duality by means of the synthetic concept of the "I." As a result, a whole chain of erroneous conclusions, and, consequently, false evaluations have become attached to the will, – to such an extent that the one who wills believes, in good faith, that willing *suffices* for action. Since it is almost always the case that there is will only where the effect of command, and therefore obedience, and therefore action, may be *expected*, the *appearance* translates into the feeling, as if there were a *necessity of effect*. In short, the one who wills believes with a reasonable degree of certainty that will and action are somehow one; he attributes the success, the performance of the willing to the will itself, and consequently enjoys an increase in the feeling of power that accompanies all success. "Freedom of the will" – that is the word for the multi-faceted state of pleasure of one who commands and, at the same time, identifies himself with the accomplished act of willing. As such, he enjoys the triumph over resistances, but thinks to himself that it was his will alone that truly overcame the resistance. Accordingly, the one who wills takes his feeling of pleasure as the commander, and adds to it the feelings of pleasure from the successful instruments that carry out the task, as well as from the useful "under-wills" or under-souls – our body is, after all, only a society constructed out of many souls –. *L'effet c'est moi*:[18] what happens here is what happens in every well-constructed and

---

[18] The effect is I.

happy community: the ruling class identifies itself with the successes of the community. All willing is simply a matter of commanding and obeying, on the groundwork, as I have said, of a society constructed out of many "souls": from which a philosopher should claim the right to understand willing itself within the framework of morality: morality understood as a doctrine of the power relations under which the phenomenon of "life" arises. –

20

That individual philosophical concepts are not arbitrary and do not grow up on their own, but rather grow in reference and relation to each other; that however suddenly and randomly they seem to emerge in the history of thought, they still belong to a system just as much as all the members of the fauna of a continent do: this is ultimately revealed by the certainty with which the most diverse philosophers will always fill out a definite basic scheme of *possible* philosophies. Under an invisible spell, they will each start out anew, only to end up revolving in the same orbit once again. However independent of each other they might feel themselves to be, with their critical or systematic wills, something inside of them drives them on, something leads them into a particular order, one after the other, and this something is precisely the innate systematicity and relationship of concepts. In fact, their thinking is not nearly as much a discovery as it is a recognition, remembrance, a returning and homecoming into a distant, primordial, total economy of the soul, from which each concept once grew: – to this extent, philosophizing is a type of atavism of the highest order. The strange family resemblance of all Indian, Greek, and German philosophizing speaks for itself clearly enough. Where there are linguistic affinities, then because of the common philosophy of grammar (I mean: due to the unconscious domination and direction through similar grammatical functions), it is obvious that everything lies ready from the very start for a similar development and sequence of philosophical systems; on the other hand, the way seems as good as blocked for certain other possibilities of interpreting the world. Philosophers of the Ural-Altaic language group (where the concept of the subject is the most poorly developed) are more likely to "see the world" differently, and to be found on paths different from those taken by the Indo-Germans or Muslims: the spell of particular grammatical functions is in the last analysis the spell of *physiological* value judgments and racial conditioning. – So much towards a rejection of Locke's superficiality with regard to the origin of ideas.

21

The *causa sui*[19] is the best self-contradiction that has ever been conceived, a type of logical rape and abomination. But humanity's excessive pride has got itself profoundly and horribly entangled with precisely this piece of nonsense. The longing for "freedom of the will" in the superlative metaphysical sense (which, unfortunately, still rules in the heads of the half-educated), the longing to bear the entire and ultimate responsibility for your actions yourself and to relieve God, world, ancestors, chance, and society of the burden – all this means nothing less than being that very *causa sui* and, with a courage greater than Münchhausen's, pulling yourself by the hair from the swamp of nothingness up into existence. Suppose someone sees through the boorish naiveté of this famous concept of "free will" and manages to get it out of his mind; I would then ask him to carry his "enlightenment" a step further and to rid his mind of the reversal of this misconceived concept of "free will": I mean the "un-free will," which is basically an abuse of cause and effect. We should not erroneously *objectify* "cause" and "effect" like the natural scientists do (and whoever else thinks naturalistically these days –) in accordance with the dominant mechanistic stupidity which would have the cause push and shove until it "effects" something; we should use "cause" and "effect" only as pure *concepts,* which is to say as conventional fictions for the purpose of description and communication, *not* explanation. In the "in-itself" there is nothing like "causal association," "necessity," or "psychological un-freedom." There, the "effect" does *not* follow "from the cause," there is no rule of "law." *We* are the ones who invented causation, succession, for-each-other, relativity, compulsion, numbers, law, freedom, grounds, purpose; and if we project and inscribe this symbol world onto things as an "in-itself," then this is the way we have always done things, namely *mythologically*. The "un-free will" is mythology; in real life it is only a matter of *strong* and *weak* wills. It is almost always a symptom of what is lacking in a thinker when he senses some compulsion, need, having-to-follow, pressure, un-freedom in every "causal connection" and "psychological necessity." It is

[19] Cause of itself.

very telling to feel this way – the person tells on himself. And in general, if I have observed correctly, "un-freedom of the will" is regarded as a problem by two completely opposed parties, but always in a profoundly *personal* manner. The one party would never dream of relinquishing their "responsibility," a belief in *themselves*, a personal right to *their own* merit (the vain races belong to this group –). Those in the other party, on the contrary, do not want to be responsible for anything or to be guilty of anything; driven by an inner self-contempt, they long to be able to *shift the blame* for themselves to something else. When they write books these days, this latter group tends to side with the criminal; a type of socialist pity is their most attractive disguise. And, in fact, the fatalism of the weak of will starts to look surprisingly attractive when it can present itself as *"la religion de la souffrance humaine"*:[20] this is *its* "good taste."

22

You must forgive an old philologist like me who cannot help maliciously putting his finger on bad tricks of interpretation: but this "conformity of nature to law," which you physicists are so proud of, just as if – – exists only because of your interpretation and bad "philology." It is not a matter of fact, not a "text," but instead only a naive humanitarian correction and a distortion of meaning that you use in order to comfortably accommodate the democratic instincts of the modern soul! "Everywhere, equality before the law, – in this respect, nature is no different and no better off than we are": a lovely case of ulterior motivation; and it serves once more to disguise the plebeian antagonism against all privilege and autocracy together with a second and more refined atheism. *"Ni dieu, ni maître"*[21] – you want this too: and therefore "hurray for the laws of nature!" – right? But, as I have said, this is interpretation, not text; and somebody with an opposite intention and mode of interpretation could come along and be able to read from the same nature, and with reference to the same set of appearances, a tyrannically ruthless and pitiless execution of power claims. This sort of interpreter would show the unequivocal and unconditional nature of all "will to power" so vividly and graphically that almost every word, and even the word "tyranny," would ultimately seem useless or like weakening and mollifying metaphors – and too humanizing. Yet this

[20] The religion of human suffering.

[21] Neither God nor master.

interpreter might nevertheless end up claiming the same thing about this world as you, namely that it follows a "necessary" and "calculable" course, although *not* because laws are dominant in it, but rather because laws are totally *absent*, and every power draws its final consequences at every moment. Granted, this is only an interpretation too – and you will be eager enough to make this objection? – well then, so much the better.

23

All psychology so far has been stuck in moral prejudices and fears: it has not ventured into the depths. To grasp psychology as morphology and the *doctrine of the development of the will to power*, which is what I have done – nobody has ever come close to this, not even in thought: this, of course, to the extent that we are permitted to regard what has been written so far as a symptom of what has not been said until now. The power of moral prejudice has deeply affected the most spiritual world, which seems like the coldest world, the one most likely to be devoid of any presuppositions – and the effect has been manifestly harmful, hindering, dazzling, and distorting. A genuine physio-psychology has to contend with unconscious resistances in the heart of the researcher, it has "the heart" against it. Even a doctrine of the reciprocal dependence of the "good" and the "bad" drives will (as a refined immorality) cause distress and aversion in a strong and sturdy conscience – as will, to an even greater extent, a doctrine of the derivation of all the good drives from the bad. But suppose somebody considers even the affects of hatred, envy, greed, and power-lust as the conditioning affects of life, as elements that fundamentally and essentially need to be present in the total economy of life, and consequently need to be enhanced where life is enhanced, – this person will suffer from such a train of thought as if from sea-sickness. And yet even this hypothesis is far from being the most uncomfortable and unfamiliar in this enormous, practically untouched realm of dangerous knowledge: – and there are hundreds of good reasons for people to keep out of it, if they – *can*! On the other hand, if you are ever cast loose here with your ship, well now! come on! clench your teeth! open your eyes! and grab hold of the helm! – we are sailing straight over and *away from* morality; we are crushing and perhaps destroying the remnants of our own morality by daring to travel there – but what do *we* matter! Never before have intrepid voyagers and adventurers opened up a *more profound* world of insight: and the psychologist who "makes sacrifices" (they are *not* the *sacrifizio dell'intelletto*[22] – to the contrary!) can at least demand in return that psychology again be recognized as queen of the sciences,[23] and that the rest of the sciences exist to serve and prepare for it. Because, from now on, psychology is again the path to the fundamental problems.

[22] Sacrifice of the intellect.

[23] In German: *Wissenschaften. Wissenschaft* has generally been translated as "science" throughout the text, but the German term is broader than the English, and includes the humanities as well as the natural and social sciences.

Part 2   The free spirit[1]

24

O sancta simplicitas![2] What a strange simplification and falsification people
live in! The wonders never cease, for those who devote their eyes to such
wondering. How we have made everything around us so bright and easy
and free and simple! How we have given our senses a *carte blanche* for everything superficial, given our thoughts a divine craving for high-spirited
leaps and false inferences! – How we have known from the start to hold
on to our ignorance in order to enjoy a barely comprehensible freedom,
thoughtlessness, recklessness, bravery, and joy in life; to delight in life
itself! And, until now, science could arise only on this solidified, granite
foundation of ignorance, the will to know rising up on the foundation of a
much more powerful will, the will to not know, to uncertainty, to untruth!
Not as its opposite, but rather – as its refinement! Even when *language*,
here as elsewhere, cannot get over its crassness and keeps talking about
opposites where there are only degrees and multiple, subtle shades of
gradation; even when the ingrained tartuffery of morals (which is now
part of our "flesh and blood," and cannot be overcome) twists the words
in our mouths (we who should know better); now and then we still realize
what is happening, and laugh about how it is precisely the best science
that will best know how to keep us in this *simplified*, utterly artificial,

[1] In German: *der freie Geist*. I have generally rendered *Geist* and words using *Geist* (such as *geistig*,
Geistigkeit) as "spirit" and words using spirit (so: spiritual and spirituality). However, *Geist* is a
broader term than spirit, meaning mind or intellect as well.

[2] O holy simplicity.

25

well-invented, well-falsified world, how unwillingly willing science loves error because, being alive, – it loves life!

25

After such a joyful entrance, there is a serious word that I want heard; it is intended for those who are most serious. Stand tall, you philosophers and friends of knowledge, and beware of martyrdom! Of suffering "for the sake of truth"! Even of defending yourselves! You will ruin the innocence and fine objectivity of your conscience, you will be stubborn towards objections and red rags, you will become stupid, brutish, bullish if, while fighting against danger, viciousness, suspicion, ostracism, and even nastier consequences of animosity, you also have to pose as the worldwide defenders of truth. As if "the Truth" were such a harmless and bungling little thing that she needed defenders! And you of all people, her Knights of the Most Sorrowful Countenance,[3] my Lord Slacker and Lord Webweaver of the Spirit! In the end, you know very well that it does not matter whether *you*, of all people, are proved right, and furthermore, that no philosopher so far has *ever* been proved right. You also know that every little question-mark you put after your special slogans and favorite doctrines (and occasionally after yourselves) might contain more truth than all the solemn gestures and trump cards laid before accusers and courts of law! So step aside instead! Run away and hide! And be sure to have your masks and your finesse so people will mistake you for something else, or be a bit scared of you! And do not forget the garden, the garden with golden trelliswork! And have people around you who are like a garden, – or like music over the waters when evening sets and the day is just a memory. Choose the *good* solitude, the free, high-spirited, light-hearted solitude that, in some sense, gives you the right to stay good yourself! How poisonous, how cunning, how bad you become in every long war that cannot be waged out in the open! How *personal* you become when you have been afraid for a long time, keeping your eye on enemies, on possible enemies! These outcasts of society (the long-persecuted, the badly harassed, as well as those forced to become hermits, the Spinozas or Giordano Brunos): they may work under a spiritual guise, and might not even know what they are doing, but they will always end up subtly seeking

3 A reference to Miguel de Cervantes' *Don Quixote* (1615).

vengeance and mixing their poisons (just try digging up the foundation of Spinoza's ethics and theology!). Not to mention the absurd spectacle of moral indignation, which is an unmistakable sign that a philosopher has lost his philosophical sense of humor. The philosopher's martyrdom, his "self-sacrifice for the truth," brings to light the agitator and actor in him; and since we have only ever regarded him with artistic curiosity, it is easy to understand the dangerous wish to see many of these philosophers in their degeneration for once (degenerated into "martyrs" or loud-mouths on their stage or soap-box). It's just that, with this sort of wish we have to be clear about *what* we will be seeing: – only a satyr-play, only a satirical epilogue, only the continuing proof that the long, real tragedy *has come to an end* (assuming that every philosophy was originally a long tragedy –).

26

Every choice human being strives instinctively for a citadel and secrecy where he is *rescued* from the crowds, the many, the vast majority; where, as the exception, he can forget the human norm. The only exception is when he is driven straight towards this norm by an even stronger instinct, in search of knowledge in the great and exceptional sense. Anybody who, in dealing with people, does not occasionally glisten in all the shades of distress, green and gray with disgust, weariness, pity, gloominess, and loneliness – he is certainly not a person of higher taste. But if he does not freely take on all this effort and pain, if he keeps avoiding it and remains, as I said, placid and proud and hidden in his citadel, well then one thing is certain: he is not made for knowledge, not predestined for it. Because if he were, he would eventually have to say to himself: "To hell with good taste! The norm is more interesting than the exception – than me, the exception!" – and he would wend his way *downwards*, and, above all, "inwards." The long and serious study of the *average* man requires a great deal of disguise, self-overcoming, confidentiality, bad company (all company is bad company except with your equals); still, this is all a necessary part of the life story of every philosopher, perhaps the least pleasant, most foul-smelling part and the one richest in disappointments. But if he is lucky, as befits knowledge's child of fortune, the philosopher will find real shortcuts and aids to make his work easier. I mean he will find so-called cynics – people who easily recognize the animal, the commonplace, the "norm" within themselves, and yet still have a degree of spiritedness and an urge to talk about themselves and their peers *in front of witnesses:* – sometimes they even wallow in books as if in their own filth. Cynicism is the only form in which base souls touch upon that thing which is genuine honesty. And the higher man needs to open his ears to all cynicism, crude or refined, and congratulate himself every time the buffoon speaks up without shame, or the scientific satyr is heard right in front of him. There are even cases where enchantment mixes with disgust: namely, where genius, by a whim of nature, is tied to some indiscreet billy-goat and ape, like the Abbé Galiani, the most profound, discerning, and perhaps also the filthiest man of his century. He was much more profound than Voltaire, and consequently a lot quieter. But, as I have already suggested, what happens more often is that the scientific head is placed on an ape's body, a more subtle and exceptional understanding is put in a base soul. This is not a rare phenomenon, particularly among physicians and phys-iologists of morals. And wherever even one person is speaking about man without any bitterness but instead quite innocuously, describing him as a stomach with dual needs and a head with one; wherever someone sees and seeks and *wants* to see only hunger, sex-drive and vanity, as if these were the sole and genuine motivating forces of human action; in short, wherever somebody is speaking "badly" of people – and not even *wickedly* – this is where the lover of knowledge should listen with subtle and studious atten-tion. He should keep his ears open wherever people are speaking without anger. Because the angry man, and anyone who is constantly tearing and shredding himself with his own teeth (or, in place of himself, the world, or God, or society), may very well stand higher than the laughing and self-satisfied satyr, considered morally. But considered in any other way, he is the more ordinary, more indifferent, less instructive case. And nobody *lies* as much as the angry man. –

27

It is hard to be understood, particularly when you think and live *gangasro-togati*[4] among people who think and live differently, namely *kurmagati*[5] or at best "walking like frogs," *mandeikagati* (am I doing everything I can to be hard to understand myself?), and you should give heartfelt thanks for

---

[4] Sanskrit for "as the current of the [river] Ganges moves."

[5] Sanskrit for "as the tortoise moves."

the goodwill apparent in any subtlety of interpretation. But as far as "good friends" are concerned, they are always too easy-going and think that they have a right to be easy-going, just because they are friends. So it is best to grant them some leeway from the very start, and leave some latitude for misunderstandings: – and then you can even laugh. Or, alternatively, get rid of them altogether, these good friends, – and then laugh some more!

28

The hardest thing to translate from one language into another is the tempo of its style, which is grounded in the character of the race, or – to be more physiological – in the average tempo of its "metabolism." There are well-meaning interpretations that are practically falsifications; they involuntarily debase the original, simply because it has a tempo that cannot be translated – a tempo that is brave and cheerful and leaps over and out of every danger in things and in words. Germans are almost incapable of a *presto* in their language: and so it is easy to see that they are incapable of many of the most delightful and daring nuances of free, free-spirited thought. Since the *buffo* and the satyr are alien to the German in body and in conscience, Aristophanes and Petronius are as good as untranslatable. Everything ponderous, lumbering, solemnly awkward, every long-winded and boring type of style is developed by the Germans in over-abundant diversity. Forgive me for pointing out that even Goethe's prose, with its mixture of the stiff and the delicate, is no exception; it is both a reflection of the "good old days" to which it belonged and an expression of the German taste back when there still was a "German taste": it was a Rococo taste, in *moribus et artibus*.[6] Lessing is an exception, thanks to his actor's nature that understood and excelled at so much. He was not the translator of Bayle for nothing; he gladly took refuge in the company of Diderot and Voltaire, and still more gladly among the Roman writers of comedy. Even in tempo, Lessing loved free-thinking[7] and the escape from Germany. But how could the German language – even in the prose of a Lessing – imitate Machiavelli's tempo – Machiavelli who, in his *Principe*,[8] lets us breathe the fine, dry air of Florence? He cannot help presenting the most serious concerns in a boisterous *allegrissimo*, and is, perhaps, not without

[6] In customs and arts.

[7] In German: *Freigeisterei*.

[8] *Il Principe* (*The Prince*) (1532).

a malicious, artistic sense for the contrast he is risking: thoughts that are long, hard, tough, and dangerous, and a galloping tempo and the very best and most mischievous mood. Who, finally, would dare to translate Petronius into German, a man who, more than any great musician so far, was the master of the *presto* in inventions, ideas, and words. What do all the swamps of the sick and wicked world – even the "ancient world" – matter in the end for someone like him, with feet of wind, with the breath and the force and the liberating scorn of a wind that makes everything healthy by making everything *run*! And as for Aristophanes, that transfiguring, complementary spirit for whose sake we can *forgive* the whole Greek world for existing (as long as we have realized in full depth and profundity *what* needs to be forgiven and transfigured here): – nothing I know has given me a better vision of *Plato's* secrecy and Sphinx nature than that happily preserved *petit fait*:[9] under the pillow of his deathbed they did not find a "Bible" or anything Egyptian, Pythagorean, or Platonic – but instead, Aristophanes. How would even a Plato have endured life – a Greek life that he said No to – without an Aristophanes! –

29

Independence is an issue that concerns very few people: – it is a prerogative of the strong. And even when somebody has every right to be independent, if he attempts such a thing without *having* to do so, he proves that he is probably not only strong, but brave to the point of madness. He enters a labyrinth, he multiplies by a thousand the dangers already inherent in the very act of living, not the least of which is the fact that no one with eyes will see how and where he gets lost and lonely and is torn limb from limb by some cave-Minotaur of conscience. And assuming a man like this is destroyed, it is an event so far from human comprehension that people do not feel it or feel for him: – and he cannot go back again! He cannot go back to their pity again! – –

30

Our highest insights must – and should! – sound like stupidities, or possibly crimes, when they come without permission to people whose ears have

---

9 Little fact.

no affinity[10] for them and were not predestined for them. The distinction between the exoteric and the esoteric, once made by philosophers, was found among the Indians as well as among Greeks, Persians, and Muslims. Basically, it was found everywhere that people believed in an order of rank and *not* in equality and equal rights. The difference between these terms is not that the exoteric stands outside and sees, values, measures, and judges from this external position rather than from some internal one. What is more essential is that the exoteric sees things up from below – while the esoteric sees them *down from above!* There are heights of the soul from whose vantage point even tragedy stops having tragic effects; and who would dare to decide whether the collective sight of the world's many woes would *necessarily* compel and seduce us into a feeling of pity, a feeling that would only serve to double these woes? . . . What helps feed or nourish the higher type of man must be almost poisonous to a very different and lesser type. The virtues of a base man could indicate vices and weaknesses in a philosopher. If a higher type of man were to degenerate[11] and be destroyed, this very destruction could give him the qualities needed to make people honor him as a saint down in the lower realm where he has sunk. There are books that have inverse values for soul and for health, depending on whether they are used by the lower souls and lowlier life-forces, or by the higher and more powerful ones. In the first case, these books are dangerous and cause deterioration and dissolution; in the second case, they are the heralds' calls that summon the most courageous to *their* courage. Books for the general public always smell foul: the stench of petty people clings to them. It usually stinks in places where the people eat and drink, even where they worship. You should not go to church if you want to breath *clean* air. – –

31

When people are young, they admire and despise without any of that art of nuance which is life's greatest reward; so it is only fair that they will come to pay dearly for having assaulted people and things like this, with a Yes and a No. Everything is set up so that the worst possible taste, the

---

[10] In German: *nicht dafür geartet.* The term *geartet* is related to the German word *Art* (type), which appears frequently in this section as well as throughout the text.

[11] In German: *dass er entartete.*

taste for the unconditional, gets cruelly and foolishly abused until people learn to put some art into their feelings, and prefer the risk they run with artifice, just like real artists of life do. It seems as if the wrath and reverence that characterize youth will not rest easy until they have falsified people and things thoroughly enough to be able to vent themselves on these targets. Youth is itself intrinsically falsifying and deceitful. Later, after the young soul has been tortured by constant disappointments, it ends up turning suspiciously on itself, still raging and wild, even in the force of its suspicion and the pangs of its conscience. How furious it is with itself now, how impatiently it tears itself apart, what revenge it exacts for having blinded itself for so long, as if its blindness had been voluntary! In this transitional state, we punish ourselves by distrusting our feelings, we torture our enthusiasm with doubts, we experience even a good conscience as a danger, as if it were a veil wrapped around us, something marking the depletion of a more subtle, genuine honesty. And, above all, we become partisan, partisan on principle *against* "youth." – A decade later, we realize that all this – was youthfulness too!

32

During the longest epoch of human history (which is called the prehistoric age) an action's value or lack of value was derived from its consequences; the action itself was taken as little into account as its origin. Instead, the situation was something like that of present-day China, where the honor or dishonor of a child reflects back on the parents. In the same way, it was the retroactive force of success or failure that showed people whether to think of an action as good or bad. We can call this period the *pre-moral* period of humanity. At that point, the imperative "know thyself!" was still unknown. By contrast, over the course of the last ten millennia, people across a large part of the earth have gradually come far enough to see the origin, not the consequence, as decisive for the value of an action. By and large, this was a great event, a considerable refinement of outlook and criterion, an unconscious after-effect of the dominance of aristocratic values and the belief in "origin," and the sign of a period that we can signify as *moral* in a narrow sense. This marks the first attempt at self-knowledge. Origin rather than consequence: what a reversal of perspective! And, certainly, this reversal was only accomplished after long struggles and fluctuations! Granted: this meant that a disastrous

new superstition, a distinctive narrowness of interpretation gained dominance. The origin of the action was interpreted in the most determinate
sense possible, as origin out of an *intention*. People were united in the belief that the value of an action was exhausted by the value of its intention.
Intention as the entire origin and prehistory of an action: under this prejudice people have issued moral praise, censure, judgment, and philosophy almost to this day. – But today, thanks to a renewed self-contemplation
and deepening of humanity, shouldn't we be facing a renewed necessity
to effect a reversal and fundamental displacement of values? Shouldn't
we be standing on the threshold of a period that would be designated,
negatively at first, as *extra-moral*? Today, when we immoralists, at least,
suspect that the decisive value is conferred by what is specifically *unin-
tentional* about an action, and that all its intentionality, everything about
it that can be seen, known, or raised to "conscious awareness," only belongs to its surface and skin – which, like every skin, reveals something
but *conceals* even more? In short, we believe that the intention is only a
sign and symptom that first needs to be interpreted, and that, moreover,
it is a sign that means too many things and consequently means almost
nothing by itself. We believe that morality in the sense it has had up to now
(the morality of intentions) was a prejudice, a precipitousness, perhaps
a preliminary, a thing on about the same level as astrology and alchemy,
but in any case something that must be overcome. The overcoming of
morality – even the self-overcoming of morality, in a certain sense: let this
be the name for that long and secret labor which is reserved for the most
subtle, genuinely honest, and also the most malicious consciences of the
day, who are living touchstones of the soul. –

33

There is nothing else to be done: the feelings of utter devotion, of sacrifice
for your neighbor, and the entire morality of self-abnegation have to
be mercilessly taken to court and made to account for themselves. And
the same holds for the aesthetic of "disinterested contemplation," the
seductive guise under which the castration of art is presently trying to
create a good conscience for itself. These feelings of "for others," of
"*not* for myself," contain far too much sugar and sorcery for us not to
need to become doubly suspicious here and ask: "Aren't these perhaps –
seductions?" To say that these feelings are *pleasing* (for the one who has

them, for the one who enjoys their fruits, and even for the mere onlooker) is not yet an argument in their *favor*, but rather constitutes a demand for caution. So let us be cautious!

34

It does not matter what philosophical standpoint you might take these days: any way you look at it, the *erroneousness* of the world we think we live in is the most certain and solid fact that our eyes can still grab hold of. We find reason after reason for it, reasons that might lure us into speculations about a deceptive principle in "the essence of things." But anyone who makes thinking itself (and therefore "the spirit") responsible for the falseness of the world (an honorable way out, taken by every conscious or unconscious *advocatus dei*[12]), anyone who considers this world, together with space, time, form, and motion, to be falsely *inferred* – such a person would at the very least have ample cause to grow suspicious of thinking altogether. Hasn't it played the biggest joke on us to date? And what guarantee would there be that it wouldn't keep doing what it has always done? In all seriousness, there is something touching and awe-inspiring about the innocence that, to this day, lets a thinker place himself in front of consciousness with the request that it please give him *honest* answers: for example, whether or not it is "real," and why it so resolutely keeps the external world at arm's length, and other questions like that. The belief in "immediate certainties" is a moral naiveté that does credit to us philosophers: but – we should stop being "merely moral," for once! Aside from morality, the belief in immediate certainties is a stupidity that does us little credit! In bourgeois life, a suspicious disposition might be a sign of "bad character" and consequently considered unwise. But here with us, beyond the bourgeois sphere with its Yeses and Noes, – what is to stop us from being unwise and saying: "As the creature who has been the biggest dupe the earth has ever seen, the philosopher pretty much has a *right* to a 'bad character.' It is his *duty* to be suspicious these days, to squint as maliciously as possible out of every abyss of mistrust." – Forgive me for playing jokes with this gloomy grimace and expression: because when it comes to betrayal and being betrayed, I myself learned a long time ago to think differently and evaluate differently; and my elbow is ready with at

[12] Advocate of God (as opposed to the devil's advocate).

least a couple of nudges for the blind rage of philosophers as they struggle not to be betrayed. Why *not*? It is no more than a moral prejudice that the truth is worth more than appearance; in fact, it is the world's most poorly proven assumption. Let us admit this much: that life could not exist except on the basis of perspectival valuations and appearances; and if, with the virtuous enthusiasm and inanity of many philosophers, someone wanted to completely abolish the "world of appearances," – well, assuming *you* could do that, – at least there would not be any of your "truth" left either! Actually, why do we even assume that "true" and "false" are intrinsically opposed? Isn't it enough to assume that there are levels of appearance and, as it were, lighter and darker shades and tones of appearance – different *valeurs*,[13] to use the language of painters? Why shouldn't the world *that is relevant to us* – be a fiction? And if someone asks: "But doesn't fiction belong with an author?" – couldn't we shoot back: "*Why?* Doesn't this 'belonging' belong, perhaps, to fiction as well? Aren't we allowed to be a bit ironic with the subject, as we are with the predicate and object? Shouldn't philosophers rise above the belief in grammar? With all due respect to governesses, isn't it about time philosophy renounced governess-beliefs?" –

35

O Voltaire! O humanity! O nonsense! There is something to "truth," to the *search* for truth; and when a human being is too humane about it – when "*il ne cherche le vrai que pour faire le bien*"[14] – I bet he won't find anything!

36

Assuming that our world of desires and passions is the only thing "given" as real, that we cannot get down or up to any "reality" except the reality of our drives (since thinking is only a relation between these drives) – aren't we allowed to make the attempt and pose the question as to whether something like this "given" isn't *enough* to render the so-called mechanistic (and thus material) world comprehensible as well? I do not mean comprehensible as a deception, a "mere appearance," a "representation"

[13] Values.

[14] "He looks for truth only to do good."

(in the sense of Berkeley and Schopenhauer); I mean it might allow us to understand the mechanistic world as belonging to the same plane of reality as our affects themselves –, as a primitive form of the world of affect, where everything is contained in a powerful unity before branching off and organizing itself in the organic process (and, of course, being softened and weakened –). We would be able to understand the mechanistic world as a kind of life of the drives, where all the organic functions (self-regulation, assimilation, nutrition, excretion, and metabolism) are still synthetically bound together – as a *pre-form* of life? – In the end, we are not only allowed to make such an attempt: the conscience of *method* demands it. Multiple varieties of causation should not be postulated until the attempt to make do with a single one has been taken as far as it will go (– *ad absurdum*, if you will). This is a moral of method that cannot be escaped these days; – it follows "from the definition," as a mathematician would say. The question is ultimately whether we recognize the will as, in effect, *efficacious*, whether we believe in the causality of the will. If we do (and *this* belief is really just our belief in causality itself –), then we *must* make the attempt to hypothetically posit the causality of the will as the only type of causality there is. "Will" can naturally have effects only on "will" – and not on "matter" (not on "nerves" for instance –). Enough: we must venture the hypothesis that everywhere "effects" are recognized, will is effecting will – and that every mechanistic event in which a force is active is really a force and effect of the will. – Assuming, finally, that we succeeded in explaining our entire life of drives as the organization and outgrowth of one basic form of will (namely, of the will to power, which is *my* claim); assuming we could trace all organic functions back to this will to power and find that it even solved the problem of procreation and nutrition (which is a single problem); then we will have earned the right to clearly designate *all* efficacious force as: *will to power*. The world seen from inside, the world determined and described with respect to its "intelligible character" – would be just this "will to power" and nothing else. –

37

"What? Doesn't that mean, to use a popular idiom: God is refuted but the devil is not – ?" On the contrary! On the contrary, my friends! And who the devil is forcing you to use popular idioms! –

38

This is what has finally happened, in the bright light of more recent times, to the French Revolution, that gruesome and (on close consideration) pointless farce: noble and enthusiastic spectators across Europe have, from a distance, interpreted their own indignations and enthusiasms into it, and for so long and with such passion *that the text has finally disappeared under the interpretation.* In the same way, a noble posterity could again misunderstand the entire past, and in so doing, perhaps, begin to make it tolerable to look at. – Or rather: hasn't this happened already? weren't we ourselves this "noble posterity"? And right now, since we're realizing this to be the case – hasn't it stopped being so?

39

No one would consider a doctrine to be true just because it makes people happy or virtuous, with the possible exception of the darling "Idealists," who wax enthusiastic over the Good, the True, and the Beautiful, and let all sorts of colorful, clumsy, and good-natured *desiderata* swim through their pond in utter confusion. Happiness and virtue are not arguments. But we like to forget (even thoughtful spirits like to forget) that being made unhappy and evil are not counter-arguments either. Something could be true even if it is harmful and dangerous to the highest degree. It could even be part of the fundamental character of existence that people with complete knowledge get destroyed, – so that the strength of a spirit would be proportionate to how much of the "truth" he could withstand – or, to put it more clearly, to what extent he *needs* it to be thinned out, veiled over, sweetened up, dumbed down, and lied about. But there is no doubt that when it comes to discovering certain *aspects* of the truth, people who are evil and unhappy are more fortunate and have a greater probability of success (not to mention those who are both evil and happy – a species that the moralists don't discuss). Perhaps harshness and cunning provide more favorable conditions for the origin of the strong, independent spirit and philosopher than that gentle, fine, yielding good nature and art of taking things lightly that people value, and value rightly, in a scholar. Assuming first of all that we do not limit our notion of the "philosopher" to the philosophers who write books – or put *their own* philosophy into books! – One last feature for the picture of the free-spirited philosopher is provided by Stendhal; and for the sake of the German taste, I will not overlook the chance to underscore this character – since it goes *against* the German taste. "*Pour être bon philosophe*," says this last, great psychologist, "*il faut être sec, clair, sans illusion. Un banquier, qui a fait fortune, a une partie du caractère requis pour faire des découvertes en philosophie, c'est-à-dire pour voir clair dans ce qui est.*"[15]

40

Everything profound loves masks; the most profound things go so far as to hate images and likenesses. Wouldn't just the *opposite* be a proper disguise for the shame of a god? A questionable question: it would be odd if some mystic hadn't already risked something similar himself. There are events that are so delicate that it is best to cover them up with some coarseness and make them unrecognizable. There are acts of love and extravagant generosity in whose aftermath nothing is more advisable than to take a stick and give the eye-witnesses a good beating: this will obscure any memory traces. Many people are excellent at obscuring and abusing their own memory, so they can take revenge on at least this one accessory: – shame is highly resourceful. It is not the worst things that we are the most ashamed of. Malicious cunning is not the only thing behind a mask – there is so much goodness in cunning. I could imagine that a man with something precious and vulnerable to hide would roll through life, rough and round like an old, green, heavy-hooped wine cask; the subtlety of his shame will want it this way. A man with something profound in his shame encounters even his fate and delicate decisions along paths that few people have ever found, paths whose existence must be concealed from his closest and most trusted friends. His mortal danger is hidden from their eyes, and so is his regained sense of confidence in life. Somebody hidden in this way – who instinctively needs speech in order to be silent and concealed, and is tireless in evading communication – *wants* and encourages a mask of himself to wander around, in his place, through the hearts and heads of his friends. And even if this is not what he wants, he will eventually realize that a mask of him has been there all the same, – and that this is for the best.

---

[15] "To be a good philosopher you have to be dry, clear, and without illusions. A banker who has made a fortune has to a certain degree the right sort of character for making philosophical discoveries, i.e. for seeing clearly into what is." From Stendhal's *Correspondance inédite* (*Unedited Correspondence*) (1855).

Every profound spirit needs a mask: what's more, a mask is constantly growing around every profound spirit, thanks to the consistently false (which is to say *shallow*) interpretation of every word, every step, every sign of life he displays. –

41

We have to test ourselves to see whether we are destined for independence and command, and we have to do it at the right time. We should not sidestep our tests, even though they may well be the most dangerous game we can play, and, in the last analysis, can be witnessed by no judge other than ourselves. Not to be stuck to any person, not even somebody we love best – every person is a prison and a corner. Not to be stuck in any homeland, even the neediest and most oppressed – it is not as hard to tear your heart away from a victorious homeland. Not to be stuck in some pity: even for higher men, whose rare torture and helplessness we ourselves have accidentally glimpsed. Not to be stuck in some field of study: however much it tempts us with priceless discoveries, reserved, it seems, for us alone. Not to be stuck in our own detachment, in the ecstasy of those foreign vistas where birds keep flying higher so that they can keep seeing more below them: – the danger of those who fly. Not to be stuck to our own virtues and let our whole self be sacrificed for some one of our details, our "hospitality," for instance: this is the danger of dangers for rich souls of a higher type, who spend themselves extravagantly, almost indifferently, pushing the virtue of liberality to the point of vice. We must know *to conserve ourselves*: the greatest test of independence.

42

A new breed of philosophers is approaching. I will risk christening them with a name not lacking in dangers. From what I can guess about them, from what they allow to be guessed (since it is typical of them to *want* to remain riddles in some respect), these philosophers of the future might have the right (and perhaps also the wrong) to be described as *those who attempt*.[16] Ultimately, this name is itself only an attempt, and, if you will, a temptation.

[16] In German: *Versucher*. Nietzsche frequently uses the terms *Versuch* (attempt or experiment) and *Versuchung* (temptation), and plays on their similarity.

43

Are they new friends of "truth," these upcoming philosophers? Probably, since all philosophers so far have loved their truths. But they certainly will not be dogmatists. It would offend their pride, as well as their taste, if their truth were a truth for everyone (which has been the secret wish and hidden meaning of all dogmatic aspirations so far). "My judgment is *my* judgment: other people don't have an obvious right to it too" – perhaps this is what such a philosopher of the future will say. We must do away with the bad taste of wanting to be in agreement with the majority. "Good" is no longer good when it comes from your neighbor's mouth. And how could there ever be a "common good"! The term is self-contradictory: whatever can be common will never have much value. In the end, it has to be as it is and has always been: great things are left for the great, abysses for the profound, delicacy and trembling for the subtle, and, all in all, everything rare for those who are rare themselves. –

44

After all this, do I really need to add that they will be free, *very* free spirits, these philosophers of the future – and that they certainly will not *just* be free spirits, but rather something more, higher, greater, and funda-mentally different, something that does not want to be misunderstood or mistaken for anything else? But, in saying this, I feel – towards them almost as much as towards ourselves (who are their heralds and precursors, we free spirits!) – an *obligation* to sweep away a stupid old prejudice and misunderstanding about all of us that has hung like a fog around the concept of the "free spirit" for far too long, leaving it completely opaque. In all the countries of Europe, and in America as well, there is now something that abuses this name: a very narrow, restricted, chained-up type of spirit whose inclinations are pretty much the opposite of our own intentions and instincts (not to mention the fact that this restricted type will be a fully shut window and bolted door with respect to these approaching *new* philosophers). In a word (but a bad one): they belong to the *levelers*, these misnamed "free spirits" – as eloquent and prolifically scribbling slaves of the democratic taste and its "modern ideas." They are all people without solitude, without their own solitude, clumsy, solid folks whose courage and honest decency cannot be denied – it's just that they are un-free and ridiculously superficial, particularly given their basic tendency to think that *all* human misery and wrongdoing is caused by traditional social structures: which lands truth happily on its head! What they want to strive for with all their might is the universal, green pasture happiness of the herd, with security, safety, contentment, and an easier life for all. Their two most well-sung songs and doctrines are called: "equal rights" and "sympathy for all that suffers" – and they view suffering itself as something that needs to be *abolished*. We, who are quite the reverse, have kept an *eye* and a conscience open to the question of where and how the plant "man" has grown the strongest, and we think that this has always happened under conditions that are quite the reverse. We think that the danger of the human condition has first had to grow to terrible heights, its power to invent and dissimulate (its "spirit" –) has had to develop under prolonged pressure and compulsion into something refined and daring, its life-will has had to be intensified to an unconditional power-will. We think that harshness, violence, slavery, danger in the streets and in the heart, concealment, Stoicism, the art of experiment,[17] and devilry of every sort; that everything evil, terrible, tyrannical, predatory, and snakelike in humanity serves just as well as its opposite to enhance the species "humanity." But to say this much is to not say enough, and, in any event, this is the point we have reached with our speaking and our silence, at the *other* end of all modern ideology and herd desires: perhaps as their antipodes? Is it any wonder that we "free spirits" are not exactly the most communicative spirits? That we do not want to fully reveal what a spirit might free himself *from* and what he will then perhaps be driven *towards*? And as to the dangerous formula "beyond good and evil," it serves to protect us, at least from being mistaken for something else. We *are* something different from "*libres-penseurs*," "*liberi pensatori*," "*Freidenker*"[18] and whatever else all these sturdy advocates of "modern ideas" like to call themselves. At home in many countries of the spirit, at least as guests; repeatedly slipping away from the musty, comfortable corners where preference and prejudice, youth, origin, accidents of people and books, and even the fatigue of traveling seem to have driven us; full of malice at the lures of dependency that lie hidden in honors, or money, or duties, or enthusiasms of the senses; grateful even for difficulties and inconstant health, because they have always freed us from some rule and

---

[17] In German: *Versucherkunst* (see note 16 above).

[18] These are terms meaning "free thinker" in French, Italian, and German.

its "prejudice," grateful to the god, devil, sheep, and maggot in us, curious to a fault, researchers to the point of cruelty, with unmindful fingers for the incomprehensible, with teeth and stomachs for the indigestible, ready for any trade that requires a quick wit and sharp senses, ready for any risk, thanks to an excess of "free will," with front and back souls whose ultimate aim is clear to nobody, with fore- and backgrounds that no foot can fully traverse, hidden under the cloak of light, conquerors, even if we look like heirs and prodigals, collectors and gatherers from morning until evening, miserly with our riches and our cabinets filled to the brim, economical with what we learn and forget, inventive in schemata, sometimes proud of tables of categories, sometimes pedants, sometimes night owls at work, even in bright daylight; yes, even scarecrows when the need arises – and today the need has arisen: inasmuch as we are born, sworn, jealous friends of *solitude*, our own deepest, most midnightly, noon-likely solitude. This is the type of people we are, we free spirits! and perhaps *you* are something of this yourselves, you who are approaching? you *new* philosophers? –

Part 3   The religious character

45

[handwritten: Time line of Endless humanity? Possibilities?]

The human soul and its limits, the scope of human inner experience to date, the heights, depths, and range of these experiences, the entire history of the soul *so far* and its still unexhausted possibilities: these are the predestined hunting grounds for a born psychologist and lover of the "great hunt." But how often does he have to turn to himself in despair and say: "Only one! only a single one! and this huge forest, this primeval forest!" And then he wishes he had a few hundred hunting aides and well-trained bloodhounds he could drive into the history of the human soul to round up *his* game. To no avail: time and again he gets an ample and bitter reminder of how hard it is to find hounds and helpers for the very things that prick his curiosity. The problem with sending scholars into new and dangerous hunting grounds, where courage, intelligence, and subtlety in every sense are needed, is that they stop being useful the very moment the "*great* hunt" (but also the great danger) begins: – this is just when they lose their sharp eye and keen nose. For instance, it might take somebody who is himself as deep, as wounded, and as monstrous as Pascal's intellectual conscience to figure out the sort of history that the problem of *science and conscience* has had in the soul of *homines religiosi*[1] so far. And, even then, such a person would still need that vaulting sky of bright, malicious spirituality from whose heights this throng of dangerous and painful experiences could be surveyed, ordered, and forced into formulas. – But who would do me this service! But who would have the time to wait for such servants! – it is clear that they grow too rarely; they are so

[1] Religious people.

43

unlikely in every age! In the end, you have to do everything *yourself* if you want to know anything: which means you have *a lot* to do! – But a curiosity like mine is still the most pleasant vice of all; – oh sorry! I meant to say: the love of truth finds its reward in heaven and even on earth. –

possibility of heaven?

46

The sort of faith demanded (and often achieved) by early Christianity in the middle of a skeptical, southern, free-spirited world, a world that had century-long struggles between schools of philosophy behind and inside it, not to mention the education in tolerance given by the *imperium Romanum*[2] – this faith is *not* the simple, rude, peon's faith with which a Luther or a Cromwell or some other northern barbarian of the spirit clung to its God and its Christianity. It is much closer to Pascal's faith, which has the gruesome appearance of a protracted suicide of reason – a tough, long-lived, worm–like reason that cannot be killed all at once and with a single stroke. From the beginning, Christian faith has been sacrifice: sacrifice of all freedom, of all pride, of all self–confidence of the spirit; it is simultaneously enslavement and self–derision, self–mutilation. There is cruelty and religious Phoenicianism in this faith, which is expected of a worn–down, many–sided, badly spoiled conscience. Its presupposition is that the subjugation of spirit *causes indescribable pain*, and that the entire past and all the habits of such a spirit resist the *absurdissimum*[3] presented to it as "faith." Obtuse to all Christian terminology, modern people can no longer relate to the hideous superlative found by an ancient taste in the paradoxical formula "god on the cross." Nowhere to date has there been such a bold inversion or anything quite as horrible, questioning, and questionable as this formula. It promised a revaluation of all the values of antiquity. – This was the revenge of the Orient, the *deep* Orient, this was the revenge of the oriental slave on Rome with its noble and frivolous tolerance, on Roman "Catholicity" of faith. And what infuriated the slaves about and against their masters was never faith itself, but rather the freedom from faith, that half-stoic and smiling nonchalance when it came to the seriousness of faith. Enlightenment is infuriating. Slaves want the unconditional;

sacrifice of intellect

tribute to the power of Christianity

[2] Roman Empire.

[3] Height of absurdity.

they understand only tyranny, even in morality. They love as they hate, without nuance, into the depths, to the point of pain and sickness – their copious, *hidden* suffering makes them furious at the noble taste that seems to *deny* suffering. [Skepticism about suffering (which is basically just an affectation of aristocratic morality) played no small role in the genesis of the last great slave revolt, which began with the French Revolution]

47

Wherever the religious neurosis has appeared so far, we find it connected with three dangerous dietary prescriptions: solitude, fasting, and sexual abstinence, – but without being able to say for sure which is the cause and which is the effect and *whether* in fact there is a causal relation at all. This last doubt seems justified by the fact that another one of the most regular symptoms of the religious neurosis, in both wild and tame peoples, is the most sudden and dissipated display of voluptuousness, which then turns just as suddenly into spasms of repentance and negations of the world and will: perhaps both can be interpreted as epilepsy in disguise? But here is where interpretation must be resisted the most: no type to date has been surrounded by such an overgrowth of inanity and superstition; and none so far has seemed to hold more interest for people, or even for philosophers. It might be time to calm down a bit, as far as this topic goes, to learn some caution, or even better: to look away, *to go away*. – This gruesome question-mark of religious crisis and awakening still stands in the background of the newest arrival in philosophy (which is to say: the Schopenhauerian philosophy), almost as the problem in itself. How is negation of the will *possible*? How is the saint possible? This really seems to have been the question that started Schopenhauer off and made him into a philosopher. And so it was a true Schopenhauerian consequence that his most devoted follower (and perhaps also his last, as far as Germany was concerned –), namely Richard Wagner, finished his own life's work at this very point, and finally brought to the stage the life and times of that awful and eternal type in the character of Kundry, *type vécu*.[4] And, at the same time, psychiatrists in almost every European country had the opportunity to study this type up close, wherever the religious neurosis – or, as I call it, "the religious character" – was having its latest epidemic outbreak and

---

[4] A type that has lived. Kundry is a character from Wagner's last opera, *Parsifal*.

pageant as the "Salvation Army." – But if someone asks what it really was in the whole phenomenon of the saint that caused such inordinate interest among people of all kinds in all ages, and even among philosophers, it was undoubtedly the aura of a miracle that clung to it; it displayed the immediate *succession of opposites*, of antithetically valorized moral states of soul. It seemed palpable that here was a "bad man" turning suddenly into a good man, a "saint." Psychology to date has been shipwrecked on this spot. Wasn't this primarily because it had put itself under the dominance of morality, because it actually *believed* in opposing moral values, and saw, read, and *interpreted* these opposites into texts *and* into facts? – What? So "miracles" are just errors of interpretation? A lack of philology? –

48

The Latin races seem to have much more of an affinity to their Catholicism than we northerners do to Christianity in general. Consequently, a lack of belief means something very different in Catholic countries than in Protestant ones. In Catholic countries it is a sort of anger *against* the spirit of the race, while with us it is more like a return *to* the spirit (or un-spirit –) of the race. There is no doubt that we northerners are descended from barbarian races, even as far as our talent for religion goes – it is a *meager* talent. The Celts are an exception, which is why they also furnished the best soil for the spread of the Christian infection to the north: – the Christian ideal came into bloom in France, at least as far as the pale northern sun would allow. Even these recent French skeptics, how strangely pious they strike our tastes, to the extent that there is some Celtic blood in their lineage! How Catholic, how un-German Auguste Comte's sociology smells to us, with its Roman logic of the instincts! How Jesuitical Sainte-Beuve is, that amiable and intelligent cicerone of Port-Royal, in spite of all his hostility towards the Jesuits! And especially Ernest Renan: how inaccessible the language of such as Renan sounds to us northerners, this man with a soul that is voluptuous (in a more refined sense) and inclined to rest quite comfortably, but is always being thrown off balance by some nothingness of religious tension! Let us repeat these beautiful sentences after him, – along with the sort of malice and arrogance that stirs in our souls in immediate reply, souls that are probably harsher and not nearly as beautiful, being German souls! – "*disons donc hardiment que la religion est un produit de l'homme normal, que l'homme est le plus dans le vrai quand il est le plus religieux et le plus assuré d'une destinée infinie . . . C'est quand il est bon qu'il veut que la vertu corresponde à un ordre éternel, c'est quand il contemple les choses d'une manière désintéressée qu'il trouve la mort révoltante et absurde. Comment ne pas supposer que c'est dans ces moments-là, que l'homme voit le mieux? . . ."*[5] These sentences are so utterly *antipodal* to my ears and habits that when I found them, my initial rage wrote *"la niaiserie religieuse par excellence!"*[6] next to them – until my final rage actually started to like them, these sentences whose truth is standing on its head! It is so elegant, so distinguished, to have your own antipodes!

their luxurious life? But still suffering

49

What is amazing about the religiosity of ancient Greeks is the excessive amount of gratitude that flows out from it: – it takes a very noble type of person to face nature and life like *this*! – Later, when the rabble gained prominence in Greece, religion became overgrown with *fear* as well, and Christianity was on the horizon. –

50

The passion for God: there is the peasant type, naive and presumptuous – like Luther. The whole of Protestantism is devoid of any southern *delicatezza*.[7] It has a certain oriental ecstasy, as when an undeserving slave has been pardoned or promoted – in Augustine, for example, who is offensively lacking any nobility of demeanor and desire. It has a certain womanly tenderness and lustfulness that pushes coyly and unsuspectingly towards a *unio mystica et physica*:[8] like Madame de Guyon. It often appears, strangely enough, as a disguise for the puberty of some girl or boy; now and then it even appears as the hysteria of an old maid, and her

---

[5] "So we strongly affirm that religion is a product of the normal man, that man is most in the right when he is most religious and most assured of an infinite destiny . . . It is when he is good that he wants virtue to correspond to an eternal order, it is when he contemplates things in a disinterested manner that he finds death revolting and absurd. How could we fail to suppose that these are the moments when man sees best?"

[6] Religious silliness *par excellence*.

[7] Delicacy.

[8] Mystical and physical union.

final ambition: – in such cases, the church often declares the woman to be a saint.

51

a new possibility for human soul : saint

To this day, the most powerful people have still bowed down in venera-tion before the saint, as the riddle of self–conquest and deliberate, final renunciation: why have they bowed down like this? They sensed a supe-rior force in the saint and, as it were, behind the question-mark of his frail and pathetic appearance, a force that wants to test itself through this sort of conquest. They sensed a strength of will in which they could recognize and honor their own strength and pleasure in domi-nation. When they honored the saint, they honored something in them-selves. Furthermore, the sight of the saint made them suspicious: "No one would desire such a monstrosity of negation, of anti-nature, for nothing," they said to (and asked of) themselves. "Perhaps there is a reason for it, perhaps the ascetic has inside information about some very great danger, thanks to his secret counselors and visitors?" Enough: in front of the saint, the powerful of the world learned a new fear, they sensed a new power, an alien, still unconquered enemy: – it was the "will to power" that made them stop in front of the saint. They had to ask him – – *saint : dominate self & own instincts*

52

The Jewish "Old Testament," the book of divine justice, has people, things, and speeches in such grand style that it is without parallel in the written works of Greece and India. We stand in horror and awe before this monstrous vestige of what humanity once was, and then reflect sadly on old Asia and its protruding little peninsula of Europe that desperately wants (over and against Asia) to stand for the "progress of humanity." Of course: there will be nothing in these ruins to astonish or distress anyone who is just a dull, tame, house pet himself, and understands only house pet needs (like educated people today, including the Christians of "educated" Christianity) – the taste for the Old Testament is a touchstone for the "great" and the "small." Perhaps he will still find the New Testament, the book of mercy, more to his liking (it is full of the proper, tender, musty stench of true believers and small souls). The fact that this New

Testament (which is a type of Rococo of taste in every respect) gets pasted together with the Old Testament to make a single book, a "Bible," a "book in itself": this is probably the greatest piece of temerity and "sin against the spirit" that literary Europe has on its conscience.

53

Why atheism today? God "the Father" has been thoroughly refuted; and so has "the Judge" and "the Reward-giver." The same for God's "free will": he doesn't listen, – and even if he did, he wouldn't know how to help anyway. The worst part of it is: he seems unable to communicate in an intelligible manner: is he unclear? – After hearing, questioning, discussing many things, these are the causes I have found for the decline of European theism. [It seems to me that the religious instinct is indeed growing vigorously – but that it rejects any specifically theistic gratification with profound distrust.]

Loss of trust with religion?

54

So what is really going on with the whole of modern philosophy? Since Descartes (and, in fact, in spite of him more than because of him) all the philosophers have been out to assassinate the old concept of the soul, under the guise of critiquing the concepts of subject and predicate. In other words, they have been out to assassinate the fundamental presupposition of the Christian doctrine. As a sort of epistemological skepticism, modern philosophy is, covertly or overtly, *anti-Christian* (although, to state the point for more subtle ears, by no means anti-religious). People used to believe in "the soul" as they believed in grammar and the grammatical subject: people said that "I" was a condition and "think" was a predicate and conditioned – thinking is an activity, and a subject *must* be thought of as its cause. Now, with admirable tenacity and cunning, people are wondering whether they can get out of this net – wondering whether the reverse might be true: that "think" is the condition and "I" is conditioned, in which case "I" would be a synthesis that only gets *produced* through thought itself. *Kant* essentially wanted to prove that the subject cannot be proven on the basis of the subject – and neither can the object. The possibility that the subject (and therefore "the soul") has a *merely apparent existence* might not always have been foreign to him, this thought that, in the form of the Vedanta philosophy, has already arisen on earth once before and with enormous power.

55

There is a great ladder of religious cruelty, and, of its many rungs, three are the most important. People used to make human sacrifices to their god, perhaps even sacrificing those they loved the best – this sort of phenomenon can be found in the sacrifice of the firstborn (a practice shared by all prehistoric religions), as well as in Emperor Tiberius' sacrifice in the Mithras grotto on the Isle of Capri, that most gruesome of all Roman anachronisms. Then, during the moral epoch of humanity, people sacrificed the strongest instincts they had, their "nature," to their god; the joy of *this* particular festival shines in the cruel eyes of the ascetic, that enthusiastic piece of "anti-nature." Finally: what was left to be sacrificed? In the end, didn't people have to sacrifice all comfort and hope, everything holy or healing, any faith in a hidden harmony or a future filled with justice and bliss? Didn't people have to sacrifice God himself and worship rocks, stupidity, gravity, fate, or nothingness out of sheer cruelty to themselves? To sacrifice God for nothingness – that paradoxical mystery of the final cruelty has been reserved for the race that is now approaching: by now we all know something about this. –

56

Anyone like me, who has tried for a long time and with some enigmatic desire, to think pessimism through to its depths and to deliver it from the half-Christian, half-German narrowness and naiveté with which it has finally presented itself to this century, namely in the form of the Schopenhauerian philosophy; anyone who has ever really looked with an Asiatic and supra-Asiatic eye into and down at the most world-negating of all possible ways of thinking – beyond good and evil, and no longer, like Schopenhauer and the Buddha, under the spell and delusion of morality –; anyone who has done these things (and perhaps precisely *by* doing these things) will have inadvertently opened his eyes to the inverse ideal: to the ideal of the most high-spirited, vital, world-affirming individual, who has learned not just to accept and go along with what was and what is, but who wants it again *just as it was and is* through all eternity, insatiably shouting *da capo*[9] not just to himself but to the whole play and performance, and not just to a performance, but rather, fundamentally, to the one who needs precisely this performance – and makes it necessary: because again and again he needs himself – and makes himself necessary. – – What? and that wouldn't be – *circulus vitiosus deus?*[10]

57

As humanity's spiritual vision and insight grows stronger, the distance and, as it were, the space that surrounds us increases as well; our world gets more profound, and new stars, new riddles and images are constantly coming into view. Perhaps everything the mind's eye has used to quicken its wit and deepen its understanding was really just a chance to practice, a piece of fun, something for children and childish people. Perhaps the day will come when the concepts of "God" and "sin," which are the most solemn concepts of all and have caused the most fighting and suffering, will seem no more important to us than a child's toy and a child's pain seem to an old man, – and perhaps "the old man" will then need another toy and another pain, – still enough of a child, an eternal child!

58

Has anyone really noticed the extent to which being outwardly idle or half-idle is necessary for a genuinely religious life (and for its favorite job of microscopic self-examination just as much as for that tender state of composure which calls itself "prayer" and is a constant readiness for the "coming of God")? – I mean an idleness with a good conscience, passed down over the ages, through the bloodline, an idleness that is not entirely alien to the aristocratic feeling that work *is disgraceful*, which is to say it makes the soul and the body into something base. And has anyone noticed that, consequently, it is the modern, noisy, time-consuming, self-satisfied, stupidly proud industriousness which, more than anything else, gives people an education and preparation in "un-belief"? For example, among those in Germany today who have distanced themselves from religion,

---

[9] From the beginning. In musical scores, this directs the performer to return to an earlier point in the piece and repeat what has already been played.

[10] God as a vicious circle.

I find representatives of various types and extractions of "free-thinking"; but, above all, a majority whose industriousness has, over generations, dissolved any religious instinct, so that they no longer know what religion is good for, and only register its presence in the world with a type of dull amazement. They feel they are already busy enough, these good people, whether it is with their businesses or their pleasures, not to mention the "fatherland" and the newspapers and "familial obligations." They do not seem to have any time to spare for religion, particularly when it is unclear to them whether it would be a new business or a new pleasure – "since people can't possibly be going to church just to spoil a good mood," they tell themselves. They are not enemies of religious customs; if circumstance (or the state) requires them to take part in such customs, they do what is required, like people tend to do –, and they do it with a patient and unassuming earnestness, without much in the way of curiosity or unease: they just live too far apart and outside to even think they need a For or Against in such matters. Today, most middle-class German Protestants are also among the ranks of the indifferent, particularly in the industrious large trade and transportation centers; the same is true for the majority of industrious scholars, and the whole university apparatus (except for the theologians, whose presence and possibility here gives the psychologist increasingly many and increasingly subtle riddles to resolve). People who are devout or even just church-goers will rarely imagine *how much* goodwill (or may be "whimsical will") is required for a German scholar to take the problem of religion seriously. On the basis of his whole craft (and, as mentioned before, on the basis of the craftsman-like industriousness his modern conscience commits him to), he tends to regard religion with an air of superior, almost gracious amusement, which is sometimes mixed with a slight contempt for what he assumes to be an "uncleanliness" of spirit that exists wherever anyone still supports the church. Only with the help of history (and therefore *not* on the basis of his personal experience) does the scholar succeed in approaching religion with a reverential seriousness and a certain cautious consideration. But even if he reaches the point where he feels grateful for religion, he does not come a single step closer to what still passes for church or piety: possibly even the reverse. The practical indifference towards religious matters with which he was born and raised tends, in his case, to be sublimated into a caution and cleanliness that shuns contact with religious people and religious affairs; and it can be the very depth of his tolerance and humanity that urges him to evade the subtle crises intrinsic to toleration itself. – Every age has its own, divine type of naiveté that other ages may envy; and how much naiveté – admirable, childish, boundlessly foolish naiveté – lies in the scholar's belief in his own superiority, in the good conscience he has of his tolerance, in the clueless, simple certainty with which he instinctively treats the religious man as an inferior, lesser type, something that he himself has grown out of, away from, and *above*, – he, who is himself a presumptuous little dwarf and rabble-man, a brisk and busy brain- and handiworker of "ideas," of "modern ideas"!

59

Anyone who has looked deeply into the world will probably guess the wisdom that lies in human superficiality. An instinct of preservation has taught people to be flighty, light, and false. We occasionally find both philosophers and artists engaging in a passionate and exaggerated worship of "pure forms." Let there be no doubt that anyone who *needs* the cult of the surface this badly has at some point reached *beneath* the surface with disastrous results. Perhaps there is even an order of rank for these wounded children, the born artists, who find pleasure in life only by intending to *falsify* its image, in a sort of prolonged revenge against life –. We can infer the degree to which life has been spoiled for them from the extent to which they want to see its image distorted, diluted, deified, and cast into the beyond – considered as artists, the *homines religiosi*[11] would belong to the *highest* rank. Entire millennia sink their teeth into a religious interpretation of existence, driven by a deep, suspicious fear of an incurable pessimism; this fear comes from an instinct which senses that we could get hold of the truth *too soon*, before people have become strong enough, hard enough, artistic enough . . . Seen in this light, piety – the "life in God" – appears as the last and most subtle monstrosity produced by *fear* of the truth; it appears as the artists' worship and intoxication before the most consistent of all falsifications, as the will to invert the truth, the will to untruth at any price. Perhaps piety has been the most potent method yet for the beautification of humanity: it can turn people into art, surface, plays of colors, benevolence, and to such an extent that we can finally look at them without suffering. –

[11] Religious people.

60

To love humanity *for the sake of God* – that has been the noblest and most bizarre feeling people have attained so far. That the love of humanity, in the absence of any sanctifying ulterior motive, is one *more* stupidity and abomination; that the tendency to love humanity like this can only get its standard, its subtlety, its grain of salt and pinch of ambergris from a higher tendency: – whoever it was that first felt and "experienced" all this, however much his tongue might have stumbled as it tried to express such a tenderness, let him be forever holy and admirable to us as the man who has flown the highest so far and has got the most beautifully lost!

61

The philosopher as *we* understand him, we free spirits –, as the man with the most comprehensive responsibility, whose conscience bears the weight of the overall development of humanity, this philosopher will make use of religion for his breeding and education work, just as he will make use of the prevailing political and economic situation. The influence that can be exerted over selection and breeding with the help of religions (and this influence is always just as destructive as it is creative and formative) varies according to the type of person who falls under their spell and protection. For people who are strong, independent, prepared, and predestined for command, people who come to embody the reason and art of a governing race, religion is an additional means of overcoming resistances, of being able to rule. It binds the ruler together with the ruled, giving and handing the consciences of the ruled over to the rulers – which is to say: handing over their hidden and most interior aspect, and one which would very much like to escape obedience. And if individuals from such a noble lineage are inclined, by their high spirituality, towards a retiring and contemplative life, reserving for themselves only the finest sorts of rule (over exceptional young men or monks), then religion can even be used as a means of securing calm in the face of the turmoil and tribulations of the *cruder* forms of government, and purity in the face of the *necessary* dirt of politics. This is how the Brahmins, for instance, understood the matter. With the help of a religious organization, they assumed the power to appoint kings for the people, while they themselves kept and felt removed and outside, a people of higher, over-kingly tasks.

Meanwhile, religion also gives some fraction of the ruled the instruction and opportunity they need to prepare for eventual rule and command. This is particularly true for that slowly ascending class and station in which, through fortunate marriage practices, the strength and joy of the will, the will to self-control is always on the rise. Religion tempts and urges them to take the path to higher spirituality and try out feelings of great self-overcoming, of silence, and of solitude. Asceticism and Puritanism are almost indispensable means of educating and ennobling a race that wants to gain control over its origins among the rabble, and work its way up to eventual rule. Finally, as for the common people, the great majority, who exist and are only *allowed* to exist to serve and to be of general utility, religion gives them an invaluable sense of contentment with their situation and type; it puts their hearts greatly at ease, it glorifies their obedience, it gives them (and those like them) one more happiness and one more sorrow, it transfigures and improves them, it provides something of a justification for everything commonplace, for all the lowliness, for the whole half-bestial poverty of their souls. Religion, and the meaning [*Why is this such a bad thing?*] religion gives to life, spreads sunshine over such eternally tormented people and makes them bearable even to themselves. It has the same effect that an Epicurean philosophy usually has on the suffering of higher ranks: it refreshes, refines, and *makes the most* of suffering, as it were. In the end it even sanctifies and justifies. Perhaps there is nothing more venerable about Christianity and Buddhism than their art of teaching even the lowliest to use piety in order to situate themselves in an illusory higher order of things, and in so doing stay satisfied with the actual order, in which their lives are hard enough (in which precisely this hardness is necessary!).

Battle of philosopher v religion

62

Finally, to show the downside of these religions as well and throw light on their uncanny dangers: there is a high and horrible price to pay when religions do *not* serve as means for breeding and education in the hands of a philosopher, but instead serve themselves and become *sovereign*, when they want to be the ultimate goal instead of a means alongside other means. With humans as with every other type of animal, there is a surplus of failures and degenerates, of the diseased and infirm, of those who necessarily suffer. Even with humans, successful cases are always the exception and, since humans are *the still undetermined animals*, the infrequent exception. But it gets worse: people who represent more nobly bred types are less likely to *turn out well*. Chance, that law of nonsense in the overall economy of mankind, is most terribly apparent in its destructive effect on the higher men, whose conditions of life are subtle, multiple, and difficult to calculate. So how is this *surplus* of failures treated by the two greatest religions, those mentioned above? They try to preserve, to keep everything living that can be kept in any way alive. In fact, they take sides with the failures as a matter of principle, as religions *of the suffering*. They give rights to all those who suffer life like a disease, and they want to make every other feeling for life seem wrong and become impossible. Whatever merit we might find in this indulgent, preserving care, which was and is meant for the highest types of people (since these are the ones that, historically, have almost always suffered the most), along with everyone else – nevertheless, in the final analysis, the religions that have existed so far (which have all been *sovereign*) have played a principal role in keeping the type "man" on a lower level. They have preserved too much of *what should be destroyed*. They have done invaluable service, these religions, and who is so richly endowed with gratitude not to grow poor in the face of everything that, for instance, the "spiritual men" of Christianity have done for Europe so far! And yet, after they gave comfort to the suffering, courage to the oppressed and despairing, a staff and support to the dependent, after they found people who were inwardly destroyed or had grown wild and lured them away from society, into cloisters and spiritual prisons: what else did they have to do, to work in good conscience and conviction for the preservation of all the sick and suffering, which really means working in word and in deed for the *deterioration of the European race*? Stand all valuations *on their head – that* is what they had to do! And crush the strong, strike down the great hopes, throw suspicion on the delight in beauty, skew everything self-satisfied, manly, conquering, domineering, every instinct that belongs to the highest and best-turned-out type of "human," twist them into uncertainty, crisis of conscience, self-destruction; at the limit, invert the whole love of the earth and of earthly dominion into hatred against earth and the earthly – *that* is the task the church set and needed to set for itself until, in its estimation, "unworldly," "unsensuous," and "higher man" finally melted together into a single feeling. If you could survey the strangely painful, crude yet subtle comedy of European Christianity with the mocking and disinterested eye of an Epicurean god, I think you would find it to be a constant source of amazement and laughter. Doesn't it seem as if, for eighteen centuries, Europe was dominated by the single will to turn humanity into a *sublime abortion?* But if somebody with opposite needs were to approach the almost willful degeneration and atrophy of humanity that the Christian European (Pascal for instance) has become, somebody whose manner is no longer Epicurean, but has instead some divine hammer in hand; wouldn't he have to yell out in rage, in pity, in horror: "Oh you fools, you presumptuous, pitying fools, what have you done here! Was that work meant for your hands! Look how you've wrecked and ruined my most beautiful stone! Who gave *you* the right to do such a thing!" – What I mean is: Christianity has been the most disastrous form of arrogance so far. People who were not high and hard enough to give *human beings* artistic form; people who were not strong or far-sighted enough, who lacked the sublime self-discipline to *give* free reign to the foreground law of ruin and failure by the thousands; people who were not noble enough to see the abysmally different orders of rank and chasms in rank between different people. People like *this*, with their "equality before God" have prevailed over the fate of Europe so far, until a stunted, almost ridiculous type, a herd animal, something well-meaning, sickly, and mediocre has finally been bred: the European of today . . .

Part 4   Epigrams and entr'actes

63

Genuine teachers only take things seriously where their students are concerned – even themselves.

64

"Knowledge for its own sake" – this is the final snare morality has laid; with it, we become completely entangled in morals once again.

65

Knowledge would have little charm if there were not so much shame to be overcome in order to reach it.

65a

People are at their least honest when it comes to their God: he is not *allowed* to sin!

66

The tendency to let oneself be debased, robbed, lied to, and exploited could be the shame of a god among men.

67

It is barbaric to love one thing alone, since this one love will be pursued at the expense of all others. This includes love of God.

68

"I did that" says my memory. I couldn't have done that – says my pride, and stands its ground. Finally, memory gives in.

69

You have been a poor observer of life if you have not also seen the hand that, ever so gently – kills.

70

If you have character, you also have a typical experience that always comes back.

71

The sage as astronomer. – If you still experience the stars as something "over you," you still don't have the eyes of a knower.

72

It is not the strength but the duration of high feelings that makes for high men.

73

Precisely by attaining an ideal, we surpass it.

73a

Many peacocks hide their peacock tails – and call that their pride.

74

A man with genius is insufferable if he doesn't have at least two more things: gratitude and cleanliness.

75

The degree and type of a person's sexuality reaches up into the furthermost peaks of their spirit.

76

In peaceful conditions, the warlike man will attack himself.

77

People use their principles to try to tyrannize or justify or honor or insult or conceal their habits: – two people with the same principles will probably want utterly different things from them.

78

Anyone who despises himself will still respect himself as a despiser.

79

A soul that knows it is loved but does not itself love exposes its sediment: – its bottom-most aspect rises to the top.

80

An issue that has been resolved stops mattering to us. – What did that god[1] who counseled "Know yourself!" really mean? Was it perhaps: "Stop letting anything matter to you! Become objective!" – And Socrates? – And the "scientific man"? –

81

It is terrible to die of thirst in the ocean. So do you have to salt your truth to the point where it doesn't quench thirst anymore?

82

"Pity for all" – would be harshness and tyranny for *you*, my dear neighbor! –

[1] Apollo.

83

Instinct. – When your house is on fire, you even forget about lunch. – Yes, but you pick it out from the ashes.

84

Women learn how to hate in the same proportion that they *unlearn* how to charm.

85

The same affects have different tempos in men and in women: that is why men and women do not stop misunderstanding each other.

86

Behind all their personal vanity, women always have an impersonal contempt – for "woman."

87

Bound heart, free spirit. – If someone binds up his heart and takes it captive, he can give his spirit considerable freedom: I have said this once already. But nobody will believe me if they do not already know . . .

88

You start to mistrust very clever people when they get embarrassed.

89

Terrible experiences make you wonder if the people who have experienced them are not terrible themselves.

90

Love and hate, the very things that weigh other people down, will make heavy, heavy-hearted people lighter and momentarily superficial.

91

So icy cold you burn your finger on him! Every hand that touches him gets a shock! – and that is why many people think he glows.

92

Who, for the sake of his good name, has never – sacrificed himself? –

93

There is no hatred for mankind in affability which, for that very reason, contains all too great a contempt for mankind.

94

Human maturity: this means rediscovering the seriousness we had towards play when we were children.

95

To be ashamed of your immorality: that is a step on the stairway that ultimately leads you to be ashamed of your morality as well.

96

People should leave life like Odysseus left Nausicaa – with more blessings than ardor.

97

What? A great man? I can only see an actor of his own ideal.

98

When we discipline our conscience, it kisses us while it bites.

99

Disappointment speaks. – "I listened for an echo and heard only praise –"

100

We all pretend to ourselves that we are more naive than we are: this is how we relax from other people.

101

Today, someone with knowledge might well feel like God becoming animal.

102

When somebody discovers their love is requited, it really should temper their feelings for their beloved. "What? This person is unassuming enough to love even you? Or stupid enough? Or – or – "

103

Danger in happiness. – "Now everything is at its best, now I love every fate: – who wants to be my fate?"

104

It is not their love for humanity but rather the impotence of their love for humanity that keeps today's Christian from – burning us.

105

For free spirits, for the "pious men of knowledge" – the *pia fraus*[2] offends taste (offends *their* "piety") more than the *impia fraus*.[3] This explains their profound failure to understand the church, which is typical of "free spirits" – as *their* un-freedom.

106

Music allows the passions to enjoy themselves.

[2] Pious fraud.

[3] Impious fraud.

107

Whenever you reach a decision, close your ears to even the best objections: this is the sign of a strong character. Which means: an occasional will to stupidity.

108

There are absolutely no moral phenomena, only a moral interpretation of the phenomena . . .

109

Often enough the criminal is no match for his deed: he cheapens and slanders it.

110

Defenders of criminals are rarely artistic enough to use the beautiful horror of the deed to the advantage of the doer.

111

Our vanity is at its strongest precisely when our pride has been wounded.

112

Whoever feels himself predestined for seeing and not believing will find all believers too noisy and pushy: he will fend them off.

113

"You want him for yourself? Stand in front of him looking embarrassed – "

114

Any sense of perspective is ruined for women from the very start by enormous expectations about sexual love and by the shame these expectations bring.

115

Where neither love nor hate are in play, woman is a mediocre player.

116

The great epochs of our lives come when we gather the courage to reconceive our evils as what is best in us.

117

The will to overcome an affect is, in the end, itself only the will of another, or several other, affects.

118

There is an innocence in admiration: it is found in people who do not realize that they themselves might also be admired some day.

119

Disgust at filth can be so great that it prevents us from cleaning ourselves – from "justifying" ourselves.

120

Sensuality often hurries the growth of love so that the root stays weak and is easy to tear up.

121

It is subtle that God learned Greek when he wanted to become a writer – and that he did not learn it better.

122

Taking pleasure in praise is, for many, only a courtesy of the heart – which is quite the reverse of a vanity of the spirit.

123

Even concubinage gets corrupted: – by marriage.

124

If someone rejoices while burning at the stake it is not because he has triumphed over his pain, but rather over not feeling any pain when he expected to. A parable.

125

When we are forced to change our mind about somebody, we count against him the trouble he has put us to.

126

A people is nature's roundabout way of getting six or seven great men. – Yes: and then of getting around them.

127

All proper women find something shameful about science. They think it is too forward, as if it would let people peek under their skin – or worse! under their dress and finery.

128

The more abstract the truth you want to teach, the more you have to seduce the senses to it.

129

The devil has the broadest perspective on God, which is why he keeps so far away from God: – the devil, that is, as the oldest friend of knowledge.

130

What someone *is* begins to reveal itself when his talent diminishes – when he stops showing what he *can* do. So talent is also a piece of finery; and finery is also a hiding place.

131

The sexes deceive themselves about each other: which means they basically only love and honor themselves (or their own ideal, to say it more nicely –). So men would have it that women are placid – but women above all are *essentially* not placid, just like cats, however much they have rehearsed the appearance of placidity.

132

We are best punished for our virtues.

133

Someone who does not know how to find the path to *his* ideal lives more carelessly and impudently than someone without an ideal.

134

All credibility, good conscience, and evidence of truth first come from the senses.

135

Pharisaism is not a degeneration in good people: rather, a good part of it is the condition of any being good.

136

The first one looks for a midwife for his thoughts – the other, for someone he can help: this is how a good conversation begins.

137

In dealing with scholars and artists, people are easily led in the wrong direction: behind a remarkable scholar you will not infrequently find a mediocre person, and behind a mediocre artist quite often – someone really remarkable.

138

When we are awake we do the same thing as when we are dreaming: we first invent and create the people we are dealing with – and then forget it immediately.

139

In revenge and in love, woman is more barbaric than man.

140

Advice as riddle. " – If the bond does not split, – then it first must be bit."

141

The <u>abdomen</u> is the reason why people are not so quick to consider themselves gods.

142

The chastest saying I ever have heard: "*Dans le véritable amour c'est l'âme qui enveloppe le corps.*"[4]

143

Our vanity would have it that the things we do best are the very things that are most difficult for us. On the origin of many morals.

---

[4] "In true love, it is the soul that envelops the body."

144

When a woman has scholarly inclinations, there is usually something wrong with her sexuality. Even sterility makes her prone to a certain masculinity of taste; man is, if you will, "the sterile animal."

145

Comparing man and woman overall, you could say: woman would not have a genius for finery if she did not have an instinct for the *secondary* role.

146

Whoever fights with monsters should see to it that he does not become one himself. And when you stare for a long time into an abyss, the abyss stares back into you.

147

From old Florentine novellas: but also – from life: *buona femmina e mala femmina vuol bastone.*[5] Sacchetti, Nov. 86.

148

To seduce those nearest to you into a good opinion, and then credit the credibility of this opinion: who can equal women in this piece of art? –

149

What an age perceives as evil is usually an untimely after-effect of something that used to be perceived as good – the atavism of an older ideal.

---

[5] "Both good and bad women need the stick." From Franco Sacchetti, *Novelle* (written in the late fourteenth century, but published in 1724).

150

Around the hero everything turns into tragedy; around the demigod everything turns into a satyr play; and around God everything turns into – what? Perhaps "world"? –

151

It is not enough to have a talent: we also need to have your permission for it, – right? my friends?

152

"Paradise is wherever the tree of knowledge stands": that is what the oldest and youngest serpents say.

153

Whatever is done out of love takes place beyond good and evil.

154

Objections, minor infidelities, cheerful mistrust, a delight in mockery – these are symptoms of health. Everything unconditional belongs to pathology.

155

A sense for the tragic grows and declines along with sensuousness.

156

Madness is rare in the individual – but with groups, parties, peoples, and ages it is the rule.

157

The thought of suicide is a strong means of comfort: it helps get us through many an evil night.

158

Our strongest drives, the tyrants in us, subjugate not only our reason but our conscience as well.

159

We *have to* repay good and bad: but why do we have to repay precisely those people who did us the good or bad?

160

You do not love your knowledge enough anymore, as soon as you communicate it.

161

Poets are shameless with their experiences: they exploit them.

162

"Our 'neighbors'[6] are not the ones next door to us, but rather the ones next door to *them*" – this is what all peoples believe.

163

Love brings to light the high and the hidden qualities of the lover – what is rare and exceptional about him: to this extent, love easily misleads about his ordinary traits.

164

Jesus said to his Jews: "The law was for servants, – love God as I do, as his son! Why should we care about morals, we sons of God?" –

---

[6] In German: *Unser Nächster*. This means "neighbor" in the Biblical sense, which Nietzsche is contrasting with *Nachbar* (the ones next door), a more general term for "neighbor."

165

Regarding all parties. – A shepherd always needs another bellwether, – or sometimes he has to be the wether himself.

166

Lies come through our mouths – but the face that accompanies them tells the truth.

167

With hard people, intimacy is a source of shame – and something precious.

168

Christianity gave Eros poison to drink: – he did not die from it, but degenerated into a vice.

169

Talking frequently about yourself can also be a way of hiding.

170

There is more intrusiveness in praise than in censure.

171

Pity is almost laughable in a man of knowledge, like tender hands on a Cyclops.

172

Every once in a while, a love of humanity will inspire us to embrace some arbitrary person (because we cannot embrace everyone): but that is precisely what we cannot let the arbitrary person know . . .

173

We do not hate what we accord little value, but only what we consider equal or superior.

174

You utilitarians, even you love everything *utile*[7] only as a *vehicle* for your inclinations, – and even you really cannot stand the noise of its wheels?

175

In the end, we love our desires and not the thing desired.

176

Other people's vanity offends our taste only when it offends our vanity.

177

Perhaps nobody has ever been truthful enough about what "truthfulness" is.

178

No one believes in the stupidities of clever people: what a loss of human rights!

179

The consequences of our acts grab us by the hair, regardless of the fact that we have "improved" ourselves in the meantime.

180

There is an innocence in lying that is the sign of good faith in a cause.

---

[7] Useful.

181

It is inhuman to bless where you are cursed.

182

The confidences of our superiors enrage us because they cannot be reciprocated. –

183

"I'm not upset because you lied to me, I'm upset because I don't believe you any more." –

184

Goodness has a high-spiritedness that looks like malice.

185

"I dislike him." – Why? – "I'm no match for him." – Has anyone ever given this sort of an answer?

Part 5   On the natural history of morals

186

In Europe these days, moral sentiment is just as refined, late, multiple, sensitive, and subtle as the "science of morals" (which belongs with it) is young, neophyte, clumsy, and crude: – an attractive contrast, and one that occasionally becomes visible, embodied in the person of the moralist himself. Considering what it signifies, the very phrase "science of morals" is much too arrogant and offends *good* taste, which always tends to prefer more modest terms. We should admit to ourselves with all due severity exactly *what* will be necessary for a long time to come and *what* is provisionally correct, namely: collecting material, formulating concepts, and putting into order the tremendous realm of tender value feelings and value distinctions that live, grow, reproduce, and are destroyed, – and, perhaps, attempting to illustrate the recurring and more frequent shapes of this living crystallization, – all of which would be a preparation for a *typology* of morals. Of course, people have not generally been this modest. Philosophers have all demanded (with ridiculously stubborn seriousness) something much more exalted, ambitious, and solemn as soon as they took up morality as a science: they wanted morality to be *grounded*, – and every philosopher so far has thought that he has provided a ground for morality. Morality itself, however, was thought to be "given." What a distance between this sort of crass pride and that supposedly modest little descriptive project, left in rot and ruin, even though the subtlest hands and senses could hardly be subtle enough for it. Precisely because moral philosophers had only a crude knowledge of moral *facta*, selected arbitrarily and abbreviated at random – for instance, as the morality of their surroundings, their class, their church, their *Zeitgeist*,[1] their climate and region, – precisely because they were poorly informed (and not particularly eager to learn more) about peoples, ages, and histories, they completely missed out on the genuine problems involved in morality, problems that only emerge from a comparison of many *different* moralities. As strange as it may sound, the problem of morality itself has been *missing* from every "science of morals" so far: there was no suspicion that anything was really a problem. Viewed properly, the "grounding of morals" (as philosophers called it, as they demanded it of themselves) was only an erudite form of good *faith* in the dominant morality, a new way of *expressing* it; as such, it was itself already situated within the terms of a certain morality. In the last analysis, it even constitutes a type of denial that these morals *can* be regarded as a problem. But, in any event, it is the opposite of an examination, dissection, interrogation, vivisection of precisely this article of faith. For example, let us listen to the almost admirable innocence with which even Schopenhauer describes his own project, and then we can draw our conclusions as to how scientific a "science" could be when its ultimate masters are still talking like children or old women. "The principle," he says (p. 136 of the *Grundprobleme der Moral*), "the fundamental claim, on whose content all ethicists *actually* agree: *neminem laede, immo omnes, quantum potes, juva*[2] – this is *actually* the claim that all moralists attempt to ground . . . the *actual* foundation of ethics that people have sought for millennia, just as they have looked for the philosophers' stone."[3] – The difficulty involved in grounding the claim just cited might be great indeed – Schopenhauer himself came up famously short in this regard. And anyone who has ever truly felt how inanely false and sentimental this claim is in a world whose essence is will to power –, they might recall that Schopenhauer, pessimism notwithstanding, *actually* – played the flute . . . every day, after dinner. You can read it in his biography. And just out of curiosity: a pessimist who negates both God and world but *stops* before morality, – who affirms morality and plays his flute, affirms *laede neminem* morality: excuse me? is this really – a pessimist? ? ? ?

---

[1] Spirit of the age.

[2] "Harm no one, but rather help everyone as much as you can."

[3] Schopenhauer's "Preisschrift über die Grundlage der Moral" (Prize Essay on the Basis of Morals), part two of *Die beiden Grundprobleme der Ethik* (*The Two Fundamental Problems of Ethics*) (1841). The emphases are Nietzsche's.

187

Apart from the value of claims like "there is a categorical imperative in us," the question remains: what do claims like this tell us about the people who make them? There are moralities that are supposed to justify their creator in the eyes of others, and other moralities that are supposed to calm him down and allow him to be content with himself; still other moralities allow him to crucify and humiliate himself. He can use some moralities to take revenge, others to hide, and still others to transfigure himself and place himself far and away. There are moralities that help their creator to forget, and others that let him – or something about him – be forgotten. Many moralists would like to wield power and impose their creative whims on humanity; many others (perhaps even Kant himself) want to make it clear through their morality that "the worthy thing about me is that I can obey – and it *should* be the same for you as it is for me!" – in short, even morality is just a *sign language of the affects*!

188

Every morality, as opposed to *laisser-aller*,[4] is a piece of tyranny against both "nature" and "reason." But this in itself is no objection; for that, we would have to issue yet another decree based on some other moral-ity forbidding every sort of tyranny and unreason. What is essential and invaluable about every morality is that it is a long compulsion. In order to understand Stoicism or Port-Royal or Puritanism, just remember the compulsion under which every language so far has developed strength and freedom: the compulsion of meter, the tyranny of rhyme and rhythm. Look at how much trouble the poets and the orators of every country have to go through! (including some of today's prose writers, who have an inexorable conscience in their ear) – and all "for the sake of some stu-pidity," as utilitarian fools say (and think they are clever for saying it) – or "in obsequious submission to arbitrary laws," as anarchists say (and then imagine themselves "free," even free-spirited). But the strange fact is that everything there is, or was, of freedom, subtlety, boldness, dance, or masterly assurance on earth, whether in thinking itself, or in ruling, or in speaking and persuading, in artistic just as in ethical practices, has only developed by virtue of the "tyranny of such arbitrary laws." And, in all

---

4 Letting go.

seriousness, it is not at all improbable that *this* is what is "nature" and "natural" – and *not* that *laisser-aller*! Every artist knows how far removed this feeling of letting go is from his "most natural" state, the free ordering, placing, disposing and shaping in the moment of "inspiration" – he knows how strictly and subtly he obeys thousands of laws at this very moment, laws that defy conceptual formulation precisely because of their hardness and determinateness (compared with these laws, there is something floundering, multiple, and ambiguous about even the most solid concept –). I will say it again: what seems to be essential "in heaven and on earth" is that there be *obedience* in one direction for a long time. In the long term, this always brings and has brought about something that makes life on earth worth living – for instance: virtue, art, music, dance, reason, intellect – something that transfigures, something refined, fantastic, and divine. The long un-freedom of spirit, the mistrustful constraint in the communicability of thought, the discipline that thinkers imposed on themselves, thinking within certain guidelines imposed by the church or court or Aristotelian presuppositions, the long, spiritual will to interpret every event according to a Christian scheme and to rediscover and justify the Christian God in every chance event, – all this violence, arbitrariness, harshness, terror, and anti-reason has shown itself to be the means through which strength, reckless curiosity, and subtle agility have been bred into the European spirit. Admittedly, this also entailed an irreplaceable loss of force and spirit, which have had to be crushed, stifled, and ruined (since here, just like everywhere else, "nature," shows itself in its utterly wasteful and *indifferent* glory, which is outrageous but noble). The fact that, for thousands of years, European thinkers have been thinking only in order to prove something (these days it is the other way around: we are suspicious of any thinker who "has something to prove") – the fact that the results which were *supposed* to emerge from their most intense contemplations were in fact already firmly established (somewhat like earlier Asian astrology or even the present-day innocuous Christian-moral interpretation of the most personal events "to the glory of god" and "to save the soul"): – this tyranny, this arbitrariness, this stern and grandiose stupidity has *trained* the spirit. Slavery, in both the crude and refined senses of the term, seems to be the indispensable means of disciplining and breeding even the spirit. We can look at every morality in the following way: whatever "nature" it contains teaches us to hate the *laisser-aller*, the all-too-great freedom, and plants in us the need for limited horizons and the closest tasks. It teaches a *narrowing* of *perspective* and so, in a certain sense, stupidity as a condition for life and growth. "You should obey someone, anyone, and for a long time: *or else* you will deteriorate and lose all respect for yourself" – this seems to me to be the moral imperative of nature, which is clearly neither "categorical," as the old Kant demanded it to be (hence the "or else" –), nor directed to the individual (what does nature care about the individual!), but rather to peoples, races, ages, classes, and above all to the whole "human" animal, to *the* human.

189

The industrious races find it extremely difficult to tolerate idleness: it was a stroke of genius on the part of the *English* instinct to spend Sundays in tedium with a *te deum* so that the English people would unconsciously lust for their week- and workdays. It is the same type of cleverly invented, cleverly interpolated period of *fasting* that you find all over the ancient world (although there, as is often the case with southern peoples, it is not exactly associated with work –). There need to be many types of fasts; and wherever powerful drives and habits rule, the law-makers have to be sure to put in leap days when these drives are chained up and made to relearn what hunger feels like. Entire generations or epochs, emerging in the grips of some moral fanaticism or another, seem (from a higher viewpoint) to be just such interposed periods of compulsion and fasting, the times when a drive learns to cower and submit, but also to keep itself *clean* and *sharp*. Some philosophical sects can be interpreted in this way as well (like the Stoa in the midst of a Hellenistic culture whose air had become heavy and lascivious with the fragrance of aphrodisiacs). – This also suggests an explanation for the paradox of why it was precisely during Europe's Christian period and only under the pressure of Christian value judgments that the sex drive sublimated itself into love (*amour-passion*[5]).

190

There is something in Plato's moral philosophy that does not really belong to him, but is there in spite of him, as it were: namely, the Socratism that

---

[5] Love as passion.

he was really too noble for. "Nobody wants to harm himself, and therefore everything bad happens involuntarily. The bad man brings harm to himself, and he would not do so if he knew badness was bad. Accordingly, people are bad only through error; if the error is removed, they will necessarily become – good." – This type of inference stinks of the *rabble*, who see only the disagreeable effects of bad actions and are in fact judging: "it is stupid to act badly," while assuming that "good" is identical with "useful and pleasant." If you start off with the assumption that this is the origin of every utilitarian morality and then follow your nose, you will rarely go wrong. – Plato did everything he could to interpret something refined and noble into his teacher's claim: above all, himself –, him, the most daring of all interpreters, who treated the whole of Socrates just like someone might treat a popular theme or folksong from the streets, varying it to the point of infinity and impossibility, into all his own masks and multitudes. As a joke (and a Homeric one at that), what is the Platonic Socrates if not:

$$\pi\varrho\acute{o}\sigma\vartheta\varepsilon\ \Pi\lambda\acute{\alpha}\tau\omega\nu\ \acute{o}\pi\iota\vartheta\acute{\varepsilon}\nu\ \tau\varepsilon\ \Pi\lambda\acute{\alpha}\tau\omega\nu\ \mu\acute{\varepsilon}\sigma\sigma\eta\ \tau\varepsilon\ X\acute{\iota}\mu\alpha\iota\varrho\alpha.\text{[6]}$$

191

The old theological problem of "faith" and "knowledge" – or, to be more precise, of instinct and reason – and so, the question of whether, with respect to the value of things, the instincts deserve more authority than reason (reason wants some ground or "what for?", some purpose or utility behind our values and actions) – this is the same old moral problem that first emerged in the person of Socrates and divided opinions long before Christianity came along. Socrates of course had initially sided with reason, given the taste of his talent – that of a superior dialectician. And, in point of fact, didn't he spend his whole life laughing at the shortcomings of his clumsy, noble Athenians, who, like all noble people, were men of instinct and could never really account for why they acted the way they did? But in the end, silently and secretly, he laughed at himself as well; with his acute conscience and self-scrutiny, he discovered the same difficulty and shortcoming in himself. "Why free ourselves from the instincts?" he asked himself; "We should give them their fair dues,

---

[6] "Plato at the front, Plato at the back, Chimaera in the middle."

along with reason – we have to follow our instincts but persuade reason to come to their aid with good motives." This was the genuine *falseness* of that great, secretive ironist; he made his conscience seem satisfied with a type of self-deceit. Basically, he had seen through to the irrationality of moral judgments. – Plato, who was more innocent in such matters and lacked Socrates' plebeian craftiness, wanted to use all his strength (the greatest strength a philosopher had ever had at his disposal!) to prove to himself that reason and the instincts converge independently on a single goal, on the Good, or "God"; and, ever since Plato, all theologians and philosophers have been on the same track. Which is to say: in matters of morality, it has been instinct, or (as the Christians say) "faith," or (as I say) "the herd" that has had the upper hand so far. Descartes was an exception, as the father of rationalism (and consequently grandfather of the Revolution) who granted authority to reason alone. But reason is only a tool and Descartes was superficial.

192

Anyone who investigates the history of a particular science will find in its development a clue to understanding the oldest and most secret processes of all "knowledge and cognition": there as here, rash hypotheses, fictions, the dumb good will to "believe," and a lack of mistrust and patience develop first – our senses learn late and never fully learn to be refined, trusty, careful organs of knowledge. Given some stimulus, our eyes find it more convenient to reproduce an image that they have often produced before than to register what is different and new about an impression: the latter requires more strength, more "morality." It is awkward and difficult for the ear to hear something new; we are bad at listening to unfamiliar music. When we hear another language, we involuntarily try to form the sounds we hear into words that sound more comfortable and familiar to us: so, for instance, German people at one point heard "*arcubalista*" and made it into the word "*Armbrust*."[7] Even our senses greet everything novel with reluctance and hostility; and affects like fear, love, and hate, as well as passive affects of laziness, will be *dominant* during even the "simplest" processes of sensibility. – Just as little as today's

---

[7] Both words mean "crossbow." The German term *Armbrust* literally means "arm-breast" and so mimics the sound but not the sense of the Latin.

reader takes in all the individual words (or especially syllables) on a page (he catches maybe five out of twenty words and "guesses" what these five arbitrary words might possibly mean) – just as little do we see a tree precisely and completely, with respect to leaves, branches, colors, and shape. We find it so much easier to imagine an approximate tree instead. Even in the middle of the strangest experiences we do the same thing: we invent most of the experience and can barely be made *not* to regard ourselves as the "inventor" of some process. – What all this amounts to is: we are, from the bottom up and across the ages, *used to lying*. Or, to put the point more virtuously, more hypocritically and, in short, more pleasantly: people are much more artistic than they think. – In the middle of a lively conversation I will often see the other person's face expressing his thoughts (or the thoughts I attribute to him) with a degree of clarity and detail that far exceeds the power of my visual ability: – such subtlety of muscle movement and ocular expression *must* have come from my own imagination. In all likelihood the person had an entirely different expression, or none at all.

193

Quidquid luce fuit, tenebris agit:[8] but vice versa too. What we experience in dreams, as long as we experience it often enough, ends up belonging to the total economy of our soul just as much as anything we have "really" experienced. Such experiences make us richer or poorer, we have one need more or less, and finally, in the bright light of day and even in the clearest moments when minds are wide awake, we are coddled a little by the habits of our dreams. Suppose someone frequently dreams that he is flying, and as soon as he starts dreaming he becomes aware of the art and ability of flight as his privilege as well as his most particular, most enviable happiness – someone like this, who thinks he can negotiate every type of curve and corner with the slightest impulse, who knows the feeling of an assured, divine ease, an "upwards" without tension or force, a "downwards" without condescension or abasement – without *heaviness*! – how could someone with dream experiences and dream habits like these *not* see that the word "happiness" is colored and determined differently in his waking day too! how could his demands for happiness not be *different*?

---

[8] "What happened in the light goes on in the dark."

Compared to this "flying," the "soaring upwards" that the poets describe will have to be too terrestrial, muscular, violent, even too "heavy" for him. ???

194

Human diversity is apparent not only in the variety of people's tables of goods – which is to say the fact that they consider different goods worthwhile and that they disagree with each other as to the more or less of values, the rank order of commonly acknowledged goods: – diversity is much more evident in what they think counts as actually *owning* and *possessing* a good. When it comes to a woman, for instance, a more modest person might consider disposal over her body and sexual usage as sufficient and satisfactory signs of possession, of ownership. Someone else with a more suspicious and demanding thirst for possession will see the "question-mark" here, the fact that this is only the appearance of possession; such a person will want to examine more closely in order to be particularly clear as to whether the woman will give not only herself to him, but also give up what she has or wants for the sake of him –: only *this* will count as "possession" for him. But even this would not satisfy the mistrust and possessive desires of a third person, who asks himself whether the woman who gives up everything for his sake is not doing this for some sort of a fantasized version of him. He wants to be thoroughly (even meticulously) well known before he is able to be loved at all; he does not dare to let anyone figure him out –. He will not feel that he possesses his beloved fully until she harbors no illusions about him, until she loves him just as much for his devilishness and hidden inexhaustibility as for his goodness, patience, and spirituality. Someone might want to possess a people, and he finds all the higher arts of the Cagliostro and Catilina suited to this goal. Someone else with a more subtle thirst for possession will say to himself "one should not deceive where one wants to possess" –. He becomes irritated and impatient at the thought that a mask of himself rules the hearts of the people: "which is why I have to *let* myself be known, and above all know myself!" Among helpful and charitable people you typically discover that clumsy piece of deceit that makes somebody ready before helping him: for instance, acting as if he "deserves" help, requires precisely *their* help, and will prove to be deeply grateful, devoted, and obsequious for any help they give him, – with these fantasies they treat the needy like their own property, since they are helpful and charitable out of a desire for property. You will find them jealous if you cross them while they are being charitable, or beat them to it. Parents involuntarily make children into something similar to themselves and call it "bringing them up." No mother doubts at the bottom of her heart that, in the child, she has given birth to a piece of property; no father questions his right to subject the child to *his own* ideas and valuations. In fact, there was a time (among the ancient Germans, for instance) when it seemed fair that the father should dispose of the life and death of the newborn as he saw fit. And now it is the teacher, the social class, the priest, and the prince who, like the father, see every new person as an incontrovertible opportunity for a new possession. And it follows from this . . .

195

The Jews – a people "born for slavery" as Tacitus[9] and the entire ancient world say, "the people chosen of all peoples" as they themselves say and think – the Jews have achieved that miraculous thing, an inversion of values, thanks to which life on earth has had a new and dangerous charm for several millennia: – their prophets melted together "rich," "godless," "evil," "violent," "sensual" and for the first time coined an insult out of the word "world." The significance of the Jewish people lies in this inversion of values (which includes using the word for "poor" as a synonym for "holy" and "friend"): the *slave revolt in morality* begins with the Jews.

196

We *infer* the existence of innumerable dark bodies lying close to the sun, – ones that we will never see. Between you and me, this is a parable; and a psychologist of morals will read the entire book of the stars only as a language of signs and parables in which much is left silent.

197

You utterly fail to understand beasts of prey and men of prey (like Cesare Borgia), you fail to understand "nature" if you are still looking for a

---

[9] Tacitus, *Historiae*, V, 8.

"disease" at the heart of these healthiest of all tropical monsters and growths, or particularly if you are looking for some innate "hell" in them –: as almost all moralists so far have done. Does it seem that moralists harbor a hatred against tropics and primeval forests? And that they need to discredit the "tropical man" at all cost, whether as a disease or degeneration of man, or as his own hell and self-martyrdom? But why? In favor of "temperate zones?" In favor of temperate men? Of "moralists"? Of the mediocre? – This for the chapter: "Morality as Timidity." –

198

All these morals directed at the individual person to promote what people call his "happiness" – are they anything other than recommendations for constraint, in proportion to the degree of *danger* in which the individual person lives his life? or cures for his passions, his good and bad tendencies to the extent that they have will to power and want to play master? or large or small acts of cleverness and artifice, tainted with the stale smell of old folk-remedies and old wives' wisdom? They are all baroque in form and unreasonable (because they are directed at "everyone," because they generalize what should not be generalized); they all speak unconditionally, consider themselves unconditional; they are all seasoned with more than just one grain of salt – in fact, they only become tolerable, and occasionally even seductive, when they learn to smell over-spiced, dangerous, and, above all, "other-worldly." – On an intellectual scale, all this is of little value and not even remotely "scientific" let alone "wise"; instead, to say it again (and again and again), it is clever, clever, clever mixed with stupid, stupid, stupid, – whether we are talking about that indifference and stone column coldness which the Stoics prescribed and applied as a cure for the feverish idiocy of the affects; or that no-more-laughter, no-more-tears of Spinoza, who so naively champions the destruction of the affects through analysis and vivisection; or that method of tuning down the affects to a harmless mean where they might be satisfied, the Aristotelianism of morals; or even morality as the enjoyment of affects, intentionally watered down and spiritualized through the symbolism of art, like music, for instance, or the love of God and the love of men for the sake of God – since in religion the passions regain their civil rights, provided that . . . ; and finally, even that easy and high-spirited surrender to the affects taught by Hafiz and

Goethe, that bold slackening of the reins, that spiritual-physical *licentia morum*[10] in the special cases of smart old eccentrics and drunks, where there "isn't much danger anymore." This also for the chapter: "Morality as Timidity."

199

For as long as there have been people, there have been herds of people as well (racial groups, communities, tribes, folk, states, churches), and a very large number of people who obey compared to relatively few who command. So, considering the fact that humanity has been the best and most long-standing breeding ground for the cultivation of obedience so far, it is reasonable to suppose that the average person has an innate need to obey as a type of *formal conscience* that commands: "Thou shalt unconditionally do something, unconditionally not do something," in short: "Thou shalt." This need tries to satisfy itself and give its form a content, so, like a crude appetite, it indiscriminately grabs hold and accepts whatever gets screamed into its ear by some commander or another – a parent, teacher, the law, class prejudice, public opinion – according to its strength, impatience, and tension. The oddly limited character of human development – its hesitancy and lengthiness, its frequent regressions and reversals – is due to the fact that the herd instinct of obedience is inherited the best and at the cost of the art of commanding. If we imagine this instinct ever advancing to its furthest excesses, in the end there will be nobody with independence or the ability to command; or, such people will suffer inwardly from bad consciences and need to fool themselves into thinking that they too are only obeying before they are able to command. This is in fact the situation in Europe today; I call it the moral hypocrisy of the commanders. They do not know how to protect themselves from their bad consciences except by acting like executors of older or higher commands (from their ancestors, constitution, justice system, laws, or God himself) or even by borrowing herd maxims from the herd mentality, such as the "first servants of the people," or the "instruments of the commonweal." For his part, the herd man of today's Europe gives himself the appearance of being the only permissible type of man and glorifies those

---

[10] Moral license.

characteristics that make him tame, easy-going and useful to the herd as the true human virtues, namely: public spirit, goodwill, consideration, industry, moderation, modesty, clemency, and pity. But in those cases where people think they cannot do without a leader and bellwether, they keep trying to replace the commander with an agglomeration of clever herd men: this is the origin of all representative constitutions, for example. What a relief it is for these European herd animals, what a deliverance from an increasingly intolerable pressure, when, in spite of everything, someone appears who can issue unconditional commands; the impact of Napoleon's appearance is the last major piece of evidence for this: – the history of Napoleon's impact is practically the history of the higher happiness attained by this whole century in its most worthwhile people and moments.

200

In an age of disintegration where the races are mixed together, a person will have the legacy of multiple lineages in his body, which means conflicting (and often not merely conflicting) drives and value standards that fight with each other and rarely leave each other alone. A man like this, of late cultures and refracted lights, will typically be a weaker person: his most basic desire is for an end to the war that he *is*. His notion of happiness corresponds to that of a medicine and mentality of pacification (for instance the Epicurean or Christian); it is a notion of happiness as primarily rest, lack of disturbance, repletion, unity at last and the "Sabbath of Sabbaths," to speak with the holy rhetorician Augustine, who was himself this sort of person. – But if conflict and war affect such a nature as one *more* stimulus and goad to life –, and if genuine proficiency and finesse in waging war with himself (which is to say: the ability to control and outwit himself) are inherited and cultivated along with his most powerful and irreconcilable drives, then what emerge are those amazing, incomprehensible, and unthinkable ones, those human riddles destined for victory and for seduction; Alcibiades and Caesar are the most exquisite expressions of this type (– and I will gladly set by their side that *first* European after my taste, the Hohenstaufen Frederick II), and among artists perhaps Leonardo da Vinci. They appear in exactly those ages when that weaker type, with his longing for peace, comes to the fore. These types belong together and derive from the same set of causes.

201

As long as herd utility is the only utility governing moral value judgments, as long as the preservation of the community is the only thing in view and questions concerning immorality are limited to those things that seem to threaten the survival of the community; as long as this is the case, there cannot yet be a "morality of neighbor love." Suppose that even here, consideration, pity, propriety, gentleness, and reciprocity of aid are already practiced in a small but steady way; suppose that even in this state of society, all the drives that would later come to be called by the honorable name of "virtues" (and, in the end, basically coincide with the concept of "morality") – suppose that they are already active: at this point they still do not belong to the realm of moral valuations at all – they are still *extra-moral*. During the best days of Rome, for instance, an act done out of pity was not called either good or evil, moral or immoral; and if it were praised on its own, the praise would be perfectly compatible with a type of reluctant disdain as soon as it was held up against any action that served to promote the common good, the *res publica*.[11] Ultimately, the "love of the neighbor" is always somewhat conventional, willfully feigned and beside the point compared to *fear of the neighbor*. After the structure of society seems on the whole to be established and secured against external dangers, it is this fear of the neighbor that again creates new perspectives of moral valuation. Until now, in the spirit of common utility, certain strong and dangerous drives such as enterprise, daring, vindictiveness, cunning, rapacity, and a domineering spirit must have been not only honored (under different names than these of course), but nurtured and cultivated (since, given the threats to the group, they were constantly needed against the common enemies). Now, however, since there are no more escape valves for these drives, they are seen as twice as dangerous and, one by one, they are denounced as immoral and abandoned to slander. Now the opposite drives and inclinations come into moral favor; step by step, the herd instinct draws its conclusion. How much or how little danger there is to the community or to equality in an opinion, in a condition or affect, in a will, in a talent, this is now the moral perspective: and fear is once again the mother of morality. When the highest and strongest drives erupt in passion, driving the individual up and out and far above the average, over the depths of the herd conscience, the self-esteem of the community is

[11] Commonwealth.

destroyed – its faith in itself, its backbone, as it were, is broken: as a result, these are the very drives that will be denounced and slandered the most. A high, independent spiritedness, a will to stand alone, even an excellent faculty of reason, will be perceived as a threat. Everything that raises the individual over the herd and frightens the neighbor will henceforth be called *evil*; the proper, modest, unobtrusive, equalizing attitude and the *mediocrity* of desires acquire moral names and honors. Finally, in very peaceable circumstances there are fewer and fewer opportunities and less and less need to nurture an instinct for severity or hardness; and now every severity starts disturbing the conscience, even where justice is concerned. A high and hard nobility and self-reliance is almost offensive, and provokes suspicion; "the lamb," and "the sheep" even more, gains respect. – There is a point in the history of a society when it becomes pathologically enervated and tenderized and it takes sides, quite honestly and earnestly, with those who do it harm, with *criminals*. Punishment: that seems somehow unjust to this society, – it certainly finds the thoughts of "punishment" and "needing to punish" both painful and frightening. "Isn't it enough to render him *unthreatening*? Why punish him as well? Punishment is itself fearful!" – with these questions, the herd morality, the morality of timidity, draws its final consequences. If the threat, the reason for the fear, could be totally abolished, this morality would be abolished as well: it would not be necessary any more, it would not *consider itself* necessary any more! Anyone who probes the conscience of today's European will have to extract the very same imperative from a thousand moral folds and hiding places, the imperative of herd timidity: "we want the day to come when there is *nothing more to fear*!" The day to come – the will and way *to that day* is now called "progress" everywhere in Europe.

202

Let us immediately repeat what we have already said a hundred times before, since there are no ready ears for such truths – for *our* truths – these days. We know all too well how offensive it sounds when someone classifies human beings as animals, without disguises or allegory; and we are considered almost *sinful* for constantly using expressions like "herd," and "herd instinct" with direct reference to people of "modern ideas." So what? We cannot help ourselves, since this is where our new insights happen to lie. Europe, we have found, has become unanimous in all major moral judgments; and this includes the countries under Europe's influence. People in Europe clearly *know* what Socrates claimed not to know, and what that famous old snake once promised to teach, – people these days "know" what is good and evil. Now it must sound harsh and strike the ear quite badly when we keep insisting on the following point: what it is that claims to know here, what glorifies itself with its praise and reproach and calls itself good is the instinct of the herd animal man, which has come to the fore, gaining and continuing to gain predominance and supremacy over the other instincts, in accordance with the growing physiological approach and approximation whose symptom it is. *Morality in Europe these days is the morality of herd animals*: – and therefore, as we understand things, it is only one type of human morality beside which, before which, and after which many other (and especially *higher*) moralities are or should be possible. But this morality fights tooth and nail against such a "possibility" and such a "should": it stubbornly and ruthlessly declares "I am morality itself and nothing else is moral!" And in fact, with the aid of a religion that indulged and flattered the loftiest herd desires, things have reached the point where this morality is increasingly apparent in even political and social institutions: the *democratic* movement is the heir to Christianity. But there are indications that the tempo of this morality is still much too slow and lethargic for those who have less patience, those who are sick or addicted to the above-mentioned instinct. This is attested to by the increasingly frantic howling, the increasingly undisguised snarling of the anarchist dogs that now wander the alleyways of European culture, in apparent opposition to the peaceable and industrious democrats and ideologists of revolution, and still more to the silly philosophasters and brotherhood enthusiasts who call themselves socialists and want a "free society." But, in fact, they are one and all united in thorough and instinctive hostility towards all forms of society besides that of the *autonomous* herd (even to the point of rejecting the concepts of "master" and "slave" – *ni dieu ni maître*[12] reads a socialist formula –); they are united in their dogged opposition to any special claims, special rights, or privileges (which means, in the last analysis, that they are opposed to *any* rights: since when everyone is equal, no one will need "rights" anymore –); they are united in their mistrust of punitive justice (as if it were a violation of those who are weaker, a wrong against the *necessary*

---

[12] Neither God nor master.

result of all earlier societies –); but they are likewise united in the religion of pity, in sympathy for whatever feels, lives, suffers (down to the animal and up to "God": – the excessive notion of "pity for God" belongs in a democratic age –); they are all united in the cries and the impatience of pity, in deadly hatred against suffering in general, in the almost feminine inability to sit watching, to *let* suffering happen; they are united in the way they involuntarily raise the general level of sensitivity and gloom under whose spell Europe seems threatened with a new Buddhism; they are united in their faith in the morality of *communal* pity, as if it were morality in itself, the height, the *achieved* height of humanity, the sole hope for the future, the solace of the present, the great redemption of all guilt from the past: – they are all united in their faith in the community as *Redeemer*, which is to say: in the herd, in "themselves"...

203

We who have a different faith –, we who consider the democratic movement to be not merely an abased form of political organization, but rather an abased (more specifically a diminished) form of humanity, a mediocritization and depreciation of humanity in value: where do *we* need to reach with our hopes? – Towards *new philosophers*, there is no alternative; towards spirits who are strong and original enough to give impetus to opposed valuations and initiate a revaluation and reversal of "eternal values"; towards those sent out ahead; towards the men of the future who in the present tie the knots and gather the force that compels the will of millennia into *new* channels. To teach humanity its future as its *will*, as dependent on a human will, to prepare for the great risk and wholesale attempt at breeding and cultivation and so to put an end to the gruesome rule of chance and nonsense that has passed for "history" so far (the nonsense of the "greatest number" is only its latest form): a new type of philosopher and commander will be needed for this some day, and whatever hidden, dreadful, or benevolent spirits have existed on earth will pale into insignificance beside the image of this type. The image of such leaders hovers before *our* eyes: – may I say this out loud, you free spirits? The conditions that would have to be partly created and partly exploited for them to come into being; the probable paths and trials that would enable a soul to grow tall and strong enough to feel the *compulsion* for these tasks; a revaluation of values whose new pressure and hammer will steel a conscience and transform a heart into bronze to bear the weight of a responsibility like this; and, on the other hand, the necessity of such leaders, the terrible danger that they could fail to appear or simply fail and degenerate – these are *our* real worries and dark clouds, do you know this, you free spirits? These are the heavy, distant thoughts and storms that traverse the sky of *our* lives. There are few pains as intense as ever having seen, guessed, or sympathized while an extraordinary person ran off course and degenerated: but someone with an uncommon eye for the overall danger that "humanity" itself will *degenerate*, someone like us, who has recognized the outrageous contingency that has been playing games with the future of humanity so far – games in which no hand and not even a "finger of God" has taken part! – someone who has sensed the disaster that lies hidden in the idiotic guilelessness and credulity of "modern ideas," and still more in the whole of Christian-European morality: someone like this will suffer from an unparalleled sense of alarm. In a single glance he will comprehend everything that *could be bred from humanity*, given a favorable accumulation and intensification of forces and tasks; he will know with all the prescience of his conscience how humanity has still not exhausted its greatest possibilities, and how often the type man has already faced mysterious decisions and new paths: – he will know even better, from his most painful memories, the sorts of miserable things that generally shatter, crush, sink, and turn a development of the highest rank into a miserable affair. The *total degeneration of humanity* down to what today's socialist fools and nitwits see as their "man of the future" – as their ideal! – this degeneration and diminution of humanity into the perfect herd animal (or, as they say, into man in a "free society"), this brutalizing process of turning humanity into stunted little animals with equal rights and equal claims is no doubt *possible*! Anyone who has ever thought this possibility through to the end knows one more disgust than other men, – and perhaps a new *task* as well! . . .

Part 6   We scholars

204

At the risk that moralizing will prove once again to be what it always was (namely, an undismayed *montrer ses plaies*,[1] in the words of Balzac), I will dare to speak out against an inappropriate and harmful shift in the rank order between science and philosophy; this shift has gone completely unnoticed and now threatens to settle in with what looks like the clearest of consciences. I mean: people need to speak from *experience* (and experience always seems to mean bad experience, doesn't it?) when it comes to such lofty questions of rank, or else they are like blind people talking about colors or like women and artists speaking out *against* science ("Oh, this awful science," their instincts and shame will sigh, "it always gets to the *bottom* of things!" −). The scientific man's declaration of independence, his emancipation from philosophy, is one of the more subtle effects of the democratic way of life (and death): this self-glorification and presumptuousness of the scholar is in the full bloom of spring, flowering everywhere you look, − which isn't to say that this self-importance has a pleasant smell. "Away with all masters!" − that's what the rabble instinct wants, even here. And now that science has been so utterly successful in fending off theology, after having been its "handmaiden" for far too long, it is so high in spirits and low on sense that it wants to lay down laws for philosophy and, for once, play at being "master" − what am I saying! play at being *philosopher*. My memory (the memory of a scientific man, if you will!) is teeming with the arrogantly naive comments about philosophy and philosophers that I have heard from young natural scientists and old physicians (not to

[1] "Showing one's wounds."

93

mention from the most erudite and conceited scholars of all, the philologists and schoolmen, who are both by profession –). Sometimes it was
the specialists and the pigeon-hole dwellers who instinctively resisted
all synthetic tasks and skills; at other times it was the diligent workers
who smelled the *otium*[2] and the noble opulence of the philosopher's psychic economy and consequently felt themselves restricted and belittled.
Sometimes it was that color-blindness of utilitarian-minded people who
considered philosophy to be just a series of *refuted* systems and a wasteful expenditure that never did anybody "any good." Sometimes a fear of
disguised mysticism and changes to the limits of knowledge sprang up; at
other times, there was disdain for particular philosophers that had unwit-
tingly become a disdain for philosophy in general. In the end, I have found
that what usually lies behind young scholars' arrogant devalorizations of
philosophy is the nasty after-effect of some philosopher himself. These
scholars had, for the most part, stopped listening to this philosopher, but
without having emerged from under the spell of his dismissive valuations
of other philosophers: – and this resulted in a generalized ill will against
all philosophy. (The after-affects of Schopenhauer on Germany in the
most recent past seem to me an example of this sort of thing: – with his
unintelligent ranting against Hegel, he has caused the whole of the last
generation of Germans to break off its ties to German culture, a culture
that, all things considered, represented a supreme and divinatory refinement of the *historical sense*. But Schopenhauer was himself impoverished,
insensitive, un-German to the point of genius on precisely this point.)
Looking at the overall picture, the damage done to the respectability of
philosophy might be primarily due to the human, all-too-human, and,
in short, miserable condition of more recent philosophy itself, which has
held open the door to the rabble instinct. We have to admit the degree
to which our modern world has departed from the whole Heraclitean,
Platonic, Empedoclean type (or whatever names all these princely and
magnificent hermits of the spirit might have had); and with what justice
a worthy man of science *can* feel that he is of a better type and a better lineage, given the sort of representatives of philosophy who, thanks
to current fashions, are just as much talked up these days as they are
washed up (in Germany, for instance, the two lions of Berlin: the anarchist Eugen Dühring and the amalgamist Eduard von Hartmann). And

---

[2] Leisure.

especially those hodgepodge philosophers who call themselves "philosophers of reality" or "positivists" – just the sight of them is enough to
instill a dangerous mistrust in the soul of an ambitious young scholar.
They are, at best, scholars and specialists themselves – you can just feel
it! They have all been defeated but then *brought back* under the domination of science; they had wanted something *more* of themselves at one
time (without any right to this "more" and its responsibility) – and now,
in word and in deed, they respectably, wrathfully, vengefully represent a
skepticism concerning philosophy's master task and authority. In the end:
how could it be any other way! Science is thriving these days, its good
conscience shines in its face; meanwhile whatever state recent philosophy
has gradually sunk to, whatever is left of philosophy today, inspires mistrust and displeasure, if not ridicule and pity. A philosophy reduced to
"epistemology," which is really no more than a timid epochism and doctrine of abstinence; a philosophy that does not even get over the threshold
and scrupulously *denies* itself the right of entry – that is a philosophy in
its last gasps, an end, an agony, something to be pitied. How could such a
philosophy – *dominate?*

205

There are so many different kinds of dangers involved in the development
of a philosopher these days that it can be doubted whether this fruit is still
capable of ripening at all. The height and width of the tower of science have
grown to be so monstrously vast that the philosopher is that much more
likely to become exhausted before he has even finished his education, or
to let himself grab hold of something and "specialize." And so he is never
at his best, never reaches a high point in his development from which he
would be able to look over, look around, and *look down.* Or he gets there
too late, when he is already past his prime and his strength has started
to fade; or he gets there disabled, having become coarse and degenerate,
so that his gaze, his overall value judgment is largely meaningless. Perhaps the very refinement of his intellectual conscience lets him hesitate
and be slowed down while underway; he is afraid of being seduced into
becoming a dilettante, a millipede with a thousand feet and a thousand
feelers; he knows too well that someone who has lost his self-respect will
no longer command or *lead*, even in the field of knowledge: unless he wants
to become a great actor, a philosophical Cagliostro and rabble-rouser of

spirits, in short, a seducer. In the end, this is a question of taste, even if it is not a question of conscience. And just to double the philosopher's difficulties again, there is the additional fact that he demands a judgment of himself, a Yes or a No, not about science but about life and the value of life. It is only with reluctance that he comes to believe he has a right or even a duty to render this sort of a judgment, and he has to draw on the most wide-ranging (and perhaps the most disturbing and destructive) experiences so that he can look – hesitantly, skeptically, silently – for a path to this right and this belief. In fact, the masses have misjudged and mistaken the philosopher for a long time, sometimes confusing him with the scientific man and ideal scholar, and sometimes with the religiously elevated, desensualized, desecularized enthusiasts and intoxicated men of God. If you hear anyone praised these days for living "wisely" or "like a philosopher" it basically just means he is "clever and keeps out of the way." To the rabble, wisdom seems like a kind of escape, a device or trick for pulling yourself out of the game when things get rough. But the real philosopher (and isn't this how it seems to *us*, my friends?) lives "un-philosophically," "unwisely," in a manner which is above all *not clever*, and feels the weight and duty of a hundred experiments and temptations[3] of life: – he constantly puts *himself* at risk, he plays *the* rough game . . .

206

Compared to a genius, which is to say: compared to a being that either *begets* or *gives birth* (taking both words in their widest scope –), the scholar, the average man of science, is somewhat like an old maid. Like her, he has no expertise in the two most valuable acts performed by humanity. And, as a sort of compensation, both the scholar and the old maid are admitted to be respectable – respectability is always emphasized – although in both cases we are annoyed by the obligatory nature of this admission. Let us look more closely: what is the scientific man? In the first place, he is an ignoble type of person with the virtues that an ignoble type will have: this type is not dominant, authoritative, or self-sufficient. He is industrious, he is patiently lined up in an orderly array, he is regular and moderate in his abilities and needs, he has an instinct for his own kind and for the needs of his kind. These needs include: that piece of

---

[3] In German: *Versuchen und Versuchungen* (see note 16, p. 39 above).

independence and green pasture without which there is no quiet for him to work in, that claim to honor and acknowledgment (whose first and foremost presupposition is recognition and being recognizable –), that sunshine of a good name, that constant seal on his value and his utility which is needed, time and again, in order to overcome the inner *mistrust* that lies at the bottom of the heart of all dependent men and herd animals. It is only fair that the scholar has the diseases and bad habits of an ignoble type as well. He is full of petty jealousies and has eyes like a hawk for the base aspects of natures whose heights he cannot attain. He is friendly, but only like someone who lets himself go without letting himself really *flow* out; and just when he is standing in front of people who really do flow out, he will act all the more cold and reserved, – at times like this, his eye is like a smooth and unwilling lake that will no longer allow a single ripple of joy or sympathy. The worst and most dangerous thing that a scholar is capable of doing comes from his type's instinct for mediocrity: from that Jesuitism of mediocrity that instinctively works towards the annihilation of the exceptional man and tries to break every taut bow or – even better! – to unbend it. Unbending it with consideration, and, of course, a gentle hand –, *unbending* it with friendly pity: that is the true art of Jesuitism, which has always known how to introduce itself as a religion of pity. –

207

However gratefully we might approach the *objective* spirit – and who hasn't been sick to death at least once of everything subjective, with its damned *ipsissimosity*![4] – nevertheless, in the end we even have to be cautious of our gratitude, and put an end to the exaggerated terms in which people have recently been celebrating the desubjectivization and depersonification of spirit, as if this were some sort of goal in itself, some sort of redemption or transfiguration. This kind of thing tends to happen within the pessimist school, which has reasons of its own for regarding "disinterested know-ing" with the greatest respect. The objective man who no longer swears or complains like the pessimist does, the *ideal* scholar who expresses the scientific instinct as it finally blossoms and blooms all the way (after things have gone partly or wholly wrong a thousand times over) – he is certainly

---

4 Nietzsche's coinage from the Latin "*ipsissima*" meaning "very own."

one of the most expensive tools there is: but he belongs in the hands of someone more powerful. He is only a tool, we will say: he is a *mirror*, – he is not an "end in himself." The objective man is really a mirror: he is used to subordinating himself in front of anything that wants to be known, without any other pleasure than that of knowing, of "mirroring forth." He waits until something comes along and then spreads himself gently towards it, so that even light footsteps and the passing by of a ghostly being are not lost on his surface and skin. He has so thoroughly become a passageway and reflection of strange shapes and events, that whatever is left in him of a "person" strikes him as accidental, often arbitrary, and still more often as disruptive. It takes an effort for him to think back on "himself," and he is not infrequently mistaken when he does. He easily confuses himself with others, he is wrong about his own basic needs, and this is the only respect in which he is crude and careless. Maybe his health is making him suffer, or the pettiness and provincial airs of a wife or a friend, or the lack of companions and company, – all right then, he makes himself think about his sufferings: but to no avail! His thoughts have already wandered off, towards *more general* issues, and by the next day he does not know how to help himself any more than he knew the day before. He has lost any serious engagement with the issue as well as the time to spend on it: he is cheerful, *not* for lack of needs but for lack of hands to grasp *his* neediness. The obliging manner in which he typically approaches things and experiences, the sunny and natural hospitality with which he accepts everything that comes at him, his type of thoughtless goodwill, of dangerous lack of concern for Yeses and Noes: oh, there are plenty of times when he has to pay for these virtues of his! – and being human, he all too easily becomes the *caput mortuum*[5] of these virtues. If you want him to love or hate (I mean love and hate as a god, woman, or animal would understand the terms –) he will do what he can and give what he can. But do not be surprised if it is not much, – if this is where he comes across as fake, fragile, questionable, and brittle. His love is forced, his hatred artificial and more like *un tour de force*, a little piece of vanity and exaggeration. He is sincere only to the extent that he is allowed to be objective: he is "nature" and "natural" only in his cheerful totality. His mirror-like soul is forever smoothing itself out; it does not know how to affirm or negate any more. He does not command; and neither does he destroy.

[5] Worthless residue.

"*Je ne méprise presque rien*,"[6] he says with Leibniz: that *presque* should not be overlooked or underestimated! He is no paragon of humanity; he does not go in front of anyone or behind. In general, he puts himself at too great a distance to have any basis for choosing between good or evil. If people have mistaken him for a *philosopher* for so long, for a Caesar-like man who cultivates and breeds, for the brutal man of culture – then they have paid him much too high an honor and overlooked what is most essential about him, – he is a tool, a piece of slave (although, without a doubt, the most sublime type of slave) but nothing in himself, – *presque rien*! The objective person is a tool, an expensive measuring instrument and piece of mirror art that is easily injured and spoiled and should be honored and protected; but he is not a goal, not a departure or a fresh start, he is not the sort of complementary person in which the *rest* of existence justifies itself. He is not a conclusion – and still less a beginning, begetter or first cause; there is nothing tough, powerful or self-supporting that wants to dominate. Rather, he is only a gentle, brushed-off, refined, agile pot of forms, who first has to wait for some sort of content or substance in order "to shape" himself accordingly, – he is generally a man without substance or content, a "selfless" man. And consequently, *in parenthesi*, nothing for women. –

208

When a philosopher these days makes it known that he is not a skeptic, – and I hope that this could be detected in the account of the objective spirit just given – everyone gets upset. People look at him apprehensively, they have so many questions, questions . . . in fact, frightened eavesdroppers (and there are crowds of them these days) will begin to consider him dangerous. It is as if they could hear, in his rejection of skepticism, some sort of evil and ominous sound in the distance, as if a new explosive were being tested somewhere, a dynamite of the spirit, perhaps a newly discovered Russian *nihiline*,[7] a pessimism *bonae voluntatis*[8] that does not just *say* No or *will* No, but – the very thought is terrible! – *does* No. It is generally acknowledged nowadays that no tranquilizer or sedative works

---

[6] "I despise almost nothing." In lines that follow, *presque* means "almost" and *presque rien* means "almost nothing."

[7] A neologism coined from "nihilism."

[8] Of goodwill.

better against this type of "goodwill" – a will to the actual, violent negation of life – than skepticism, the soft, sweet, soothing, poppy flower of
skepticism; and even *Hamlet* is prescribed by physicians today as a protection against "spirit" and its underground rumblings. "Aren't people's
ears already filled with enough bad sounds?" the skeptic asks, being a
friend of peace and almost a type of security police: "This subterranean
No is awful! Be quiet already, you pessimistic moles!" Which is to say: the
skeptic, that gentle creature, is all too easily frightened. His conscience
has been trained to jump at every no, or even at a decisive and hardened
yes, and to feel it like a bite. Yes! and No! – this is contrary to morality, as
far as he is concerned. Conversely, he loves to treat his virtues to a feast of
noble abstinence, when, for instance, he says, with Montaigne: "What do I
know?" Or with Socrates: "I know that I don't know anything." Or "I don't
trust myself here, there aren't any doors open to me." Or: "Even if one
were open, why go in right away!" Or: "What good are rash hypotheses?
It might very well be good taste not to formulate any hypotheses at all.
When something is crooked, do you people really need to straighten it
right away? or plug something into every hole? Isn't there plenty of time
for that? Doesn't time have plenty of time? Oh, you fiends, why can't you
just *wait* a while? Even uncertainty has its charms, even the Sphinx is a
Circe, even Circe was a philosopher." – This is how a skeptic comforts
himself; and it is true that he needs some comfort. Skepticism is the most
spiritual expression of a certain complex physiological condition which in
layman's terms is called weak nerves or a sickly constitution. It originates
whenever races or classes that have been separated for a long time are
suddenly and decisively interbred. The different standards and values,
as it were, get passed down through the bloodline to the next generation
where everything is in a state of restlessness, disorder, doubt, experimen-
tation. The best forces have inhibitory effects, the virtues themselves do
not let each other strengthen and grow, both body and soul lack a center of balance, a center of gravity and the assurance of a pendulum. But
what is most profoundly sick and degenerate about such hybrids is the
will: they no longer have any sense of independence in decision-making,
or the bold feeling of pleasure in willing, – they doubt whether there is
"freedom of will," even in their dreams. Our contemporary Europe, the
site of an absurdly sudden experiment in the radical mixing of classes and
consequently of races, is therefore skeptical from its heights to its depths,
sometimes with that agile kind of skepticism that leaps impatiently and

licentiously from one branch to another; at other times it is gloomy like a cloud overloaded with question-marks – and often sick to death of its will! Paralysis of the will: where *won't* you find this cripple today? And often how nicely dressed! How seductively dressed! This illness has the prettiest fancy-dress clothes and liar's outfits. And most of what presents itself in the shop windows these days as "objectivity," for instance, or "scientificity," "*l'art pour l'art*,"[9] or "pure, will-less knowing," is only dressed–up skepticism and paralysis of the will, – I will vouch for this diagnosis of the European disease. – The disease of the will has spread unevenly across Europe. It appears greatest and most varied where the culture has been at home for the longest period of time; and it becomes increasingly faint to the extent that "the barbarian" still – or once again – asserts his rights under the sagging robes of occidental cultivation. This is why the will is most sick in present-day France, a fact which can be logically concluded as easily as it can be palpably felt. France has always had the brilliant historical sense to turn even disastrous changes of its spirit into something charming and seductive. Now, it clearly indicates its culturally dominant position within Europe by being the school and showcase for all the magic spells of skepticism. The strength to will and, in fact, a will to will at length, is somewhat more vigorous in Germany, and stronger in the north of Germany than in the center. It is considerably stronger in England, Spain, and Corsica; in one place it is bound up with apathy, in another, with hard heads, – not to mention Italy, which is too young to know what it wants, and which first needs to prove that it *can* will –. But it is the strongest of all and the most amazing in that vast intermediary zone where Europe, as it were, flows back into Asia: in Russia. There, the strength to will has been laid aside and stored up over a long time; there, the will is waiting threateningly (uncertain whether as a will of negation or of affirmation), to be discharged (to borrow a favorite term from today's physicists). More than just Indian wars and Asian intrigues might be needed to relieve Europe of its greatest danger – inner rebellions might be needed as well, the dispersion of the empire into small bodies, and, above all, the introduction of parliamentary nonsense, added to which would be the requirement that every man read his newspaper over breakfast. This is not something I am hoping for. I would prefer the opposite, – I mean the sort of increase in the threat Russia poses that

9 "Art for art's sake."

would force Europe into choosing to become equally threatening and, specifically, *to acquire a single will* by means of a new caste that would rule over Europe, a long, terrible will of its own, that could give itself millennia-long goals: – so that the long, spun-out comedy of Europe's petty provincialism and its dynastic as well as democratic fragmentation of the will could finally come to an end. The time for petty politics is over: the next century will bring the struggle for the domination of the earth – the *compulsion* to great politics.

209

The extent to which the new, warlike age that we Europeans have obviously entered into may, perhaps, also be favorable to the development of another, stronger type of skepticism – for the time being, I would like to restrict my remarks on this matter to a parable that the friends of German history will already understand. That completely unscrupulous devotee of tall, handsome grenadiers who, as king of Prussia, brought a military and skeptical genius into being (and with it, fundamentally, that new type of German which is only now approaching in triumph), the questionable, mad father of Frederick the Great,[10] had the grasp and lucky claw of a genius too, although on one point only: he knew what was missing in Germany in those days, and which lack was a hundred times more urgent and anxiety-provoking than the lack of something like education or social decorum, – his dislike for young Frederick came from the anguish of a profound instinct. *Men were lacking*; and he suspected, to his most bitter distress, that his own son was not man enough. He was wrong about this, but who wouldn't have been wrong in his place? He saw his son falling prey to atheism, *esprit*, and the entertaining, happy-go-lucky spirit of clever Frenchmen: he saw that enormous bloodsucker, the spider of skepticism, in the background, and he suspected the incurable misery of a heart that was no longer hard enough for evil or for good, of a shattered will that no longer commanded, that was no longer *able* to command. Meanwhile, however, a harsher and more dangerous new type of skepticism was growing in his son (and who knows how much it was encouraged precisely *by* his father's hatred and the icy melancholy of an isolated will?) – the

---

[10] Frederick William I.

skepticism of a bold masculinity, which is most closely related to the genius for war and conquest, and which first entered Germany in the shape of the great Frederick. This skepticism despises and nevertheless appropriates; it undermines and takes possession; it does not believe but does not die out on this account; it gives the spirit a dangerous freedom, but is severe on the heart. The *German* form of skepticism (being a continued Frederickianism that has been intensified to the most spiritual degree) has put Europe under the dominion of German spirit with its critical and historical mistrust for a long time. Thanks to the unyielding strength and tenacity in the masculine character of the great German philologists and critical historians (seen properly, they were also all artists of decay and destruction), and in spite of all the romanticism in music and philosophy, a *new* concept of the German spirit is gradually emerging, and it clearly tends towards a masculine skepticism: it might be the intrepidity of the gaze, the courage and severity of the dissecting hand, or the tenacious will to dangerous voyages of discovery, to spiritualized North Pole expeditions under desolate and dangerous skies. Warm-blooded and superficial humanitarians may have good reasons for crossing themselves in front of this spirit; *cet esprit fataliste, ironique, méphistophélique*[11] as Michelet calls it, not without a shudder. But this "man" in the German spirit, which has awoken Europe from its "dogmatic slumber,"[12] – if you want to understand how distinctive the fear of this "man" really is, just remember the earlier conception that this one had to overcome, – and how it was not so long ago that a masculinized woman[13] could dare, with boundless presumption, to commend the Germans to European sympathies as gentle, good-hearted, weak-willed, poetic fools. You can really understand Napoleon's surprise when he got to see Goethe:[14] it showed what people had understood by the term "German spirit" for centuries. "*Voilà un homme!*" – which was to say: "Now there's a *man*! And I'd only expected a German!" –

---

[11] "This fatalistic, ironical, Mephistophelian spirit."

[12] An allusion to Kant's claim in the *Prolegomena zu einer jeden künftigen Metaphysik* (*Prolegomena to any Future Metaphysics*) (1783) that Hume's empiricism awoke him from the dogmatic slumber of rationalism.

[13] Madame de Staël in her *De l'Allemagne* (*On Germany*) (1810).

[14] See Goethe's *Unterredung mit Napoleon* (*Discussion with Napoleon*) (2 October 1808).

So, if something in the image of future philosophers makes us suspect that they will, perhaps, be skeptics (in the sense just mentioned), then it would only indicate some aspect of them and *not* who they themselves really are. They could be called critics with equal justification; and they will certainly be engaged in experiments. I have already laid particular emphasis on the notions of tempting, attempting, and the joy of experimenting in the name that I have dared to christen them with: is this because, as critics in body and soul, they love to experiment in a new, perhaps broader, perhaps more dangerous sense? In their passion for knowledge, won't they need to go further, with bold and painful experiments, than the faint-hearted, pampered taste of a democratic century can think proper? – Without a doubt: these coming philosophers will be least able to dispense with the qualities that distinguish the critic from the skeptic – qualities that are rather serious and by no means harmless. I mean: the certainty of value standards, the conscious implementation of a unity of method, a sly courage, a solitary stance, and capacity for responsibility. In fact, these philosophers admit to taking *pleasure* in saying no, in dissecting, and in a certain level-headed cruelty that knows how to guide a knife with assurance and subtlety, even when the heart is bleeding. They will be *more severe* (and perhaps not always with themselves alone) than humane people might wish them to be. They will not engage with "truth" in such a way that it "pleases" or "elevates" or "inspires" them; they will hardly believe that the *truth*, of all things, would keep the feelings this amused. These severe spirits will smile when they hear someone say: "This thought elevates me: how could it fail to be true?" Or: "This work charms me: how could it fail to be beautiful?" Or: "That artist ennobles me: how could he fail to be noble?" – they might be ready not just with a smile but with a genuine disgust for all these over-enthusiasms, idealisms, femininities, hermaphrodisms. And anyone who knows how to follow these spirits down into the secret chambers of their heart is not likely to discover any intention to reconcile "Christian feelings" with "ancient taste" or with anything like "modern parliamentarianism" (although these sorts of conciliatory overtures are said to take place in our very uncertain and consequently very conciliatory century, even among philosophers). These philosophers of the future will demand (and not only of themselves) critical discipline and every habit that leads to cleanliness and rigor in matters of the spirit. They might even wear these like a type of jewel they have on display, – nevertheless, they still do not want to be called critics. They think it is no small disgrace for philosophy these days, when people are so happy to announce: "Philosophy itself is criticism and critical science – and nothing else whatsoever!" However much all the French and German positivists might approve of this evaluation of philosophy (– and it might even have flattered *Kant's* heart and taste: just think of the titles of his major works –), our new philosophers will nevertheless say: critics are tools of philosophy and that is precisely why, being tools, they are so far from being philosophers! Even the great Chinaman of Königsberg[15] was only a great critic. –

211

I am going to insist that people finally stop mistaking philosophical laborers and scientific men in general for philosophers, – that here, of all places, people be strict about giving "each his due" and not too much to the one, and much too little to the other. In the course of his education, the genuine philosopher might have been required to stand on each of the steps where his servants, the philosophical scientific laborers, have come to a stop, – have *had to* come to a stop. Perhaps the philosopher has had to be a critic and a skeptic and a dogmatist and historian and, moreover, a poet and collector and traveler and guesser of riddles and moralist and seer and "free spirit" and practically everything, in order to run through the range of human values and value feelings and *be able* to gaze with many eyes and consciences from the heights into every distance, from the depths up to every height, from the corner onto every expanse. But all these are only preconditions for his task: the task itself has another will, – it calls for him to *create values*. The project for philosophical laborers on the noble model of Kant and Hegel is to establish some large class of given values (which is to say: values that were once *posited* and created but have come to dominate and have been called "truths" for a long time) and press it into formulas, whether in the realm of *logic* or *politics* (morality) or *art*. It is up to these researchers to make everything that has happened or been valued so far look clear, obvious, comprehensible, and manageable, to abbreviate everything long, even "time" itself, and to *overwhelm* the entire past. This is an enormous and wonderful task, in whose service any subtle

[15] An allusion to Kant, who spent his life in Königsberg.

pride or tough will can certainly find satisfaction. *But true philosophers are commanders and legislators*: they say "That is how it *should* be!" they are the ones who first determine the "where to?" and "what for?" of people, which puts at their disposal the preliminary labor of all philosophical laborers, all those who overwhelm the past. True philosophers reach for the future with a creative hand and everything that is and was becomes a means, a tool, a hammer for them. Their "knowing" is *creating*, their creating is a legislating, their will to truth is – *will to power*. – Are there philosophers like this today? Have there ever been philosophers like this? Won't there *have to be* philosophers like this? . . .

212

It seems increasingly clear to me that the philosopher, being *necessarily* a person of tomorrow and the day after tomorrow, has, in every age, been and has *needed* to be at odds with his today: his enemy has always been the ideal of today. So far, all these extraordinary patrons of humanity who are called philosophers (and who have seldom felt like friends of wisdom, but like disagreeable fools and dangerous question-marks instead –) have found that their task, their harsh, unwanted, undeniable task (though in the end, the *greatness* of their task) lay in being the bad conscience of their age. In applying a vivisecting knife directly to the chest of the *virtues of the age*, they gave away their own secret: to know a *new* greatness in humanity, a new, untraveled path to human greatness. Every time they have done this, they have shown how much hypocrisy and laziness, how much letting yourself go and letting go of yourself, how many lies are hidden beneath the most highly honored type of their present-day morality, and how much virtue is *out of date*. Every time, they have said: "We need to go there, out there, out where *you* feel least at home today." When encountering a world of "modern ideas" which would gladly banish everyone into a corner and "specialization," a philosopher (if there could be philosophers today) would be compelled to locate the greatness of humanity, the concept of "greatness," in the very scope and variety of humanity, in its unity in multiplicity. He would determine even value and rank according to how much and how many things someone could carry and take upon himself, how *far* someone could stretch his responsibility. Today, the will is weakened and diluted by the tastes and virtues of the times, and nothing is as timely as weakness of will: this is why precisely strength of will and the hardness and capacity for long-term resolutions must belong to the concept of "greatness," in the philosopher's ideal. With equal justice, the opposite doctrine and the ideal of a stupid, self-abnegating, humble, selfless humanity was suited to an opposite age, to an age like the sixteenth century that suffered from its accumulated energy of the will and from the most savage floods and storm tides of egoism. In the age of Socrates, among honest people with tired instincts, among conservatives of ancient Athens who let themselves go – "toward happiness," as they put it, toward pleasure, as they did it – and who kept mouthing old, magnificent words (words that they had absolutely no right to use any more, given the lives they were leading), – here, perhaps, *irony* was needed for greatness of soul, that malicious, Socratic certainty of the old physician and man of the rabble who cut brutally into his own flesh like he cut into the flesh and heart of the "noble," with a glance that spoke clearly enough: "Don't act some part in front of me! Here – we are equals!" These days, by contrast, when only the herd animal gets and gives honor in Europe, when "equal rights" could all too easily end up as equal wrongs (I mean, in waging a joint war on everything rare, strange, privileged, on the higher man, higher soul, higher duty, higher responsibility, on creative power and mastery) – these days, the concept of "greatness" will include: being noble, wanting to be for yourself, the ability to be different, standing alone and needing to live by your own fists. And the philosopher will be revealing something of his own ideal when he proposes: "Greatest of all is the one who can be the most solitary, the most hidden, the most different, the person beyond good and evil, the master of his virtues, the one with an abundance of will. Only this should be called *greatness*: the ability to be just as multiple as whole, just as wide as full." And to ask once again: is greatness *possible* today?

213

It is difficult to learn what a philosopher is, because it cannot be taught: you have to "know" by experience, – or you should be proud that you do *not* know it at all. But nowadays everyone talks about things that they *cannot* experience, and most especially (and most terribly) when it comes to philosophers and philosophical matters. Hardly anyone knows about them or is allowed to know, and all popular opinions about them are false. So, for instance, the genuinely philosophical compatibility between a bold and lively spirituality that runs along at a *presto*, and a dialectical rigor and necessity that does not take a single false step – this is an experience most thinkers and scholars would find unfamiliar and, if someone were to mention it, unbelievable. They think of every necessity as a need, a painstaking having-to-follow and being-forced; and they consider thinking itself as something slow and sluggish, almost a toil and often enough "worth the *sweat* of the noble." Not in their wildest dreams would they think of it as light, divine, and closely related to dance and high spirits! "Thinking" and "treating an issue seriously," "with gravity" – these belong together, according to most thinkers and scholars: that is the only way they have "experienced" it –. Artists might have a better sense of smell even in this matter: they are the ones who know only too well that their feeling of freedom, finesse and authority, of creation, formation, and control only reaches its apex when they have stopped doing anything "voluntarily" and instead do everything necessarily, – in short, they know that inside themselves necessity and "freedom of the will" have become one. In the last analysis, there is a rank order of psychic states which corresponds to the rank order of problems; and the highest problems will ruthlessly repel anyone who dares to get close without being predestined by sheer stature and power of spirituality to reach a solution. What good is it if, as happens so often these days, agile, ordinary minds or clumsy, worthy mechanists and empiricists throng with their plebeian ambition to these problems and into, as it were, the "inner courtyard"! But crude feet would never be allowed on a carpet like this: this has already been provided for in the primordial laws of things. The door will stay barred against these intruders, however much they push or pound their heads against it! You need to have been born for any higher world; to say it more clearly, you need to have been *bred* for it: only your descent, your ancestry can give you a right to philosophy – taking that word in its highest sense. Even here, "bloodline" is decisive. The preparatory labor of many generations is needed for a philosopher to come about; each of his virtues needs to have been individually acquired, cared for, passed down, and incorporated: and not only the bright, light, gentle gait and course of his thoughts, but above all the eagerness for great responsibilities, the sovereignty of his ruling gazes and downward gazes, the feeling of separation from the crowd with its duties and virtues, the genial protection and defense of anything misunderstood and slandered, whether it is god or devil, the pleasure and practice in great justice, the art of command, the expanse of the will, the slow eye that hardly ever admires, hardly ever looks up, hardly ever loves . . .

Part 7 Our virtues

214

Our virtues? – We probably still have our virtues too, although of course they will not be those trusting and muscular virtues for which we hold our grandfathers in honor – but also slightly at arm's length. We Europeans from the day after tomorrow, we firstborn of the twentieth century, – with all of our dangerous curiosity, our diversity and art of disguises, our worn-out and, as it were, saccharine cruelty in sense and in spirit, – *if* we happen to have virtues, they will presumably only be the ones that have learned best how to get along with our most secret and heartfelt propensities, with our most fervent desires. So let us look for them in our labyrinths! where, as we know, so many things lose their way, so many things get entirely lost. And is there anything more beautiful than *looking for* your own virtues? Doesn't this almost mean: *believing* in your own virtue? But this "believing in your own virtue" – isn't this basically what people used to call their "good conscience," that venerable, long-haired pigtail of a concept that hung on the back of our grandfathers' heads, and often enough behind their intellects too? And so it seems that however up-to-date and unworthy of grandfatherly honor we might otherwise appear, there is nevertheless one respect in which we are the worthy grandchildren of these grandfathers, we last Europeans with a good conscience: we still wear their pigtail. – Oh! If you knew how soon, so soon now – things will be different! . . .

215

Just as in the celestial realm, the track of one planet will sometimes be determined by two suns; just as, in certain cases, suns of different colors will shine on a single planet with red light one moment and green light the next, and then strike it again, inundating it with many colors all at once: in the same way, thanks to the complex mechanics of *our* "starry skies," we modern men are determined by a *diversity* of morals; our actions shine with different colors in turn, they are rarely unambiguous, – and it happens often enough that we perform *multi-colored* actions.

216

To love your enemies? I think this has been learned quite well: it happens thousands of times these days, in large and small ways; in fact, something even higher and more sublime happens every once in a while – we learn to *despise* when we love and precisely when we love the most. But all of this is unconscious, noiseless, lacking in pomp or pageantry but possessing that shame and concealed goodness which forbids the mouth from using any solemn words or virtuous formulas. Morality as posturing – offends our taste these days. This is progress too, just as it was progress for our fathers when religion as posturing finally offended *their* taste, including the hostility and Voltairean bitterness towards religion (and everything that used to belong to the sign language of free spirits). No puritan litany, moral homily, or petty bourgeois respectability wants to resonate with the music in our conscience and the dance in our spirit.

217

Watch out for people who put a high value on being credited with moral tact and with subtlety in making moral distinctions! They will never forgive us if they ever make a mistake in front of us (or especially *about* us), – they will inevitably become our instinctive slanderers and detractors, even if they still remain our "friends." Blessed are the forgetful: for they will "have done" with their stupidities too.

218

The French psychologists – and where else are there still psychologists today? – have never grown tired of their bitter and manifold delight in the *bêtise bourgeoise*,[1] somewhat as if . . . enough, this reveals something about them. For instance, Flaubert, the good citizen of Rouen, ultimately stopped seeing, hearing, or tasting anything else: this was his brand of self-torture and subtler cruelty. Now – because this is getting boring – I recommend another source of amusement for a change: the unconscious cunning that all good, fat, well-behaved, mediocre spirits have shown towards higher spirits and their tasks, that subtle, intricate, Jesuitical cunning that is a thousand times more subtle than any taste or understanding evinced by this middle class in its best moments – it is even more subtle than its victims' understanding (which is on-going proof that "instinct" is the most intelligent type of intelligence discovered so far). In short, you psychologists should study the philosophy of the "rule" in its struggle against the "exception": there you will see drama good enough for gods and divine malice! Or, to be even more up to date: vivisect the "good man," the "*homo bonae voluntatis*"[2] . . . *yourselves*!

219

Moral judgment and condemnation is the favorite revenge of the spiritually limited on those who are less so, as well as a type of compensation for having been slighted by nature, and an opportunity to finally acquire spirit and *become* refined: – malice spiritualizes. It warms the bottom of their hearts for there to be a standard that makes them the equal of even people who are teeming with all the qualities and privileges of spirit: – they fight for the "equality of all before God" and almost *need* to believe in God for this reason alone. Among them are the strongest opponents of atheism. If anyone were to tell them that "a high spirituality is beyond comparison with any sort of good behavior or worthiness of a merely moral man," they would be livid: – I certainly would not do it. I would rather flatter them by claiming that a high spirituality is itself only the final, monstrous product of moral qualities; that it is a synthesis of all the states attributed to the "merely moral" men after they had been acquired individually, through long discipline and practice, perhaps through whole series of generations; that high spirituality is just the spiritualization of justice and a benevolent severity that knows how to charge itself with the preservation of the

---

[1] Bourgeois stupidity.

[2] "Man of goodwill."

order of rank in the world among things themselves – and not just among people.

220

Given the popularity of the term "disinterested" in praising people these days, we need to be aware (although this might prove dangerous) of *what* it is that really interests the people and what sorts of things the common man cares truly and deeply about (including educated people and even scholars and, unless I am badly mistaken, the philosophers as well). The fact then emerges that the overwhelming majority of things that interest and appeal to the more refined and discriminating tastes, to every higher nature, will strike the average person as utterly "uninteresting." If he notices a devotion to it anyway, then he calls it "*désintéressé*" and wonders how it is possible to act in a "disinterested" fashion. There have been philosophers who have even known how to express this popular perplexity in a seductive and mystico–otherworldly way (– perhaps because they did not have first-hand knowledge of higher natures?) – instead of laying down the naked and fully proper truth that a "disinterested" action is a *very* interesting and interested action, provided . . . "And love?" – What? Even an action done out of love is supposed to be "unegoistic"? But you fools – ! "And praise for the self-sacrificing?" But anyone who has really made sacrifices knows that he wanted and got something in return, – perhaps something of himself in return for something of himself – that he gave up here in order to have more there, perhaps in order to be more in general, or just to feel like "more." But this is a realm of questions and answers in which a more discriminating spirit will not want to stay for very long: the truth is already desperate to keep herself from yawning when she is required to respond. In the end, she is a woman: we should not do violence to her.

221

"It sometimes happens," said a moralistic pedant and stickler for detail, "that I honor and esteem an altruistic person. Not because he is altruistic, however, but because it seems to me that he has the right to help another person at his own expense. Enough, it is always a question of who *he* is and who that *other* is. For instance, in a person who was made and determined for command, self-denial and modest retreat would not be a virtue but the waste of a virtue: that is how it seems to me. Every unegoistic morality that considers itself unconditional and is directed toward everyone does not just sin against taste: it is a provocation to sins of omission, and one *more* temptation under a mask of benevolence – a temptation and injury to precisely the higher, the rarer, the privileged. Morals must be compelled from the very start to bow before *rank order*, their presumptuousness must be forced onto their conscience, – until they are finally in agreement with each other that it is *immoral* to say: 'What's right for the one is fair for the other.'" – So says my moralistic pedant and *bonhomme*:[3] does he really deserve to be laughed at for urging morals to morality in this way? But you should not be too right if you want to get a laugh; a kernel of wrong belongs to even a good taste.

222

Wherever pity is preached these days – and if you are listening properly, no other religion is preached any more – let the psychologist open up his ears. Through all the vanity, through all the noise that this preacher (like all preachers) intrinsically possesses, the psychologist will hear the genuine, rasping, groaning sound of *self-hatred*. This self-hatred belongs to the darkening and increasing ugliness of Europe, which have been growing for a hundred years now (and whose first symptoms were already documented in Galiani's thought-provoking letter to Madame d'Epinay): *if it is not the cause!* The man of "modern ideas," this proud ape, is exceedingly unhappy with himself: this is clear. He suffers: and his vanity would have it that he only pities . . . [4]

223

The hybrid mixed man of Europe – a fairly ugly plebeian, all in all – absolutely must have a costume: he needs history as a storage closet of costumes. Of course, he notices that nothing really looks right on him, – he keeps changing. Just look at these rapid preferences and changes in the masquerade of styles over the course of the nineteenth century; and at the moments of despair over the fact that "nothing suits" us –. It is pointless to

---

[3] Good man.

[4] In German: *mit leidet* (literally: "suffers with"). Here as elsewhere, Nietzsche is playing on the similarities between the terms *leiden* (to suffer) and *Mitleid* (pity).

dress up as romantic or classical or Christian or Florentine or Baroque or "national," in *moribus et artibus*:[5] it "doesn't look good"! But the "spirit," and particularly the "historical spirit," finds that even this despair is to its own advantage: again and again, a new piece of prehistory or foreign country will be tried out, turned over, filed away, packed up, and above all *studied*. We are the first age to be educated *in puncto*[6] of "costumes," I mean of morals, articles of faith, artistic tastes, and religions, and prepared as no age has ever been for a carnival in the grand style, for the most spiritually carnivalesque laughter and high spirits, for the transcendental heights of the highest inanity and Aristophanean world mockery. Perhaps it's that we still discover a realm of our *invention* here, a realm where we can still be original too, as parodists of world history or buffoons of God, or something like that, – perhaps it's that, when nothing else from today has a future, our *laughter* is the one thing that does!

224

The *historical sense* (or the ability quickly to guess the rank order of the valuations that a people, a society, an individual has lived by, the "divinatory instinct" for the connections between these valuations, for the relationship between the authority of values and the authority of effective forces): this historical sense that we Europeans claim as our distinguishing characteristic comes to us as a result of that enchanting and crazy *half-barbarism* into which Europe has been plunged through the democratic mixing of classes and races, – only the nineteenth century sees this sense as its sixth sense. Thanks to this mixture, the past of every form and way of life, of cultures that used to lie side by side or on top of each other, radiates into us, we "modern souls." At this point, our instincts are running back everywhere and we ourselves are a type of chaos –. "Spirit," as I have said, eventually finds that this is to its own advantage. Because of the half-barbarism in our bodies and desires, we have secret entrances everywhere, like no noble age has ever had, and, above all, access to the labyrinths of unfinished cultures and to every half-barbarism that has ever existed on earth. And since the most considerable part of human culture to date has been just such half-barbarism, the "historical sense" practically amounts to a sense and

[5] In customs and arts.

[6] With respect to.

instinct for everything, a taste and tongue for everything: by which it immediately shows itself to be an *ignoble* sense. For instance, we are enjoying
Homer again: knowing how to taste Homer might be our greatest advantage, one that people from a noble culture (such as seventeenth-century
Frenchmen, like Saint-Evremond, who reproached Homer for an *esprit
vaste*,[7] and even Voltaire, their concluding note) do not and did not find
very easy to acquire – and one that they would hardly allow themselves
to enjoy. The very precise Yes and No of their palate, their ready disgust,
their hesitant reserve about everything strange or exotic, their fear of the
poor taste of even a lively curiosity, and in general that unwillingness seen
in every noble and self-sufficient culture to admit to itself a new lust, a
dissatisfaction with its own, an admiration of something foreign: all this
prejudices a noble culture and puts it at odds with even the best things
in the world, if they are not its property and *could not* become its spoils.
And no sense is more incomprehensible to such people than precisely
this historical sense with its obsequious plebeian curiosity. It is no different with Shakespeare, that amazing Spanish-Moorish-Saxon synthesis of
tastes that would have almost killed one of Aeschylus' ancient Athenian
friends with either rage or laughter: but we – accept precisely this wild
burst of colors, this confusion of the most delicate, the crudest, and the
most artificial with a secret familiarity and warmth. We enjoy him as the
artistic refinement that has been reserved just for us, and meanwhile we
do not let ourselves be bothered by the noxious fumes and the proximity
of the English rabble in which Shakespeare's art and taste lives, any more
than we do on the Chiaja of Naples, for instance: where we go on our way
with all of our senses, enchanted and willing, however much the sewers
of the rabble districts are in the air. We men of "historical sense," we do
have our virtues – this cannot be denied. We are unassuming, selfless,
modest, brave, full of self-overcoming, full of dedication, very grateful,
very patient, very accommodating: – but for all that we are, perhaps, not
very "tasteful." Finally, let us admit to ourselves: what we men of "historical sense" find the most difficult to grasp, to feel, to taste again and
love again, what we are fundamentally biased against and almost hostile
towards, is just that perfected and newly ripened aspect of every art and
culture, the genuinely noble element in works and people, their moment
of smooth seas and halcyon self-sufficiency, the gold and the coldness

---

[7] Enormous spirit.

seen in all things that have perfected themselves. Perhaps our great virtue of historical sense is necessarily opposed to *good* taste, at least to the very best taste, and it is only poorly and haltingly, only with effort that we are able to reproduce in ourselves the trivial as well as greatest serendipities and transfigurations of human life as they light up every now and then: those moments and marvels when a great force stands voluntarily still in front of the boundless and limitless –, the enjoyment of an abundance of subtle pleasure in suddenly harnessing and fossilizing, in settling down and establishing yourself on ground that is still shaking. *Moderation* is foreign to us, let us admit this to ourselves; our thrill is precisely the thrill of the infinite, the unmeasured. Like the rider on a steed snorting to go further onward, we let the reins drop before the infinite, we modern men, we half-barbarians – and *we* feel supremely happy only when we are in the most – *danger*.

225

Hedonism, pessimism, utilitarianism, eudamonianism: these are all ways of thinking that measure the value of things according to *pleasure* and *pain*, which is to say according to incidental states and trivialities. They are all foreground ways of thinking and naivetés, and nobody who is conscious of both *formative* powers and an artist's conscience will fail to regard them with scorn as well as pity. Pity for *you*! That is certainly not pity as you understand it: it is not pity for social "distress," for "society" with its sick and injured, for people depraved and destroyed from the beginning as they lie around us on the ground; even less is it pity for the grumbling, dejected, rebellious slave strata who strive for dominance – they call it "freedom." *Our* pity is a higher, more far-sighted pity: – we see how humanity is becoming smaller, how *you* are making it smaller! – and there are moments when we look on *your* pity with indescribable alarm, when we fight this pity –, when we find your seriousness more dangerous than any sort of thoughtlessness. You want, if possible (and no "if possible" is crazier) *to abolish suffering*. And us? – it looks as though *we* would prefer it to be heightened and made even worse than it has ever been! Well-being as you understand it – that is no goal; it looks to us like an *end*! – a condition that immediately renders people ridiculous and despicable – that makes their decline into something *desirable*! The discipline of suffering, of *great* suffering – don't you know that *this* discipline has been the sole cause of every enhancement in humanity so far? The tension that breeds strength into the unhappy soul, its shudder at the sight of great destruction, its inventiveness and courage in enduring, surviving, interpreting, and exploiting unhappiness, and whatever depth, secrecy, whatever masks, spirit, cunning, greatness it has been given: – weren't these the gifts of suffering, of the disciple of great suffering? In human beings, *creature* and *creator* are combined: in humans there is material, fragments, abundance, clay, dirt, nonsense, chaos; but in humans there is also creator, maker, hammer-hardness, spectator-divinity and seventh day: – do you understand this contrast? And that *your* pity is aimed at the "creature in humans," at what needs to be molded, broken, forged, torn, burnt, seared and purified, – at what necessarily needs to *suffer* and *should* suffer? And *our* pity – don't you realize who our *inverted* pity is aimed at when it fights against your pity as the worst of all pampering and weaknesses? – Pity *against* pity, then! – But to say it again: there are problems that are higher than any problems of pleasure, pain, or pity; and any philosophy that stops with these is a piece of naiveté. –

226

We immoralists! – This world as it concerns *us*, in which *we* need to love and be afraid, this almost invisible, inaudible world of subtle command, subtle obedience, a world of the "almost" in every respect, twisted, tricky, barbed, and loving: yes, it is well defended against clumsy spectators and friendly curiosity! We have been woven into a strong net and shirt of duties, and *cannot* get out of it –, in this sense we are "people of duty," – even us! It is true that we sometimes dance quite well in our "chains" and between our "swords"; it is no less true that *more* often we grind our teeth and feel impatient at all the secret harshness of our fate. But we can do as we please: fools and appearances will speak up against us, claiming "those are people *without* duties" – fools and appearances are always against us!

227

Genuine honesty,[8] assuming that this is our virtue and we cannot get rid of it, we free spirits – well then, we will want to work on it with all the

---

[8] In German: *Redlichkeit*.

love and malice at our disposal, and not get tired of "perfecting" ourselves in *our* virtue, the only one we have left: may its glory come to rest like a gilded, blue evening glow of mockery over this aging culture and its dull and dismal seriousness! And if our genuine honesty nevertheless gets tired one day and sighs and stretches its limbs and finds us too harsh and would rather things were better, easier, gentler, like an agreeable vice: we will stay *harsh*, we, who are the last of the Stoics! And we will help it out with whatever devilishness we have – our disgust at clumsiness and approximation, our *"nitimur in vetitum,"*[9] our adventurer's courage, our sly and discriminating curiosity, our subtlest, most hidden, most spiritual will to power and world-overcoming which greedily rambles and raves over every realm of the future, – we will bring all of our "devils" to help out our "god"! People will probably misjudge us and misconstrue us on account of this: so what! People will say: "this 'genuine honesty' – this is devilishness and absolutely nothing else!" So what! And even if they were right! Haven't all gods so far been devils like this, who have became holy and been re-baptized? And, ultimately, what do we know about ourselves? And what the spirit that leads us wants to be *called*? (It is a question of names.) And how many spirits we are hiding? Our genuine honesty, we free spirits, – let us make sure that it does not become our vanity, our pomp and finery, our limitation, our stupidity! Every virtue tends towards stupidity, every stupidity towards virtue; "stupid to the point of holiness" they say in Russia, – let us make sure we do not end up becoming saints or tedious bores out of genuine honesty! Isn't life a hundred times too short to be bored? You would have to believe in eternal life in order to . . .

228

You will have to forgive me for having discovered that all moral philosophy so far has been boring and should be classified as a soporific – and that nothing has done more to spoil "virtue" for my ears than this *tediousness* of its advocates; although I would not want to underestimate their general utility. It is quite important that as few people as possible think about morality – consequently, it is *really* quite important for morality not to somehow turn interesting one of these days! But there is no need to worry!

---

[9] "We strive for the forbidden" from Ovid's *Amores*, III, 4, 17.

Things today are the same as they have always been: I don't see anyone in Europe who has (or *conveys*) any idea that moral deliberation could be dangerous, insidious, seductive – that it could be *disastrous*! Just look at the indefatigable, unavoidable English utilitarians, for example, how awkwardly and honorably they walk in Bentham's footsteps, wandering to, wandering fro (a Homeric simile says it better), just as he himself had walked in the footsteps of the honorable Helvétius (no, this was not a dangerous man, this Helvétius!). No new thoughts, no sign of any subtle change or fold in an old thought, not even a real history of the earlier thought: an *impossible* literature on the whole, unless you know how to sour it with some malice. That old English vice called *cant*,[10] which is a piece of *moral tartufferie*, has insinuated itself into these moralists too (who have to be read with ulterior motives, if they have to be read at all –), hidden this time under a new form: science. And there is no lack of secret defenses against all the bites of conscience that will afflict a race of former Puritans whenever they deal with morality on a scientific level. (Isn't a moralist the opposite of a Puritan? A thinker, that is, who treats morality as something questionable, question-mark-able, in short, as a problem? Shouldn't moralists be – immoral?) Ultimately, they all want *English* morality to be given its dues: since it is best for humanity, for the "general utility" or "the happiness of the majority" – no! the happiness of *England*. They want, with all the strength they can muster, to prove to themselves that striving for English happiness, I mean for comfort and fashion[11] (and, at the highest level, for a seat in Parliament), is the proper path to virtue as well, and, in fact, that whatever virtue has existed in the world so far has involved just this sort of striving. Not one of these clumsy, conscience-stricken herd animals (who set out to treat egoism as a matter of general welfare –) wants to know or smell anything of the fact that "general welfare" is no ideal, no goal, not a concept that can somehow be grasped, but only an emetic; – that what is right for someone absolutely *cannot* be right for someone else; that the requirement that there be a single morality for everyone is harmful precisely to the higher men; in short, that there is an *order of rank* between people, and between moralities as well. They are a modest and thoroughly mediocre type of person, these utilitarian Englishmen, but, as I have said: to the extent

---

[10] Nietzsche uses the English word.

[11] Nietzsche uses the English words "comfort" and "fashion."

that they are boring, we cannot think highly enough of their utility. They should even be *encouraged*: as the following rhymes try, in part, to do.

> Good barrow pushers, we salute you,
> "More is best" will always suit you,
> Always stiff in head and knee,
> Lacking spirit, humor too,
> Mediocre through and through,
> *Sans genie et sans esprit!*[12]

229

Mature epochs that have the right to be proud of their humanity are still so full of fear, so full of *superstitious* fear of the "cruel and wild beast" (although the pride these more humane ages feel is actually caused by their mastery of this beast), that even obvious truths remain unspoken for centuries, as if by agreement, because they have the appearance of helping bring the wild beast back to life after it had finally been killed off. Perhaps I am taking a risk in allowing a truth like this to escape: let other people recapture it and make it drink the "milk of pious reflection" until it lies quiet and forgotten in its old corner. – People should rethink their ideas about cruelty and open up their eyes; they should finally learn impatience, so that big, fat, presumptuous mistakes like this will stop wandering virtuously and audaciously about. An example of this is the mistaken ideas about tragedy that have been nurtured by both ancient and modern philosophers. This is my claim: almost everything we call "higher culture" is based on the spiritualization and deepening of *cruelty*. The "wild animal" has not been killed off at all; it is alive and well, it has just – become divine. Cruelty is what constitutes the painful sensuality of tragedy. And what pleases us in so-called tragic pity as well as in everything sublime, up to the highest and most delicate of metaphysical tremblings, derives its sweetness exclusively from the intervening component of cruelty. Consider the Roman in the arena, Christ in the rapture of the cross, the Spaniard at the sight of the stake or the bullfight, the present-day Japanese flocking to tragedies, the Parisian suburban laborer who is homesick for bloody revolutions, the Wagnerienne who unfastens

---

[12] "Without genius and without spirit."

her will and lets *Tristan und Isolde* "wash over her" – what they all enjoy and crave with a mysterious thirst to pour down their throats is "cruelty," the spiced drink of the great Circe. We clearly need to drive out the silly psychology of the past; the only thing this psychology was able to teach about cruelty was that it originated from the sight of *another's* suffering. But there is abundant, overabundant pleasure in your own suffering too, in making yourself suffer, – and wherever anyone lets himself be talked into self-denial in the *religious* sense, or self-mutilation (as the Phoenicians or ascetics did), or into desensitization, disembowelment or remorse in general, or into puritanical penitential spasms, vivisections of conscience or a Pascalian *sacrifizio dell'intelletto*[13] – wherever this is the case, he is secretly being tempted and urged on by his cruelty, by that dangerous thrill of *self*-directed cruelty. Finally, people should bear in mind that even the knower, by forcing his spirit to know *against* its own inclination and, often enough, against the wishes of his heart (in other words, to say "no" when he would like to affirm, love, worship), this knower will prevail as an artist of cruelty and the agent of its transfiguration. Even treating something in a profound or thorough manner is a violation, a wanting-to-hurt the fundamental will of the spirit, which constantly tends towards semblances and surfaces, – there is a drop of cruelty even in every wanting-to-know.

230

Perhaps people will not immediately understand what I have said here about a "fundamental will of the spirit": let me explain. – The commanding element (whatever it is) that is generally called "spirit" wants to dominate itself and its surroundings, and to feel its domination: it wills simplicity out of multiplicity, it is a binding, subduing, domineering, and truly masterful will. Its needs and abilities are the same ones that physiologists have established for everything that lives, grows, and propagates. The power of spirit to appropriate foreign elements manifests itself in a strong tendency to assimilate the new to the old, to simplify the manifold, to disregard or push aside utter inconsistencies: just as it will arbitrarily select certain aspects or outlines of the foreign, of any piece of the "external world," for stronger emphasis, stress, or falsification in its own interest. Its

[13] Sacrifice of the intellect.

intention here is to incorporate new "experiences," to classify new things into old classes, – which is to say: it aims at growth, or, more particularly, the *feeling* of growth, the feeling of increasing strength. This same will is served by an apparently opposite drive of spirit, a suddenly emerging resolution in favor of ignorance and arbitrary termination, a closing of its windows, an inner nay-saying to something or other, a come-no-closer, a type of defensive state against many knowable things, a contentment with darkness, with closing horizons, a yea-saying and approval of ignorance: all of which are necessary in proportion to the degree of its appropriating force, its "digestive force," to speak metaphorically – and really, "spirit" resembles a stomach more than anything. The spirit's occasional will to be deceived belongs here too, perhaps with a playful hunch that things are *not* one way or the other, that people just accept things as one way or the other, a sense of pleasure in every uncertainty and ambiguity, a joyful self-delight at the arbitrary narrowness and secrecy of a corner, at the all-too-close, the foreground, at things made bigger, smaller, later, better, a self-delight at the sheer caprice in all these expressions of power. Finally, the spirit's not quite harmless willingness to deceive other spirits and to act a part in front of them belongs here too, that constant stress and strain of a creative, productive, mutable force. What the spirit enjoys here is its multiplicity of masks and its artfulness, and it also enjoys the feeling of security these provide, – after all, its Protean arts are the very things that protect and conceal it the best! – *This* will to appearances, to simplification, to masks, to cloaks, in short, to surfaces – since every surface is a cloak – meets *resistance* from that sublime tendency of the knower, who treats and *wants* to treat things in a profound, multiple, thorough manner. This is a type of cruelty on the part of the intellectual conscience and taste, and one that any brave thinker will acknowledge in himself, assuming that he has spent as long as he should in hardening and sharpening his eye for himself, and that he is used to strict discipline as well as strict words. He will say "There is something cruel in the tendency of my spirit": – just let kind and virtuous people try to talk him out of it! In fact, it would sound more polite if, instead of cruelty, people were to accuse, mutter about and praise us as having a sort of "wild honesty" – free, *very* free spirits that we are: – and perhaps *this* is what our reputation will really be – posthumously? In the meantime – because this won't be happening for a while – we are the least likely to dress ourselves up with these sorts of moral baubles and beads: all the work we have done so far has spoiled our taste for precisely this sort of bright opulence. These are beautiful, twinkling, tinkling, festive words: genuine honesty, love of truth, love of wisdom, sacrifice for knowledge, the heroism of truthfulness, – there is something about them that makes you swell with pride. But we hermits and marmots, we convinced ourselves a long time ago and in all the secrecy of a hermit's conscience that even this dignified verbal pageantry belongs among the false old finery, debris, and gold dust of unconscious human vanity, and that the terrible basic text of *homo natura*[14] must be recognized even underneath these fawning colors and painted surfaces. To translate humanity back into nature; to gain control of the many vain and fanciful interpretations and incidental meanings that have been scribbled and drawn over that eternal basic text of *homo natura* so far; to make sure that, from now on, the human being will stand before the human being, just as he already stands before the *rest* of nature today, hardened by the discipline of science, – with courageous Oedipus eyes and sealed up Odysseus ears, deaf to the lures of the old metaphysical bird catchers who have been whistling to him for far too long: "You are more! You are higher! You have a different origin!" – This may be a strange and insane task, but it is a *task* – who would deny it! Why do we choose it, this insane task? Or to ask it differently: "Why knowledge at all?" – Everyone will be asking us this. And we who have been prodded so much, we who have asked ourselves the same question a hundred times already, we have not found and are not finding any better answers . . .

231

Learning transforms us, it acts like all other forms of nourishment that do not just "preserve" –: as physiologists know. But at our foundation, "at the very bottom," there is clearly something that will not learn, a brick wall of spiritual *fatum*,[15] of predetermined decisions and answers to selected, predetermined questions. In any cardinal problem, an immutable "that is me" speaks up. When it comes to men and women, for instance, a thinker cannot change his views but only reinforce them, only finish discovering what, to his mind, "is established." In time, certain solutions are found to problems that inspire *our* strong beliefs in particular; perhaps they will

---

[14] Natural man.

[15] Fate.

start to be called "convictions." Later – they come to be seen as only footsteps to self-knowledge, signposts to the problems that we *are*, – or, more accurately, to the great stupidity that we are, to our spiritual *fatum*, to that thing "at the very bottom" that *will not learn*. – On account of the abundant civility that I have just extended to myself, I will perhaps be more readily allowed to pronounce a few truths about the "woman *an sich*":[16] assuming that people now know from the outset the extent to which these are only – *my* truths. –

232

Women want to become independent, so they are beginning to enlighten men about the "woman *an sich*" – *this* is one of the worst developments in Europe's general trend towards *increasing ugliness*. Just imagine what these clumsy attempts at female scientificity and self-disclosure will bring to light! Women have so much cause for shame; they contain so much that is pedantic, superficial, and schoolmarmish as well as narrowmindedly arrogant, presumptuous, and lacking in restraint (just think about their interactions with children!), all of which has been most successfully re-strained and kept under control by their *fear* of men. Look out when the "eternal tedium of woman" (which they all have in abundance!) first dares to emerge! When, on principle, they start completely forgetting their dis-cretion and their art – of grace, play, chasing-all-cares-away, of making things easier and taking them lightly, as well as their subtle skill at pleas-ant desires! Even now, female voices are becoming heard which – holy Aristophanes! – are terrifying, and threaten with medicinal clarity what, in the first and last instance, women *want* from men. Isn't it in the very worst taste when women prepare to be scientific like this? Fortunately, enlightenment had been a man's business, a man's talent until now – as such, we could remain "among ourselves." And with respect to everything that women write about "woman," we can ultimately reserve a healthy doubt as to whether women really want – and are *able* to want – to provide enlightenment about themselves . . . If this is not really all about some woman trying to find a new piece of *finery* for herself (and isn't dressing up a part of the Eternal Feminine?), well then, she wants to inspire fear of

[16] In German: *das "Weib an sich."* The term *"an sich"* means "in itself," as in Kant's *Ding an sich* (thing in itself). I have left the term in German because any English rendering is clumsy, and the German retains both the gender neutrality and the philosophical connotations of the term.

herself: – perhaps in order to dominate. But she *does not* want truth: what does truth matter for a woman! Nothing is so utterly foreign, unfavorable, hostile for women from the very start than truth, – their great art is in lying, their highest concern is appearance and beauty. Let us admit that we men love and honor precisely *this* art and *this* instinct in women: we have a rough time of it, and gladly seek relief by attaching ourselves to a being in whose hands, eyes, and gentle stupidities our seriousness, our gravity, and profundity look almost stupid to us. Finally, I will pose the question: has a woman herself ever acknowledged a female mind as profound or a female heart as just? And isn't it true that, judging overall, "woman" has historically been most despised by women themselves – and not by us at all? – We men wish that women would stop compromising themselves through enlightenment: just as male care and protection of women were at work when the church decreed: *mulier taceat in ecclesia!*[17] It was for women's own good, when Napoleon gave the all-too-eloquent Madame de Staël to understand: *mulier taceat in politicis!*[18] – and I think that it is a true friend of the ladies who calls to them today: *mulier taceat de muliere!*[19]

233

It shows corruption of the instincts – even apart from the fact that it shows bad taste – when a woman refers specifically to Madame Roland or Madame de Staël or Monsieur Georges Sand, as if that proved something in *favor* of the "woman *an sich.*" Men consider these the three *comical* women *an sich* – nothing else! – and precisely the best involuntary *counter-arguments* against emancipation and female self-determination.

234

Stupidity in the kitchen; woman as cook; the spine-chilling thoughtlessness in the feeding of the family and the head of the house! Women do not understand what food *means*: and yet want to cook! If woman were a thoughtful creature, then the fact that she has been the cook for thousands of years would surely have led her to discover the greatest physiological facts, and at the same time make the art of medicine her own! Bad cooking

[17] "Woman should be silent in church."

[18] "Woman should be silent about politics."

[19] "Woman should be silent about woman."

and the complete absence of reason in the kitchen have caused the longest delays and the worst damage to the development of humanity: even today, things are hardly any better. A speech for young ladies.

235

There are phrases and masterstrokes of the spirit, there are aphorisms, a small handful of words, in which an entire culture, an entire society is suddenly crystallized. Madame de Lambert's occasional remark to her son is one of them: "*Mon ami, ne vous permettez jamais que de folies qui vous feront grand plaisir*":[20] – which, by the way, is the most motherly and astute remark that has ever been addressed to a son.

236

What Dante and Goethe believed about women – the former when he sang "*ella guardava suso, ed io in lei*,"[21] the latter when he translated it as "the Eternal Feminine draws us *upward*" –:[22] I have no doubt that any noble woman will object to this belief, since *this* is just what she believes about the Eternal Masculine.

237

Seven little maxims about women

Suddenly we're bored no more when a man crawls through the door!

* *

Age, alas! and science too gives weaker virtues strength anew.

* *

Black gowns and a silent guise make any woman look quite – wise.

* *

Who to thank for my success? God – and my own tailoress.

* *

[20] "My friend, only allow yourself the follies that will give you great pleasure."

[21] "She looked up, and I at her." From Dante's *Divina Commedia: Paradiso*, II, 22.

[22] From Goethe's *Faust* II, line 12110f.

In youth: a flower-covered lair. In age: a dragon stirs in there.

* *

His name is good, his figure's fine, a man as well – if only mine!

* *

When words are few but always sound – a she-mule walks on dangerous ground!

237

So far, men have been treating women like birds that have lost their way and flown down to them from some height or another: like something finer, more vulnerable, wilder, stranger, sweeter, more soulful, – but also like something that has to be locked up to keep it from flying away.

238

To be wrong about the fundamental problem of "man and woman"; on the one hand, to deny the most abysmal antagonism and the necessity of an eternally hostile tension; and, on the other hand, to dream, perhaps, of equal rights, equal education, equal entitlements and obligations: that is a *typical* sign of a shallow mind, and a thinker who has proven to be shallow in this dangerous area – shallow in instinct! –, can be generally regarded as suspicious, or, even more, as shown up for what he is, as exposed. He will probably be too "short" for all the fundamental questions of life, including future life, and unable to get down to them in *any* depth. On the other hand, someone who has the same depth in his spirit as he does in his desires, and also that depth of goodwill which is capable of harshness and strictness and is easily mistaken for them – that sort of man will only ever be able to think about woman in an *oriental* manner. He needs to understand the woman as a possession, as property that can be locked up, as something predestined for servitude and fulfilled by it. In this he has to adopt the position of Asia's enormous rationality, Asia's superiority of instinct, just as the Greeks once did (being Asia's best heirs and students); we know that, from Homer up to the times of Pericles, while their culture was *growing* and their strength expanding, the Greeks were gradually becoming *stricter* with women too – in short, more oriental. *How* necessary, *how* logical – in fact, *how* humanly desirable all this has been: just think about it for a while!

239

The men of our epoch treat the weaker sex with more respect than any epoch has ever done – this is part of the democratic tendency and fundamental taste, as is a lack of respect for age –: is it any wonder that this respect is immediately misused? People want more, people learn to make demands, people ultimately find this respect tax almost hurtful, people would prefer to compete for rights or, in all seriousness, wage war: enough, woman loses her shame. Let us immediately add that she also loses her taste. She forgets her *fear* of man: but the woman who "forgets fear" abandons her most feminine instincts. It is fair enough and also understandable enough for women to dare to emerge when fear of men is no longer inculcated, or, to be more exact, when the *man* in men is no longer wanted and cultivated; what is more difficult to understand is that in the process – women degenerate. This is happening today, make no mistake about it! Wherever the industrial spirit has won out over the military and aristocratic spirit, women are now striving for the economic and legal independence of a clerk: "the woman as clerk" is written on the gateway to the developing, modern society. While women are seizing new rights in this manner, trying to become "master" and writing "progress" for women on their flags and pennants, the opposite is taking place with terrifying clarity: *woman are regressing*. Ever since the French Revolution, the influence of women in Europe has *decreased* proportionately as they have gained rights and entitlements. Accordingly, the "emancipation of women," to the extent that it has been demanded and called for by women themselves (and not just by shallow-minded masculine dolts), turns out to be a strange symptom of the increased weakening and softening of the most feminine instincts of all. The *stupidity* in this movement, an almost masculine stupidity, is enough to make any woman who has turned out well (which always means a clever woman) thoroughly ashamed. To lose your sense for which ground best insures your victory; to neglect practice of your own military arts; to lose control of yourself in front of men, perhaps even "to the point of writing books," where you used to act with discipline and subtle, cunning humility; to work with virtuous courage against men's belief in any *veiled*, fundamentally different ideal in women, in any sort of Eternal or Necessary Feminine; to dissuade men, emphatically and at length, from thinking that women must by kept, cared for, protected, and looked after like gentle, strangely wild and often pleasant house pets; to collect together, in an inept and indignant manner, everything slavish and serflike that was and still is intrinsic to the position of women in the present social order (as if slavery were a counter-argument and not rather a condition of any higher culture, any elevation of culture): – what does all this mean except a crumbling away of feminine instincts, a defeminization? Of course, there are plenty of idiotic friends and corrupters of women among the scholarly asses of the male sex who recommend that women defeminize themselves like this and copy all the stupidities that the "man" in Europe, that European "manliness" suffers from, – who would like to bring women down to the level of "general education," and maybe even of reading the newspapers and taking part in politics. Every now and then, people even want to make free spirits and *literati* out of women: as if a woman without piety were anything other than absolutely repugnant or ludicrous to a profound and godless man –. Almost everywhere, women's nerves are being ruined by the most pathological and dangerous of all types of music (our most recent German music) and women are being made more hysterical by the day, and less capable of performing their first and last profession, the bearing of strong children. People want women to be more "cultivated" in general and want, as they say, to make the "weaker sex" *strong* through culture: as if history did not teach as vividly as possible that "cultivating" human beings and weakening – in particular, weakening, dissipating, afflicting the *strength of the will* – have always kept pace with each other, and that the most powerful and influential women in the world (recently even Napoleon's mother) owed their power and their dominance over men precisely to the strength of their will – and not to schoolteachers! What inspires respect and, often enough, fear of women is their *nature* (which is "more natural" than that of men), their truly predatory and cunning agility, their tiger's claws inside their glove, the naiveté of their egoism, their inner wildness and inability to be trained, the incomprehensibility, expanse, and rambling character of their desires and virtues . . . What inspires pity, in spite of all the fear, for this dangerous and beautiful cat "woman" is that she seems to suffer more, be more vulnerable, need more love, and be condemned to more disappointments than any animal. Fear and pity: these are the feelings with which men have stood before women so far, always with one foot in tragedy which tears you apart even as it delights you –. What? And that brings it to an end? The *demystification* of women is in progress? Women's tediousness comes slowly into view? Oh Europe, Europe! We are familiar with the horned animal that you always found the most attractive, who kept threatening you with more danger![23] Your old fable could become "history" once more, – once more an enormous stupidity could come to dominate you and carry you away! And there is no god hidden inside, no! only an "idea," a "modern idea"! . . .

---

[23] An allusion to the Greek myth in which Zeus, in the form of a bull, abducts Europa, daughter of the royal house of Phoenicia.

Part 8 Peoples and fatherlands

240

I heard it again for the first time – Richard Wagner's overture to *Meistersinger*: it is magnificent, ornate, heavy, late art that takes pride in presupposing two hundred years of music as still living in order to be comprehensible: – it is a credit to the Germans that this sort of pride is not mistaken! What strengths and life forces, what seasons and territories are *not* combined here! One moment the work will strike us as old-fashioned, and the next as alien, harsh, and overly young. It is just as capricious as it is pompously conventional, it is not infrequently mischievous, and more often coarse and uncouth – it has fire and courage and at the same time the loose, drab skin of fruit that ripens too late. It flows in a full and expansive manner: and then suddenly a moment of inexplicable hesitation, like a gap that springs up between cause and effect, a dream-inducing pressure, practically a nightmare – , but, even then, the old stream of contentment spreads far and wide once again, that stream of the most varied contentment, of fortunes old and new which *very much* include the artist's happiness with himself (a happiness he does not want to hide), his astonished, joyful part in knowing he has mastered the devices he employs here – new, newly acquired, untried artistic devices, as he seems to reveal to us. All told, no beauty, nothing of the south, none of the fine, southern, brilliant skies, no gracefulness or dance, barely a will to logic; a certain awkwardness, in fact, which is even emphasized, as if the artist wanted to tell us: "I meant to do that"; an unwieldy guise, something capriciously barbaric and solemn, a flurry of erudite and venerable delicacies and lace; something German in the best and the worst senses of the word, something multiple, informal and inexhaustible in a German way; a certain German powerfulness and overfullness of the soul that is not afraid to hide behind the refinements of decline (and perhaps this is where it feels best); a fair and fitting emblem of the German soul that is simultaneously young and obsolete, over-done and still overflowing with future. This type of music best expresses what I think about the Germans: they are from the day before yesterday and the day after tomorrow, – *they still have no today*.

241

We "good Europeans": even we have hours when we allow ourselves a robust fatherlandishness, a slip and backslide into old loves and confines (I have just given a sample of this), hours of national outbursts, patriotic trepidations, and all sorts of other antiquated floods of affect. But things that run their course in us in a matter of hours might take clumsier spirits longer periods of time to get over, a good half a year in some cases and half a lifetime in others, according to the speed and strength of their digestion and metabolism. In fact, I could imagine dull and hesitant races who would need half a century even in our speedy Europe to overcome such atavistic fits of fatherlandishness, to unglue themselves from the soil and return to reason, by which I mean "good Europeanism." And while digressing on this possibility, it so happens that I'm becoming an ear-witness to a conversation between two old "patriots," both obviously hard of hearing, and so speaking that much louder. "*He* thinks and knows as much about philosophy as a peasant or a fraternity student," said the one –: "He's still innocent. But who cares these days? This is the age of the masses: they lie prostrate in front of anything massive. And the same in *politicis* too. They call a statesman 'great' if he builds them a new tower of Babel or some sort of monstrosity of empire and power – who cares if we are more cautious and circumspect and keep holding on to our old belief that it takes a great thought to make a cause or action great. Suppose that a statesman puts his people in the position of needing to do 'great politics' in the future, although they are ill equipped and ill prepared by nature for this task, so that they need to sacrifice their old and reliable virtues for the sake of a new and dubious mediocrity, – suppose that such a statesman condemns his people to any 'political activity' at all, when in fact they have had better things to do and to think about until now, and at the bottom of their souls they hadn't got rid of a cautious disgust at the agitation, emptiness, and riotous brawling of truly politicized peoples: – suppose that a statesman like this incites the dormant passions and greed of his people, makes a flaw out of their former shyness and the way they enjoyed staying to the side, makes a fault out of their cosmopolitanism and secret infinity, devalues their most heart-felt tendencies, turns their conscience around, makes their spirit narrow and their taste 'national,' – what! A statesman who would do all that, whose people would have to serve him like a prison sentence for all the future (if they even had a future); this sort of a statesman is *great?*" "Without a doubt!" answered the other old patriot vehemently, "Otherwise he wouldn't have been *able* to do it! Perhaps it was crazy to want something like this? But perhaps everything great started out as simply crazy!" – "That's an abuse of language!" shouted the first speaker in reply: "– strong! strong! strong and crazy! *Not* great!" – The old men had grown visibly heated as they yelled their "truths" into each other's faces like this; but me, in my happiness and my beyond, I considered how soon the strong come to be dominated by the stronger; and also that the spiritual leveling of one people is compensated for in the deepening of another. –

242

Whatever term is used these days to try to mark what is distinctive about the European, whether it is "civilization" or "humanization" or "progress" (or whether, without implying praise or censure, it is simply labeled Europe's *democratic* movement); behind all the moral and political foregrounds that are indicated by formulas like these, an immense *physiological* process is taking place and constantly gaining ground – the process of increasing similarity between Europeans, their growing detachment from the conditions under which climate- or class-bound races originate, their increasing independence from that *determinate* milieu where for centuries the same demands would be inscribed on the soul and the body – and so the slow approach of an essentially supra-national and nomadic type of person who, physiologically speaking, is typified by a maximal degree of the art and force of adaptation. This process of the *European in a state of becoming* can be slowed down in tempo through large-scale relapses (although this might be the very thing that makes it gain and grow in vehemence and depth). The still-raging storm and

133

stress of "national feeling" belongs here, as does the anarchism that is only just approaching. This process will probably end up with results that its naive supporters and eulogists, the apostles of "modern ideas," have least expected. The same new conditions that generally lead to a leveling and mediocritization of man – a useful, industrious, abundantly serviceable, and able herd animal man – are to the highest degree suitable for giving rise to exceptional people who possess the most dangerous and attractive qualities. Considering the fact that every adaptive force which systematically tests an ever-changing set of conditions (starting over with each generation, practically with each decade) does not make the *powerfulness* of the type even remotely possible; considering the fact that the overall impression of such future Europeans will probably be of exceedingly garrulous, impotent and eminently employable workers who *need* masters and commanders like they need their daily bread; and, finally, considering the fact that Europe's democratization amounts to the creation of a type prepared for *slavery* in the most subtle sense: taking all this into account, the *strong* person will need, in particular and exceptional cases, to get stronger and richer than he has perhaps ever been so far, – thanks to a lack of prejudice in his schooling, thanks to an enormous diversity in practice, art, and masks. What I'm trying to say is: the democratization of Europe is at the same time an involuntary exercise in the breeding of *tyrants* – understanding that word in every sense, including the most spiritual.

243

I'm glad to hear that our sun is moving rapidly towards the constellation of *Hercules*, and I hope that the people of this earth will act like the sun. With us in front, we good Europeans! –

244

There was a time when it was customary to call the Germans "profound," as a term of distinction. Now that the most successful type of new Germanism desires a completely different sort of honor and has, perhaps, come to regret the absence of a certain "elan" in everything profound, it is almost timely and patriotic to ask whether people have not been fooling themselves with this praise; in short, whether German profundity is not something fundamentally different and worse – and something we are about to get rid of, thank God. So: to try to change our ideas about German profundity, all we need is a little vivisection of the German soul. – More than anything else, the German soul is multiple, it originates in different places and is more piled up and pieced together than actually constructed: this is due to its origin. A German with the audacity to claim "two souls, alas, are dwelling in my breast"[1] would be abusing the truth quite badly, or to be more accurate, would fall quite a few souls short of the truth. As a people composed of the most enormous assortment and combination of races (perhaps even with a preponderance of the pre-Aryan element), as a "people of the middle" in every sense, the Germans are more incomprehensible, comprehensive, contradictory, unfamiliar, unpredictable, surprising, and even frightening than other peoples are to themselves: – they escape *definition* which by itself makes them the despair of the French. It is characteristic of the Germans that the question "what is German?" never dies out with them. Kotzebue certainly knew his Germans well enough: "We are known" they called out to him in joy, – but *Sand* claimed to know them too. Jean Paul knew what he was doing when he came out furiously against Fichte's dishonest but patriotic flattery and exaggerations[2] – but Goethe probably felt differently from Jean Paul about the Germans, even though he thought Jean Paul was right about Fichte. What *did* Goethe really think about the Germans? – But Goethe never did speak plainly about many of the things around him, and was an expert at subtle silence all his life: – he probably had his reasons. It is clear that the "Wars of Liberation" did not raise his level of enthusiasm any more than the French Revolution had done; the event that made him rethink his *Faust* – and indeed the whole problem of "man" – was the appearance of Napoleon. There are sayings where Goethe speaks as if from abroad, disputing with impatient hardness just what Germans take pride in. He once defined the famous German *Gemüt*[3] as "tolerance towards others' weaknesses as well as your own." Was he wrong? It is characteristic of the Germans that people are rarely completely wrong about them. The German soul has passages going this way and that, it has caves, hiding places and dungeons; its disorder has much of the charm of the mysterious; the German is an expert on

---

[1] Goethe's *Faust* I, line 1112.

[2] Reference to Jean Paul's review of Fichte's *Reden an die Deutsche Nation* (*Speeches to the German Nation*), in *Heidelberger Jahrbücher* (1810).

[3] This term is difficult to translate, but suggests a soulful quality or warm-hearted disposition.

the secret paths to chaos. And just as everything loves its likeness, the German loves clouds and everything unclear, becoming, nebulous, damp and overcast: he feels that uncertainty, disorganization, displacement, and growth of every type are "profound." The German himself *is* not, he *becomes*, he "develops." "Development," then, is the truly German discovery and sensation in the great realm of philosophical formulas: – a governing concept that, in conjunction with German beer and German music, is working to Germanize all of Europe. Foreigners stand amazed and enthralled before the riddles posed to them by the contradictory nature at the base of the German soul (which Hegel brought into a system and Richard Wagner finally set to music). "Good-natured and spiteful" – a juxtaposition like this, which would be absurd in reference to any other people, is all too often justified in Germany (unfortunately: just live with Swabians for a while!). The ponderousness of German scholars, their social fatuousness, is frighteningly consistent with an inner high-wire act and easy boldness in the face of which all gods have learned fear by now. If you want a demonstration of the German soul *ad oculos*,[4] just look at German taste, German arts and customs: what a boorish indifference to "taste"! How the noblest stands right next to the most base! How disorderly and rich this whole psychic economy really is! The German *lugs* his soul around, he lugs around everything he experiences. He digests his events badly, he is never "finished" with them; German profundity is often just a weak and sluggish "digestion." And just as everyone who is chronically ill (all dyspeptics) tends toward comfortable things, the Germans love "openness" and everything "upright."[5] How *comfortable* it is to be open and upright! Today, the Germans are expert at what is perhaps the happiest and most dangerous disguise, that trusting, accommodating, all-cards-on-the-table attitude of genuine German *honesty*: this is their truly Mephistophelean art, and with it they can "still go far"![6] The German lets himself go, looks out with true, blue, empty German eyes, – and foreigners immediately mistake him for his nightshirt! – What I am trying to say is: let "German profundity" be what it will (and just between us, perhaps, we will allow ourselves a laugh at its expense?), we would do well to honor its appearance and good name in the future as well, and

---

[4] Before the eyes.

[5] In German: *Biederkeit*.

[6] From Goethe's *Faust* part I, line 370.

not to trade in our old reputation as people of profundity too cheaply for Prussian "elan" or Berliner wit and sand. It is clever of a people to pass themselves off – to *let* themselves pass – for profound, undiplomatic, good-natured, honest and un-clever: it could even be – profound! Finally: people should live up to their name, – and it's not for nothing that the Germans [*die Deutsche*] are called the "*tiusche*" people, the "*Täusche*" (deceptive) people . . .

245

The "good old days" are over – they sang themselves out in Mozart. How lucky for *us* that his Rococo still speaks to us, that his "good company," his tender enthusiasms, his childish pleasure in *Chinoiserie* and fancy flourishes, his courtesy of the heart, his longing for the delicate and the amorous, for dancing and tearful moments of bliss, his faith in the south, might still appeal to some *vestige* in us! Oh, some day all this will be gone! – but who can doubt that the understanding and taste for Beethoven will be gone even sooner! – although he was only the finale of a transitional style and stylistic discontinuity and not, like Mozart, the finale of a centuries-old, great European taste. Beethoven falls somewhere between a brittle old soul that is constantly coming apart and an overly young, future-oriented soul that is constantly *on its way*. A dusk of eternal loss and eternal, wild hope lies over his music – the same light that lay across Europe when it dreamed with Rousseau, danced around the freedom tree of the Revolution and ended up practically worshipping Napoleon. But how quickly this very feeling is now fading, how difficult it is to even *know* about this feeling these days – how foreign the language of this Rousseau, Schiller, Shelley, and Byron sounds to our ear, these men in whom, *collectively*, the same European destiny which in Beethoven knew how to sing, found its way into words! – What became of German music afterwards belongs in romanticism, which is to say in a movement that was (calculated historically), even briefer, more fleeting and more superficial than that great *entr'acte*, that European transition from Rousseau to Napoleon and the rise of democracy. Weber: but what are *Freischütz* and *Oberon* to *us* these days! Or Marschner's *Hans Heiling* and *Vampyr*! Or even Wagner's *Tannhäuser*! This music is gone, if not yet forgotten. At any rate, the whole music of romanticism was not noble enough, not music enough to have rights anywhere except in the theater and in front of crowds; it was second-rate music from the very start, and real musicians took little notice of it. Things were different with Felix Mendelssohn, that halcyon master who, thanks to his easier, purer, happier soul, was quickly honored and just as quickly forgotten, as a lovely *incident* in German music. But when it comes to Robert Schumann, who took things seriously and was from the start taken seriously himself (he is the last to have founded a school): don't we think of it today as a stroke of luck, a relief, a liberation that just this Schumannian romanticism has been overcome? Schumann, fleeing into the "Saxon Switzerland" of his soul, half Werther-ish, half Jean Paul-ine by nature, certainly not Beethoven-esque! certainly not Byronic! His *Manfred* music is a mistake and a misunderstanding to the point of injustice –; Schumann with his taste, which was fundamentally a *small* taste (being a dangerous tendency towards calm lyricism and a drunkenness of feeling, which is twice as dangerous among Germans), going constantly to the side, timidly excusing himself and retreating, a noble, tender creature, who reveled in nothing but anonymous happiness and pain, a type of little girl and *noli me tangere*[7] from the start: this Schumann was already a merely *German* event in music, no longer a European event like Beethoven, or, to a still more comprehensive extent, like Mozart. With Schumann, German music was threatened with its greatest danger, that of losing *the voice of the European soul* and descending to a mere fatherlandishness. –

246

– What torture German books are for anyone with a *third* ear! How reluctantly he stands by the slowly revolving quagmire of toneless tones and rhythms without dance that the Germans call a "book"! And the Germans who *read* books! How lazily, how grudgingly, how badly they read! How many Germans know (and require themselves to know) that there is *art* in every good sentence! Art that wants to be discerned to the extent that the sentence wants to be understood! A misunderstanding about its tempo, for instance, and the sentence itself is misunderstood! To have no doubts as to the rhythmically decisive syllables, to feel breaks in the most stringent of symmetries as deliberate and attractive, to extend a subtle and patient ear to every *staccato* and every *rubato*, guessing the

[7] Do not touch me.

meaning of the order of vowels and diphthongs and how tenderly and richly they can change color and change it again when put next to each other – who among book-reading Germans is well-meaning enough to acknowledge duties and demands like these and to listen for so much art and intent in language? In the end, people just do not have "the ear for it," and so the strongest contrasts in style go unheard and the most subtle artistry is *wasted* as if on the deaf. – These were my thoughts as I noticed two masters in the art of prose being crudely and thoughtlessly mistaken for each other, the one whose words drip down with coldness and hesitation, as if from the roof of a damp cave (he counts on their dull sound and resonance) and another who handles his language like a supple rapier and, from his fingers to his toes, feels the dangerous joy of the quivering, over-sharpened sword that wants to bite, sizzle, cut. –

247

How little the German style has to do with tones and with ears is shown by the fact that it is precisely our good musicians who write poorly. Germans do not read aloud, they do not read for the ear but only with the eye, keeping their ears in a drawer in the meantime. When ancient people read, if they read at all (it happened seldom enough), it was aloud to themselves, and moreover in a loud voice. People were surprised by someone reading quietly, and secretly wondered why. In a loud voice: that means with all the swells, inflections, sudden changes in tone, and shifts in tempo that the ancient, *public* world took pleasure in. At that time, the rules for written style were the same as those for spoken style, and those rules depended in part on the astonishing development and subtle requirements of the ear and larynx, and also, in part, on the strength, endurance, and power of the ancient lung. What the ancients meant by a period is primarily a physiological unit insofar as it is combined in a single breath. Periods like the ones that occur in Demosthenes and Cicero – swelling up twice and twice sinking down and all within a single breath – those were a delight for people of *antiquity* who knew from their own training to value the virtue of the rarity and difficulty involved in performing periods like these. *We* have no real right to the *great* period, we who are modern, we who are short-winded in every sense! On the whole, these ancients were themselves dilettantes in rhetoric, and therefore authorities, and consequently critics – this is how they drove their rhetoricians to extremes. Similarly, in the previous century, when all the men and women of Italy knew how to sing, virtuosity in song (and with it the art of melody too –) reached a high point. But in Germany there was (until very recently, when a sort of grandstand verbosity shyly and awkwardly stirred its young wings) really only one species of public and *vaguely* artistic rhetoric, and that came from the pulpit. In Germany, only the preachers knew the weight of a word or syllable, the extent to which a sentence stumbled, sprang, rang, ran, or ran away. They were the only ones with a conscience in their ears, which was often enough an evil conscience: because there was no shortage of reasons why a German of all people should achieve competence in rhetoric infrequently and almost always too late. This is why the masterpiece of German prose is by all rights the masterpiece of its greatest preacher: the *Bible* has been the best German book to date. Compared to Luther's Bible, almost everything else is merely "literature" – something that had not grown in Germany and for that reason did not grow and is not growing into German hearts like the Bible did.

248

There are two types of genius: one that fundamentally begets and wants to beget, and another that is happy to be impregnated and give birth. Similarly with peoples of genius, there are those who inherit the female problem of pregnancy and the secret task of forming, ripening, and bringing to completion – the Greeks, for instance, were this type of people as well as the French –; and others who need to impregnate and be the cause of new orders of life, – like the Jews, the Romans, and, to pose a modest question, the Germans? – peoples tortured and delighted by unknown fevers who irresistibly leave themselves, loving and lusting after foreign races (after ones who "let themselves be impregnated" –) and also domineering, like everything that knows itself to be full of creative forces and consequently knows of "God's grace." These two types of genius look for each other like men and women; but they also misunderstand each other, – like men and women.

249

Every people has its own tartufferies, and calls them its virtues. You do not know – you cannot know – what is best about yourself.

250

What Europe owes to the Jews? Many things both good and bad, but mainly one thing that is both best and worst: the grand style in morality, the horror and majesty of infinite demands, infinite meanings, the whole romanticism and sublimity of the morally questionable – and, consequently, precisely the most appealing, insidious, and exceptional aspect of those plays of colors and seductions to life in whose afterglow the sky of our present European culture, its evening sky, glows away – perhaps goes away. This is why, among the spectators and philosophers, artists like us regard the Jews with – gratitude.

251

We have to accept the fact that all sorts of clouds and disturbances (basically, small fits of stupefaction) drift over the spirit of a people who suffers and *wants* to suffer from national nervous fevers and political ambition. With today's Germans, for instance, there is the anti-French stupidity one moment and the anti-Jewish stupidity the next, now the anti-Polish stupidity, now the Christian-Romantic, the Wagnerian, the Teutonic, the Prussian (just look at these poor historians, these Sybels and Treitschkes with their thickly bandaged heads –), or whatever else they might be called, these little stupors of the German spirit and conscience. Please forgive the fact that, during a short and risky stay in a badly infected region, I did not completely escape this illness either, and like everyone else started worrying about things that were none of my business: the first sign of political infection. About the Jews, for instance: just listen. – I have yet to meet a German who was well disposed towards Jews. And however unconditional the rejection of genuine anti-Semitism might be on the part of every prudent or political person, such prudence and politics are not really aimed at anti-Semitic sentiment in general, but instead at its dangerous excess, and especially at the outrageous and disgraceful expression of this excessive sentiment – this cannot be denied. That Germany has *ample* quantities of Jews, that the German stomach and the German blood have difficulty (and will continue for a long time to have difficulty) coping with even this number of "Jews" – as the Italians, the French, the British have coped, due to a stronger digestion –: this is the clear statement and language of a universal instinct that needs to be listened to and acted on. "Don't let in any more Jews! And lock the doors to the east in particular (even to Austria)!" – so commands the instinct of a people whose type is still weak and indeterminate enough to blur easily and be easily obliterated by a stronger race. But the Jews are without a doubt the strongest, purest, most tenacious race living in Europe today. They know how to thrive in even the worst conditions (and actually do better than in favorable ones) due to some virtues that people today would like to see labeled as vices, – above all, thanks to a resolute faith that does not need to feel ashamed in the face of "modern ideas." The Jews change, *if* they change, only in the way the Russian empire makes its conquests (being an empire that has time and was not made yesterday): namely, according to the fundamental principle "as slowly as possible!" A thinker who has Europe's future on his conscience will, in every sketch he draws of this future, consider the Jews, like the Russians, to be the most certain and probable factors at present in the great play and struggle of forces. What gets called a "nation" in Europe today (and is really more a *res facta* than *nata*[8] – every once in a while a *res ficta et picta*[9] will look exactly the same –) is, in any case, something young, easily changed, and in a state of becoming, not yet a race let alone the sort of *aere perennius*[10] that the Jewish type is: these "nations" should be on a careful lookout for any hotheaded rivalry and hostility! The fact that the Jews, if they wanted (or if they were forced, as the anti-Semites seem to want), *could* already be dominant, or indeed could quite literally have control over present-day Europe – this is established. The fact that they are *not* working and making plans to this end is likewise established. Meanwhile, what they wish and want instead, with a unified assertiveness even, is to be absorbed and assimilated into Europe; they thirst for some place where they can be settled, permitted, respected at last and where they can put an end to the nomadic life, the "wandering Jew" –; and this urge and impulse (which in itself perhaps already reveals a slackening of the Jewish instincts) should be carefully noted and accommodated – in which case it might be practical and appropriate to throw the anti-Semitic hooligans out of the country. Approached selectively and with all due caution, the way it is done by the English nobility. It would clearly be unproblematic

---

[8] *Res facta* means "something made"; *res nata* means "something born."

[9] Something fictitious and unreal.

[10] More enduring than bronze.

for the stronger and more strongly delineated types of new Germanism (the officers of noble rank from the Mark,[11] for instance) to get involved with them: and it would be very interesting to see whether the genius of fortune and fortitude (and above all some spirit and spiritedness, which are in very short supply in the place just mentioned –) could not be added into, bred into, the hereditary art of commanding and obeying – both of which are classic features of the Mark these days. But I should really break off my cheerful speeches and hyper-Germania here, since I am already touching on something I take *seriously*, on the "European problem" as I understand it, on the breeding of a new caste to rule Europe. –

252

This is not a philosophical race – these Englishmen. Bacon signified an *attack* on the philosophical spirit in general; Hobbes, Hume, and Locke indicated a degradation and a depreciation in value of the concept "philosopher" for more than a century. Kant rose up and rebelled *against* Hume; and it was Locke about whom Schelling *was able* to say "*je méprise Locke.*"[12] Hegel and Schopenhauer were of one mind (along with Goethe) in the struggle against the English-mechanistic world-stupidification; those two hostile brother geniuses in philosophy who divided along the opposing poles of the German spirit and, in the process, wronged each other as only brothers can. That fatuous dolt, Carlyle, knew well enough what England lacks and has always lacked; Carlyle, that half-actor and rhetorician who tried to conceal under impassioned grimaces what he knew about himself: namely, what he *lacked* – real *power* of intellect, real *profundity* of spiritual vision, in short: philosophy. It is characteristic of an unphilosophical race like this to firmly support Christianity: they *need* its discipline to be "moralized" and in some sense humanized. It is just because the English are gloomier, stronger-willed, more sensuous, and more brutal than the Germans that they, as the baser of the two, are the more pious as well: they *need* Christianity that much more. To subtler nostrils, even this English Christianity bears the genuinely English odor of the very spleen and alcoholic dissipation against which it is rightly used as a remedy, – the subtler poison treating the cruder. In fact, a subtler poisoning is a sign of

[11] The Mark Brandenburg, the region around Berlin.

[12] "I despise Locke."

progress in crude peoples; it is a step towards spiritualization. The English crudeness and peasant-like seriousness is most tolerably disguised (or better: explained and reinterpreted) by Christian gestures, prayers, and psalm-singing. And for that herd of drunken and dissipated cows who in the past learned to grunt morally under the influence of Methodism and again more recently as a "salvation army," – for them, a penitential spasm just might be the highest level of "humanity" that they can attain: that much you can allow. But what is offensive in even the most humane Englishman is his lack of music, speaking metaphorically (and without metaphors –): there is no dance or timing in the movement of his soul and his body, not even a desire for dance or timing, for "music." Just listen to him speak; just watch the most beautiful Englishwomen *walk* – no other country on earth has more beautiful doves or swans, – finally, listen to them sing! But I am asking too much . . .

253

There are truths best known by mediocre minds, because they are best suited to mediocre minds; there are truths that have a charm and seductive allure only for mediocre spirits. We are coming up against this perhaps unpleasant proposition right now, since the spirit of worthy but mediocre Englishmen – I mean Darwin, John Stuart Mill, and Herbert Spencer – is starting to come to prominence in the middle regions of European taste. In fact, who would doubt the utility of having spirits *like these* prevail for the time being? It would be a mistake to think that far-flying spirits of the highest type would be particularly adept at detecting, collecting, and drawing conclusions from lots of common little facts: – rather, being exceptions, they are not well situated with respect to the "rule." Ultimately, they have more to do than just to know – they have to *be* something new, *mean* something new, and *present* new values! The chasm between knowing something and being able to do it is perhaps even greater and more uncanny than it is generally thought to be: people who can do things in the grand style, the creators, might need to be ignorant. On the other hand, when it comes to scientific discoveries of a Darwinian type, a certain narrowness, aridity, and diligent, painstaking care – in short, something English – is not a bad thing to have at your disposal. – Finally, let us not forget that the English have caused a total depression of the European spirit once already with their profound ordinariness. What people call "modern ideas" or "eighteenth-century ideas" or even "French ideas" – in other words, what the *German* spirit rebelled against in profound disgust –, was English in origin, there is no doubt about it. The French were just the apes and actors (as well as the best soldiers) of these ideas, and unfortunately their first and most thorough *victims* too, since the *âme française*[13] ended up so sparse and emaciated from the damned Anglomania of "modern ideas" that people these days look back at its sixteenth and seventeenth centuries, its profound impassioned strength, and its inventive nobility, with something bordering on disbelief. But we have to hold on to this statement of historical fairness with our teeth and defend it against the moment and appearances: the European *noblesse* (of feeling, of taste, of manner – in short, taking the word in all its higher senses) – is *France's* work and invention; European baseness, the plebeianism of modern ideas – is *England's*. –

254

France is still the seat of the most spiritual and sophisticated culture in Europe today, and the preeminent school of taste: but you have to know how to find this "France of taste." People belonging to it keep themselves well hidden: – there might be only a small number of people in which it loves and lives, people who might not have the sturdiest legs to stand on, some of them fatalists, somber and ill, some of them pampered and over the top, people who have the *ambition* to hide themselves. There is something they all have in common: they shut their ears to the raging stupidity and the noisy jabbering of the democratic bourgeoisie. In fact, it is a coarsened and stultified France that thrashes around in the foreground these days, – it recently celebrated a real orgy of bad taste combined with self-admiration at Victor Hugo's funeral.[14] They have something else in common too: the goodwill to ward off spiritual Germanization – and an even better inability to do it! Perhaps Schopenhauer is more at home and settled now in this France of the spirit (which is also a France of pessimism) than he ever was in Germany; not to mention Heinrich Heine, who has been in the flesh and blood of the subtler and more promising lyric poets of Paris for a while now; or Hegel who, in the form of Taine

---

[13] French soul.

[14] In 1885.

(which is to say: in the form of the *foremost* living historian), exerts an almost tyrannical influence these days. But as far as Wagner goes, the more French music learns to develop according to the real needs of the *âme moderne*,[15] the more "Wagnerianized" it becomes; this can be predicted, – it is already happening now! Nevertheless, there are three things that, even today, the French can proudly exhibit as their heir and their own and an enduring mark of an old cultural superiority over Europe, in spite of any voluntary or involuntary Germanization or vulgarization of taste. One is the capacity for artistic passions and devotion to "form," for which the phrase *l'art pour l'art* [16] (along with a thousand others) was invented. Things like this have not been absent from France for the last three hundred years and, thanks to a reverence for "small numbers," keep making possible a type of literary chamber music that is not to be found anywhere else in Europe –. The second point on which France can base a claim to superiority over Europe is its old, diverse culture of *moralism*, which means that even among little *romanciers*[17] of newspapers and chance *boulevardiers de Paris*[18] you will find, on average, a psychological sensitivity and curiosity that people in Germany, for instance, have no concept of (much less the thing itself!). For this, the Germans would need a few hundred years of moralism which, as I have said, France had not spared itself. Anyone calling the Germans "naive" on this account is dressing up a deficiency as a compliment. (As a contrast to the German inexperience and innocence in *voluptate psychologica*[19] – which is not at all unrelated to the tedium of German company –, and as the most successful expression of a genuinely French curiosity and inventiveness in this realm of delicate tremblings, we can name Henri Beyle. This remarkable, anticipatory forerunner ran with a Napoleonic tempo through *his* Europe, through several centuries of the European soul, as a pathfinder and discoverer of this soul. It took two generations to somehow *catch up* with him, to guess some of the riddles that tormented and delighted him, this strange Epicurean and question-mark of a man who was France's last great psychologist –.)

[15] Modern soul.

[16] Art for art's sake.

[17] Novelists.

[18] People on the Parisian boulevards.

[19] Taking pleasure in psychology.

There is, in addition, a third claim to superiority: at the core of the French there is a half-successful synthesis of north and south which lets them conceive many things and do many others that will never occur to an Englishman. Using a temperament that is turned periodically towards and away from the south, and whose Provençal and Ligurian blood bubbles over from time to time, the French fortify themselves against the awful northern gray on gray, the sunless concept-ghostliness and anemia, – our *German* disease of the taste, against whose excess people at the moment are strongly resolved to prescribe blood and iron:[20] I mean "great politics" (following a dangerous medical practice that teaches me to wait and wait but not, so far, to hope –). And in France there is still a predisposition to understand and accommodate those rarer and rarely satisfied people who are too far-ranging to find satisfaction in any fatherlandishness, and know how to love the south in the north and the north in the south, – the born Mediterraneans,[21] the "good Europeans." – It was for them that *Bizet* made music, this last genius to have seen a new beauty and seduction, – who discovered a piece of the *southernness of music*.

255

I recommend taking a number of precautions against German music. Suppose that someone loves the south like I do, as an immense school for convalescence of both the most spiritual and the most sensual kind, as an unbridled, sun-drenched, sun-transfiguration that spreads across a high-handed, self-assured existence: such a person will learn to be somewhat careful with German music, because, along with ruining his taste, it will ruin his health again too. If someone like this (who is southern not by descent but by *belief*) dreams about the future of music, he will also have to dream about music being redeemed from the north, and have the prelude to a more profound and powerful, perhaps more evil and mysterious music in his ears, a supra-German music that does not fade, yellow, or pale at the sight of the voluptuous blue sea or the luminous Mediterranean sky, which is what happens with all German music; a supra-European music that still stands its ground before the brown sunsets of the desert, whose soul is related to the palm tree, and that knows

[20] Bismarck's famous phrase.

[21] In German: *Mittelländler* (literally: people whose country is in the middle).

how to wander and to be at home among huge, beautiful, lonely beasts
of prey . . . I could imagine a music whose rarest magic consisted in no
longer knowing anything of good and evil – although, perhaps, some
sailor's homesickness, some golden shadow and delicate weakness might
run across it every now and then: an art that would see colors flying
towards it from a setting *moral* world – a distant world that had become almost incomprehensible – and would be hospitable and profound
enough to receive such late refugees. –

256

Thanks to the pathological manner in which nationalist nonsense has
alienated and continues to alienate the peoples of Europe from each
other; thanks as well to the short-sighted and swift-handed politicians
who have risen to the top with the help of this nonsense, and have no idea
of the extent to which the politics of dissolution that they practice can
only be *entr'acte* politics, – thanks to all this and to some things that are
strictly unmentionable today, the most unambiguous signs declaring that
Europe wants to be one are either overlooked or willfully and mendaciously
reinterpreted. The mysterious labor in the souls of all the more profound
and far-ranging people of this century has actually been focused on prepar-
ing the path to this new *synthesis* and on experimentally[22] anticipating the
Europeans of the future. Only in their foregrounds or in hours of weakness
(like old age) were they "fatherlanders," – they only became "patriots"
when they were resting from themselves. I am thinking about people like
Napoleon, Goethe, Beethoven, Stendhal, Heinrich Heine, Schopenhauer:
and do not blame me for including Richard Wagner as well; we should not
let his own self-misunderstanding lead us astray – geniuses of his type do
not often have the right to understand themselves. Although, admittedly,
it is not so apparent given the rude clamor with which Wagner is resisted
and opposed in France today, it nonetheless remains the case that *late
French romanticism* of the '40s and Richard Wagner belong most closely
and intimately together. They are related, fundamentally related, in all the
heights and depths of their needs: it is the soul of Europe, the one Europe,
that presses and yearns upwards and outwards through their multiple and

---

[22] In German: *versuchsweise* (see note 16, p. 39 above).

tumultuous art – towards what? towards a new light? a new sun? But who could really express something that all these masters of new means of language did not know how to express clearly? What is certain is that the same storm and stress tormented them, that they *searched* in the same way, these last great seekers! They were all dominated by literature, up to their eyes and ears – the first artists with an education in world literature. For the most part, they were themselves writers, poets, go-betweens and mixers of the arts and the senses (as a musician, Wagner belongs among painters, as a poet, among musicians, as an artist in general, among actors); they were all fanatics of *expression* "at any cost" (I emphasize Delacroix, Wagner's next of kin), all of them great discoverers in the realm of the sublime as well as the repugnant and repulsive, even greater discoverers in effects, in showmanship, in the art of window displays; they were all talents far above their genius –, virtuosos through and through, with uncanny access to everything tempting, seductive, compelling, and subversive, born enemies of logic and straight lines, longing for the foreign, the exotic, the monstrous, the crooked, the self-contradictory. As humans, Tantaluses of the will, plebeians on the rise who knew that they were incapable of a noble tempo, a *lento*, in their life or work (just consider Balzac, for instance), unconstrained workers, almost destroying themselves with work: antinomians and agitators when it came to customs, ambitious and insatiable without equilibrium or enjoyment; and in the end they all crumbled and sank down in front of the Christian cross (and with complete justification: which one of them would have been profound and original enough for a philosophy of the *Antichrist*? –); on the whole, an adventurously daring, splendidly violent, high-flying, high-ascending type of higher men, who first taught their century – and it is the century of the *masses*! – the concept "higher man" ... Let Richard Wagner's German friends decide whether there is something purely German about Wagner's art, or whether it is not distinguished precisely by its derivation from *supra-German* sources and drives; the extent to which Paris in particular was indispensable for the cultivation of Wagner's type should not be underestimated (the profundity of his instincts called him to Paris at the decisive moment); nor should the extent to which his whole manner and self-apostolate required the model of the French socialists. Perhaps closer comparison will reveal, to the credit of Richard Wagner's German nature, that he did everything in a stronger, bolder, harder, and higher way than a Frenchman of the nineteenth century could do, – thanks to the fact that we Germans are still closer to barbarism than the French are. The strangest thing that Richard Wagner created might even be inaccessible, incomprehensible, and inimitable to the entire, late, Latinate race, forever and not just for now: the figure of Siegfried,[23] that *very free* man, who may in fact be far too free, too hard, too cheerful, too healthy, too *anti-Catholic* for the taste of old and worn-out cultures. He might even have been a sin against romanticism, this anti-romantic Siegfried – although Wagner thoroughly atoned for this sin in his sad old age, when (anticipating a taste that has since become political) he began preaching, if not traveling, *the way to Rome* with a religious vehemence peculiar to himself. – So that you do not misunderstand these final words of mine, I want to use a few strong rhymes; and then even less subtle ears will guess what I want, – what I have *against* the "final Wagner" and his *Parsifal* music.

> – Is this still German? –
> It's from a German heart, this murky howling?
> From German flesh this self-aimed disemboweling?
> It's German then, this type of priestly feel,
> This incense-scented sensuous appeal?
> This broken, falling, swaggered swaying?
> This unassured singsong-saying?
> This nun-eyed *Ave*-chiming leavening,
> This falsely raptured heaven-overheavening?
> – Is this still German? –
> Just think! You're standing there, the doorway's near,
> *It's Rome! Rome's faith without the text, you hear.*

---

[23] Siegfried is the heroic figure of Wagner's mythological *Ring der Nibelungen* opera cycle. In his final opera, *Parsifal*, Wagner emphasized more explicitly Christian themes.

Part 9 What is noble?

257

Every enhancement so far in the type "man" has been the work of an aristocratic society – and that is how it will be, again and again, since this sort of society believes in a long ladder of rank order and value distinctions between men, and in some sense needs slavery. Without the *pathos of distance* as it grows out of the ingrained differences between stations, out of the way the ruling caste maintains an overview and keeps looking down on subservient types and tools, and out of this caste's equally continuous exercise in obeying and commanding, in keeping away and below – without *this* pathos, that *other*, more mysterious pathos could not have grown at all, that demand for new expansions of distance within the soul itself, the development of states that are increasingly high, rare, distant, tautly drawn and comprehensive, and in short, the enhancement of the type "man," the constant "self-overcoming of man" (to use a moral formula in a supra-moral sense). Of course, you cannot entertain any humanitarian illusions about how an aristocratic society originates (and any elevation of the type "man" will presuppose an aristocratic society –): the truth is harsh. Let us not be deceived about how every higher culture on earth has *begun*! Men whose nature was still natural, barbarians in every terrible sense of the word, predatory people who still possessed an unbroken strength of will and lust for power threw themselves on weaker, more civilized, more peaceful races of tradesmen perhaps, or cattle breeders; or on old and mellow cultures in which the very last life-force was flaring up in brilliant fireworks of spirit and corruption. The noble caste always started out as the barbarian caste. Their supremacy was in psychic, not physical strength, – they were *more complete* people (which at any level amounts to saying "more complete beasts" –).

258

Corruption, as an expression of the fact that anarchy threatens inside the instincts and that the foundation of the affects, which we call "life," has been shaken: corruption means fundamentally different things, depending on the life-form in which it manifests itself. When, for instance, an aristocracy like that in France at the beginning of the Revolution throws away its privileges with a sublime disgust and sacrifices itself to an excess of its moral feeling, then this is corruption. It was really just the final act of that centuries-long corruption in which the aristocracy gradually relinquished its dominant authority and was reduced to a mere *function* of the kingdom (and, in the end, to its trinket and showpiece). But the essential feature of a good, healthy aristocracy is that it does *not* feel that it is a function (whether of the kingdom or of the community) but instead feels itself to be the *meaning* and highest justification (of the kingdom or community), – and, consequently, that it accepts in good conscience the sacrifice of countless people who have to be pushed down and shrunk into incomplete human beings, into slaves, into tools, all *for the sake of the aristocracy*. Its fundamental belief must always be that society *cannot* exist for the sake of society, but only as the substructure and framework for raising an exceptional type of being up to its higher duty and to a higher state of *being*. In the same way, the sun-seeking, Javanese climbing plant called the *sipo matador* will wrap its arms around an oak tree so often and for such a long time that finally, high above the oak, although still supported by it, the plant will be able to unfold its highest crown of foliage and show its happiness in the full, clear light.

259

Mutually refraining from injury, violence, and exploitation, placing your will on par with the other's: in a certain, crude sense, these practices can become good manners between individuals when the right conditions are present (namely, that the individuals have genuinely similar quantities of force and measures of value, and belong together within a single body). But as soon as this principle is taken any further, and maybe even held to be the *fundamental principle of society,* it immediately shows itself for what it is: the will to *negate* life, the principle of disintegration and decay. Here we must think things through thoroughly, and ward off any sentimental weakness: life itself is *essentially* a process of appropriating, injuring, overpowering the alien and the weaker, oppressing, being harsh, imposing your own form, incorporating, and at least, the very least, exploiting, – but what is the point of always using words that have been stamped with slanderous intentions from time immemorial? Even a body within which (as we presupposed earlier) particular individuals treat each other as equal (which happens in every healthy aristocracy): if this body is living and not dying, it will have to treat other bodies in just those ways that the individuals it contains *refrain* from treating each other. It will have to be the embodiment of will to power, it will want to grow, spread, grab, win dominance, – not out of any morality or immorality, but because it is *alive,* and because life *is* precisely will to power. But there is no issue on which the base European consciousness is less willing to be instructed than this; these days, people everywhere are lost in rapturous enthusiasms, even in scientific disguise, about a future state of society where "the exploitative character" will fall away: – to my ears, that sounds as if someone is promising to invent a life that dispenses with all organic functions. "Exploitation" does not belong to a corrupted or imperfect, primitive society: it belongs to the *essence* of being alive as a fundamental organic function; it is a result of genuine will to power, which is just the will of life. – Although this is an innovation at the level of theory, – at the level of reality, it is the *primal fact* of all history. Let us be honest with ourselves to this extent at least! –

260

As I was wandering through the many subtle and crude moralities that have been dominant or that still dominate over the face of the earth, I found certain traits regularly recurring together and linked to each other. In the end, two basic types became apparent to me and a fundamental distinction leapt out. There is a *master morality* and a *slave morality*; – I will immediately add that in all higher and more mixed cultures, attempts to negotiate between these moralities also appear, although more frequently the two are confused and there are mutual misunderstandings. In fact, you sometimes find them sharply juxtaposed – inside the same person even, within a single soul. Moral value distinctions have arisen within either a dominating type that, with a feeling of well-being, was conscious of the difference between itself and those who were dominated – or alternatively, these distinctions arose among the dominated people themselves, the slaves and dependants of every rank. In the first case, when dominating people determine the concept of "good," it is the elevated, proud states of soul that are perceived as distinctive and as determining rank order. The noble person separates himself off from creatures in which the opposite of such elevated, proud states is expressed: he despises them. It is immediately apparent that, in this first type of morality, the contrast between "good" and "bad" amounts to one between "noble" and "despicable" (the contrast between "good" and "*evil*" has a different lineage). People who were cowardly, apprehensive, and petty, people who thought narrowly in terms of utility – these were the ones despised. But the same can be said about distrustful people with their uneasy glances, about grovelers, about dog-like types of people who let themselves be mistreated, about begging flatterers and, above all, about liars: – it is a basic belief of aristocrats that base peoples are liars. "We who are truthful" – that is what the nobility of ancient Greece called themselves. It is obvious that moral expressions everywhere were first applied to *people* and then, only later and derivatively, to *actions* (which is why it is a tremendous mistake when historians of morality take their point of departure from questions such as "why do acts of pity get praised?"). The noble type of person feels that *he* determines value, he does not need anyone's approval, he judges that "what is harmful to me is harmful in itself," he knows that he is the one who gives honor to things in the first place, he *creates values*. He honors everything he sees in himself: this sort of morality is self-glorifying. In the foreground, there is the feeling of fullness, of power that wants to overflow, the happiness associated with a high state of tension, the consciousness of a wealth that wants to make gifts and give away. The noble person helps the unfortunate too, although not (or hardly ever) out of pity, but rather more out of an impulse generated by the over-abundance of power. In honoring himself, the noble man honors the powerful as well as those who have power over themselves, who know how to speak and be silent, who joyfully exercise severity and harshness over themselves, and have respect for all forms of severity and harshness. "Wotan has put a hard heart in my breast," reads a line from an old Scandinavian saga: this rightly comes from the soul of a proud Viking. This sort of a man is even proud of *not* being made for pity: which is why the hero of the saga adds, by way of warning, "If your heart is not hard when you are young, it will never be hard." The noble and brave types of people who think this way are the furthest removed from a morality that sees precisely pity, actions for others, and *désintéressement*[1] as emblematic of morality. A faith in yourself, pride in yourself, and a fundamental hostility and irony with respect to "selflessness" belong to a noble morality just as certainly as does a slight disdain and caution towards sympathetic feelings and "warm hearts." – The powerful are the ones who *know* how to honor; it is their art, their realm of invention. A profound reverence for age and origins – the whole notion of justice is based on this double reverence –, a faith and a prejudice in favor of forefathers and against future generations is typical of the morality of the powerful. And when, conversely, people with "modern ideas" believe almost instinctively in "progress" and "the future," and show a decreasing respect for age, this gives sufficient evidence of the ignoble origin of these "ideas." But, most of all, the morality of dominating types is foreign and painful to contemporary taste due to its stern axiom that people have duties only towards their own kind; that when it comes to creatures of a lower rank, to everything alien, people are allowed to act as they see fit or "from the heart," and in any event, "beyond good and evil" –: things like pity might have a place here. The capacity and duty to experience extended gratitude and vengefulness – both only among your own kind –, subtlety in retaliation, refinement in concepts of friendship, a certain need to have enemies (as flue holes, as it were, for the affects of jealousy, irascibility, arrogance, – basically, in order to be a good *friend*): all these are characteristic features of noble morality which, as I have suggested, is not the morality of "modern ideas," and this makes it difficult for us to relate to, and also difficult for us to dig it up and lay it open. – It is different with the second type of morality, *slave morality*. What if people who were violated, oppressed, suffering, unfree, exhausted, and unsure of themselves were to moralize: what type of moral valuations would they have? A pessimistic suspicion of the whole condition of humanity would probably find expression, perhaps a condemnation of humanity along with its condition. The slave's gaze resents the virtues of the powerful. It is skeptical and distrustful, it has a *subtle* mistrust of all the "good" that is honored there –, it wants to convince

---

[1] Disinterestedness.

itself that even happiness is not genuine there. Conversely, qualities that serve to alleviate existence for suffering people are pulled out and flooded with light: pity, the obliging, helpful hand, the warm heart, patience, industriousness, humility, and friendliness receive full honors here –, since these are the most useful qualities and practically the only way of holding up under the pressure of existence. Slave morality is essentially a morality of utility. Here we have the point of origin for that famous opposition between "good" and "*evil*." Evil is perceived as something powerful and dangerous; it is felt to contain a certain awesome quality, a subtlety and strength that block any incipient contempt. According to the slave morality then, "evil" inspires fear; but according to the master morality, it is "*good*" that inspires and wants to inspire fear, while the "bad" man is seen as contemptible. The opposition comes to a head when, following the logic of slave morality, a hint of contempt (however slight and well disposed) finally comes to be associated with even its idea of "good," because within the terms of slave morality, the good man must always be *unthreatening*: he is good-natured, easy to deceive, maybe a bit stupid, *un bonhomme*.[2] Wherever slave morality holds sway, language shows a tendency for the words "good" and "stupid" to come closer together. – A final fundamental distinction: the desire for *freedom*, the instinct for happiness, and subtleties in the feeling of freedom necessarily belong to slave morals and morality, just as an artistry and enthusiasm in respect and devotion are invariant symptoms of an aristocratic mode of thinking and valuing. – This clearly shows why love *as passion* (our European specialty) must have had a purely noble descent: it is known to have been invented in the knightly poetry of Provence, by those magnificent, inventive men of the "*gai saber*."[3] Europe is indebted to these men for so many things, almost for itself.

261

Vanity is perhaps one of the most difficult things for a noble person to comprehend: he will be tempted to keep denying it when a different type of man will almost be able to feel it in his hands. He has difficulty imagining creatures who would try to inspire good opinions about themselves that they themselves do not hold – and consequently do not "deserve"

---

[2] A good simple fellow.

[3] Gay science.

either –, and who would then end up *believing* these good opinions. For one thing, this strikes the noble as being so tasteless and showing such a lack of self-respect, and, for another thing, it seems so baroque and unreasonable to him, that he would gladly see vanity as an exception and stay skeptical in most of the cases where it is brought up. For example, he will say: "I can be wrong about my own worth and still insist that other people acknowledge it to be what I say it is, – but that is not vanity (instead, it is arrogance or, more frequently, it is what they call 'humility' or 'modesty')." Or alternatively: "There are many reasons why I can enjoy other people's good opinions, perhaps because I love and honor them and rejoice in each of their joys, and perhaps also because their good opinions confirm and reinforce my faith in my own good opinion of myself, perhaps because other people's good opinions are useful or look as though they could be useful to me, even when I don't agree with them, – but none of that is vanity." It is only when forced (namely with the help of history) that the noble person realizes that from time immemorial, in all strata of people who are in some way dependent, base people *were* only what they were *considered to be*: – not being at all accustomed to positing values, the only value the base person attributes to himself is the one his masters have attributed to him (creating values is the true *right of masters*). We can see it as the result of a tremendous atavism that, to this day, ordinary people still *wait* for an opinion to be pronounced about themselves before instinctively deferring to it. And this is by no means only the case with "good" opinions – they defer to bad and unfair ones as well (for instance, just think about most of the self-estimations and self-underestimations that devout women accept from their father confessors and, in general, that devout Christians accept from their church). As a matter of fact, in keeping with the slow approach of a democratic order of things (and its cause, the mixing of blood between masters and slaves), the originally rare and noble urge to ascribe to yourself a value that comes *from* yourself, and to "think well" of yourself is now increasingly widespread and encouraged. But in every age it is opposed by an older, broader, and more thoroughly ingrained tendency, – and in the phenomenon of "vanity," this older tendency gains mastery over the younger. The vain take pleasure in *every* good opinion they hear about themselves (abstracted entirely from the point of view of utility, and just as much removed from truth or falsity), just as they suffer from every bad opinion. This is because they submit – they *feel* submissive – to both good and bad opinions out of that oldest instinct of submissiveness which erupts within them. – This is "the slave" in the blood of the vain, a remnant of the mischief of the slave – and how much "slave" is still left over in women, for instance! –, they try to *seduce* people into having good opinions of them. By the same token, it is the slave who submits to these opinions immediately afterwards, as if he were not the one who had just called for them. – And to say it again: vanity is an atavism.

262

A *species*[4] originates, a type grows sturdy and strong, in the long struggle with essentially constant *unfavorable* conditions. Conversely, people know from the experience of breeders that species with overabundant diets and, in general, more than their share of protection and care, will immediately show a striking tendency towards variations of the type, and will be rich in wonders and monstrosities (including monstrous vices). You only need to see an aristocratic community (such as Venice or an ancient Greek *polis*[5]) as an organization that has been established, whether voluntarily or involuntarily, for the sake of *breeding*: the people living there together are self-reliant and want to see their species succeed, mainly because if they *do not* succeed they run a horrible risk of being eradicated. Here there are none of the advantages, excesses, and protections that are favorable to variation. The species needs itself to be a species, to be something that, by virtue of its very hardness, uniformity, and simplicity of form, can succeed and make itself persevere in constant struggle with its neighbors or with the oppressed who are or threaten to become rebellious. A tremendous range of experiences teaches it which qualities are primarily responsible for the fact that, despite all gods and men, it still exists, it keeps prevailing. It calls these qualities virtues, and these are the only virtues it fosters. It does so with harshness; in fact, it desires harshness. Every aristocratic morality is intolerant about the education of the young, disposal over women, marriage customs, relations between old and young and penal laws (which only concern deviants): – it considers intolerance itself to be a virtue, under the rubric of "justice." A type whose traits are few in number but very strong, a species of people who are strict, warlike, clever, and silent, close to each other and closed up (which gives

---

[4] In German: *Art*. In this section, *Art* is translated as "species" and *Typus* as "type."
[5] City-state.

them the most subtle feeling for the charms and nuances of association) will, in this way, establish itself (as a species) over and above the change of generations. The continuous struggle with constant *unfavorable* conditions is, as I have said, what causes a type to become sturdy and hard. But, eventually, a fortunate state will arise and the enormous tension will relax; perhaps none of the neighbors are enemies anymore, and the means of life, even of enjoying life, exist in abundance. With a single stroke, the bonds and constraints of the old discipline are torn: it does not seem to be necessary any more, to be a condition of existence, – if it wanted to continue, it could do so only as a form of *luxury*, as an archaic *taste*. Variation, whether as deviation (into something higher, finer, rarer) or as degeneration and monstrosity, suddenly comes onto the scene in the greatest abundance and splendor; the individual dares to be individual and different. At these turning points of history, a magnificent, diverse, jungle-like growth and upward striving, a kind of *tropical* tempo in the competition to grow will appear alongside (and often mixed up and tangled together with) an immense destruction and self-destruction. This is due to the wild egoisms that are turned explosively against each other, that wrestle each other "for sun and light," and can no longer derive any limitation, restraint, or refuge from morality as it has existed so far. It was this very morality that accumulated the tremendous amount of force to put such a threatening tension into the bow: – and now it is, now it is being "outlived." The dangerous and uncanny point has been reached when the greatest, most diverse, most comprehensive life *lives past* the old morality. The "individual" is left standing there, forced to give himself laws, forced to rely on his own arts and wiles of self-preservation, self-enhancement, self-redemption. There is nothing but new whys and hows; there are no longer any shared formulas; misunderstanding is allied with disregard; decay, ruin, and the highest desires are horribly entwined; the genius of the race overflows from every cornucopia of good and bad; there is a disastrous simultaneity of spring and autumn, filled with new charms and veils that are well suited to the young, still unexhausted, still indefatigable corruption. Danger has returned, the mother of morals, great danger, displaced onto the individual this time, onto the neighbor or friend, onto the street, onto your own child, onto your own heart, onto all of your own-most, secret-most wishes and wills: and the moral philosophers emerging at this time – what will they have to preach? These sharp observers and layabouts discover that everything is rapidly coming to an end, that everything around them is ruined and creates ruin, that nothing lasts as long as the day after tomorrow except one species of person, the hopelessly *mediocre*. Only the mediocre have prospects for continuing on, for propagating – they are the people of the future, the only survivors: "Be like them! Be mediocre!" is the only morality that still makes sense, that still finds ears. But this morality of mediocrity is difficult to preach! It can never admit what it is and what it wants! It has to talk about moderation and dignity and duty and loving your neighbors, – it will have a hard time *hiding its irony! –*

263

There is an *instinct for rank* that, more than anything else, is itself the sign of a *high* rank; there is a *pleasure* in nuances of respect that indicates a noble origin and noble habits. The subtlety, quality, and stature of a soul is put dangerously to the test when something of the first rank passes by before the shudders of authority are there to protect it from intrusive clutches and crudeness: something that goes on its way like a living touchstone, undiscovered, unmarked, and experimenting, perhaps voluntarily covered and disguised. Anyone whose task and exercise is the investigation of souls will use this very art, in a variety of forms, to establish the ultimate value of a soul, the unalterable, inborn order of rank it belongs to: this sort of investigator will test out the soul's *instinct for respect. Différence engendre haine:*[6] many natures have a baseness that suddenly bursts out, like dirty water, when any sort of holy vessel, any sort of treasure from a closed shrine, any sort of book that bears the mark of a great destiny is carried past. On the other hand, there is an involuntary hush, a hesitation of the eye and a quieting of every gesture, all of which indicate that the soul *feels* the presence of something deserving the highest honors. The way in which respect for the *Bible* has, on the whole, been maintained in Europe might be the best piece of discipline and refinement in manners that Europe owes to Christianity. Books with this sort of profundity and ultimate meaning need the protection of an externally imposed tyranny of authority; this way, they can *last* through the millennia that are needed to use them up and figure them out. It is a great achievement when the

---

[6] "Difference engenders hatred."

masses (people of all kinds who lack depth or have speedy bowels) have finally had the feeling bred into them that they cannot touch everything, that there are holy experiences which require them to take off their shoes and keep their dirty hands away, – and this is pretty much as high a level of humanity as they will ever reach. Conversely, what is perhaps the most disgusting thing about so-called scholars, the devout believers in "modern ideas," is their lack of shame, the careless impudence of their eyes and hands that touch, taste, and feel everything. And there might still be a greater *relative* nobility of taste and tactfulness of respect within a people these days, within a lower sort of people, namely within the peasantry, than among the newspaper-reading *demimonde* of the spirit, the educated.

264

What a man's forefathers liked doing the most, and the most often, cannot be wiped from his soul: whether they were diligent savers and accessories of some writing desk or cash box, modest and middle-class in their wants and modest in their virtues as well; or whether they lived their lives giving orders from morning to night, fond of rough pleasures and perhaps of even rougher duties and responsibilities; or whether they finally sacrificed old privileges of birth and belongings in order to live entirely for their faith – their "god" –, being people of a tender and unyielding conscience, embarrassed by any compromise. It is utterly impossible that a person might *fail* to have the qualities and propensities of his elders and ancestors in his body: however much appearances might speak against it. This is the problem of race. If you know anything about the ancestors, you can draw conclusions about the child. Some sort of harmful immoderation, some sort of corner jealousy, a clumsy insistence on always being right – together, these three elements have constituted the true "vulgar" type in every age. And something like this will be passed on to the child just as certainly as contaminated blood. With the help of the best education and culture, people will only just reach the point of being able to *lie* about a bequest like this. And what else are education and culture for these days! In our very popular, which is to say vulgar age, "education" and "culture" essentially *have* to be the art of deception – to deceive about lineage, about the inherited vulgarity in body and soul. An educator who preaches truthfulness above all else these days and constantly calls for his students to "be true! be natural! be what you are!" – after a while, even a virtuous and trusting ass like this will learn to reach for that *furca* of Horace, in order to *naturam expellere*: and with what success? "The vulgar" *usque recurret*.[7] –

265

At the risk of annoying innocent ears I will propose this: egoism belongs to the essence of the noble soul. I mean that firm belief that other beings will, by nature, have to be subordinate to a being "like us" and will have to sacrifice themselves. The noble soul accepts this fact of its egoism without any question-mark, and also without feeling any harshness, compulsion, or caprice in it, but rather as something that may well be grounded in the primordial law of things. If the noble soul were to try to name this phenomenon, it would call it "justice itself." It admits to itself, under certain circumstances (that at first give it pause), that there are others with rights equal to its own. As soon as it is clear about this question of rank, it will move among these equals and "equally righted" with an assured modesty and a gentle reverence equal to how it treats itself, in accordance with an inborn, celestial mechanics that all stars know so well. This is just *another* piece of its egoism, this finesse and self-limitation in dealing with equals – every star is an egoist of this sort. And the noble soul honors *itself* in them and in the rights that it gives them; it has no doubt that the exchange of rights and honors belongs to the natural state of things too, as the *essence* of all interaction. The noble soul gives as it takes, out of the passionate and sensitive instinct of retribution that is so fundamental to it. The concept of "mercy" is senseless and noisome *inter pares*;[8] there might be a sublime way of letting gifts fall down on you from above, as it were, and lapping them up like raindrops; but the noble soul has no talent for this art and conduct. Its egoism gets in the way: it does not generally like looking "upwards," – but rather *ahead*, horizontally and slowly, or downwards: – *it knows that it is high up*. –

266

"One can only truly admire those who do not *seek* themselves." – Goethe to Rat Schlosser.

---

[7] "Try expelling nature with a pitchfork and it keeps coming back," from Horace's *Epistolae*, I, 10, 24.

[8] Between equals.

267

The Chinese have an expression that even mothers teach their children: *siao-sin*, "make your heart *small*!" This is the true, basic tendency of late civilizations: I have no doubt that this sort of self-belittlement would be the first thing an ancient Greek would notice in us Europeans of today, – and this alone would already "offend his taste." –

268

What, in the end, is base?[9] – Words are acoustic signs for concepts; concepts, though, are more or less determinate pictorial signs for sensations that occur together and recur frequently, for groups of sensations. Using the same words is not enough to get people to understand each other: they have to use the same words for the same species of inner experiences too; ultimately, people have to have the same experience *base*. This is why a people in a community will understand each other better than they understand people belonging to other groups, even when they all use the same language. Or rather, when individuals have lived together for a long time under similar conditions (of climate, soil, danger, necessities, work), there *arises* something that "understands itself" – a people. In all souls, an equal number of frequently recurring experiences have gained an upper hand over ones that occur less frequently: understanding takes place faster and faster on this basis (the history of language is the history of a process of abbreviation); and people join closer and closer together on the basis of this understanding. The greater the danger, the greater the need to agree quickly and easily about necessities. *Not* to misunderstand each other when there is danger: people require this in order to interact with each other. In every friendship or relationship, people still put this principle to the test: nothing will last once the discovery is made that one of the two feels, means, senses, wishes, fears something different from the other when using the same words. (Fear of the "eternal misunderstanding": this is the benevolent genius that so often keeps people of the opposite sex from rushing into relationships at the insistence of their hearts and senses – and *not* some Schopenhauerian "genius of the species" –!) What

---

[9] In German: *Gemeinheit*. Another possible translation is "common," which captures the sense of the word (and the point of the passage) according to which base qualities are found among common people, or are what people have in common. I have chosen to translate *gemein* as base (both here and throughout the text) since it captures more of the derogatory connotations of the term.

group of sensations in a soul will be the first to wake up, start speaking, and making demands is decisive for the whole rank order of its values, and will ultimately determine its table of goods. A person's valuations reveal something about the *structure* of his soul and what the soul sees as its conditions of life, its genuine needs. Now, assuming that needs have only ever brought people together when they could somehow indicate similar requirements and similar experiences with similar signs, then it follows, on the whole, that the easy communicability of needs (which ultimately means having only average and *base* experiences) must have been the most forceful of the forces that have controlled people so far. People who are more alike and ordinary have always been at an advantage; while people who are more exceptional, refined, rare, and difficult to understand will easily remain alone, prone to accidents in their isolation and rarely propagating. Immense countervailing forces will have to be called upon in order to cross this natural, all-too-natural *progressus in simile*,[10] people becoming increasingly similar, ordinary, average, herd-like, – increasingly *base*!

269

The more a psychologist – a born, inevitable psychologist and unriddler of souls – turns to exceptional cases and people, the greater the danger that he will be choked with pity: he *needs* hardness and cheerfulness more than anyone else. The ruin, the destruction of higher people, of strangely constituted souls, is the rule: it is horrible always to have a rule like this in front of your eyes. The manifold torment of the psychologist who discovered this destruction, who first discovered and then kept rediscovering (in *almost* every case) the whole inner "hopelessness" of the higher person, the eternal "too late!" in every sense, throughout the entirety of history, – this torment might make him turn bitterly against his own lot one day and try to destroy himself, – to "ruin" himself. In almost every psychologist, you find a telling inclination and preference for dealing with normal, well-ordered people. This reveals that the psychologist is in constant need of a cure, of a type of forgetting and escape from the things that make his insight and incisiveness, that make his "craft" weigh heavily on his conscience. It is characteristic of him to be afraid of his

[10] Continuation of the same thing.

memory. He is easily silenced by other people's judgments: he listens with an unmoved face to how they honor, admire, love, and transfigure what he has *seen*, – or he keeps his silence hidden by expressly agreeing with some foreground opinion. Perhaps the paradox of his condition becomes so horrible that the masses, the educated, the enthusiasts, develop a profound admiration for the very things he has learned to regard with profound pity and contempt, – they admire the "great men" and prodigies who inspire people to bless and honor the fatherland, the earth, the dignity of humanity, and themselves, "great men" who are pointed out to young people for their edification . . . And who knows if this is not just what has happened in all great cases so far: the masses worshiped a God, – and that "God" was only a poor sacrificial animal! Success has always been the greatest liar, – and the "work" itself is a success. The great statesman, the conqueror, the discoverer – each one is disguised by his creations to the point of being unrecognizable. The "work" of the artist, of the philosopher, is what invents whoever has created it, whoever was supposed to have created it. "Great men," as they are honored, are minor pieces of bad literature, invented after the fact; in the world of historical values, counterfeit *rules*. These great authors, for example, this Byron, Musset, Poe, Leopardi, Kleist, Gogol, – they are, and perhaps have to be men of the moment, excited, sensual, and childish, thoughtless and sudden in trust and mistrust; with souls that generally hide some sort of crack; often taking revenge in their work for some inner corruption, often flying off in search of forgetfulness for an all-too-faithful memory, often getting lost in the mud and almost falling in love with it until they become like the will-o'-the-wisps around swamps and *pretend* to be stars (then people might call them idealists), often fighting a prolonged disgust, a recurring specter of unbelief that makes them cold and forces them to pine for *gloria*[11] and to feed on "faith in itself" from the hands of drunken flatterers. What *torture* these great artists and higher people in general are for anyone who has ever guessed what they really are! It is easy to imagine that *these* men will soon be subject to eruptions of boundless and most devoted *pity* from women in particular (who are clairvoyant in the world of suffering and whose desires to help and save far exceed their ability to actually do so). The masses, the adoring masses, above all, do not understand this pity, and they pile all sorts of nosy and smug interpretations

[11] Fame.

on it. This pity is continually deceived as to its own strength; women would like to believe that love makes *all things* possible, – this is their true *faith*. Oh, those who know hearts can guess how impoverished, stupid, helpless, presumptuous, and mistaken even the best and deepest love really is – how much more likely it is to destroy than to rescue! – It is possible that one of the most painful cases of the martyrdom of *knowledge about love* lies hidden under the holy fable and disguise of the life of Jesus: the martyrdom of the most innocent and wishful of hearts, who never had enough of human love, who asked for nothing other than to love and be loved, but who asked it with harshness, with madness, with horrible outbursts against anyone refusing to love him; the story of a poor man who was unsatisfied and insatiable in love, who had to invent hell for there to be somewhere to send people who did not *want* to love him, – and who, in the end, having learned about human love, had to invent a God who was all love and all *ability* to love, – who had mercy on human love for being so desperately poor and ignorant! – Anyone who feels this way, anyone who *knows* this about love – will *look for* death. – But why give yourself up to such painful things? Assuming you do not have to. –

270

The spiritual arrogance and disgust of anyone who has suffered deeply (order of rank is almost determined by just *how* deeply people can suffer), the trembling certainty that saturates and colors him entirely, a certainty that his sufferings have given him a *greater knowledge* than the cleverest and wisest can have, that he knows his way around and was once "at home" in many distant and terrifying worlds that "*you* don't know anything about!" . . . this spiritual, silent arrogance of the sufferer, this pride of knowledge's chosen one, its "initiate," almost its martyr, needs all kinds of disguises to protect itself from the touch of intrusive and pitying hands, and in general from everyone who is not its equal in pain. Profound suffering makes you noble; it separates. One of the most refined forms of disguise is Epicureanism, and a certain showy courage of taste that accepts suffering without a second thought and resists everything sad and profound. There are "cheerful people" who use cheerfulness because it lets them be misunderstood: – they *want* to be misunderstood. There are "scientific people" who use science because it gives a cheerful appearance, and because being scientific implies that a person is superficial: – they *want* to encourage this false inference. There are free, impudent spirits who would like to hide and deny that they are shattered, proud, incurable hearts; and sometimes even stupidity is the mask for an ill-fated, all-too-certain knowing. – From which it follows that a more refined humanity will have great respect for "masks," and will not indulge in psychology and curiosity in the wrong place.

271

The thing that separates two people the most is a difference in their sense and degree of cleanliness. All the good behavior, mutual utility, and goodwill in the world will not help: what matters, in the end, is that they "can't stand the smell of each other!" The highest instinct of cleanliness puts someone afflicted with it into the strangest and most dangerous solitude, in the form of a holy saint: because this is what holiness is – the highest spiritualization of this instinct. Some sort of shared knowledge of an indescribable abundance of joy in bathing, some sort of lust and craving that constantly drives the soul out of the night and into the morning, out of dullness and gloom into light, radiance, profundity, finesse –: however much a tendency like this *characterizes* somebody (it is a noble tendency), it *separates* him out as well. – The pity of the saint is a pity for the *filth* of the human, all-too-human. And there are degrees and heights where he feels even pity as a form of pollution, as filth . . .

272

Signs of nobility: never thinking about debasing our duties into duties for everyone, not wanting to relinquish, not wanting to share your own responsibility; considering privileges and the exercise of these privileges as a *duty*.

273

Someone who strives for greatness will regard everyone he comes across as either a means or a delay and obstacle – or as a temporary resting place. His distinctive and superior *graciousness* towards his fellow creatures is only possible when he is at his best, at his height, and dominating. Impatience and his awareness of being condemned to comedy until then (since even war is a comedy and concealment, just as every means conceals the end) ruins all company for him. This type of person knows solitude and what is most poisonous about it.

274

The problem of those who wait. Strokes of luck and many unpredictable factors are needed for a higher person, who contains the dormant solution to a problem, to go into action at the right time, "into explosion" you might say. This does *not* usually happen, and in every corner of the earth people sit waiting, hardly knowing how much they are waiting, much less that they are waiting in vain. And every once in a while, the alarm call will come too late, the chance event that gives them "permission" to act, – just when the prime of youth and strength for action has already been depleted by sitting still. And how many people have realized in horror, just as they "jump up," that their limbs have gone to sleep and their spirit is already too heavy! "It's too late" – they say, having lost faith in themselves and being useless from this point on. – What if in the realm of genius, the "Raphael without hands"[12] (taking that phrase in the broadest sense) is not the exception but, perhaps, the rule? Perhaps genius is not rare at all: what is rare is the five hundred *hands* that it needs to tyrannize the καιρός, "the right time," in order to seize hold of chance!

275

People who do not *want* to see someone's height will look all the more closely at everything about him that is low and in the foreground – in so doing, they show themselves for what they really are.

276

With every type of wound and loss, the lower, cruder soul is better off than the nobler soul. The dangers for the nobler soul must be greater; the likelihood that it will get into an accident and be destroyed is truly enormous, given the diversity of its conditions of life. – When a lizard loses a finger, it grows back: not so with people. –

[12] This phrase from Lessing's *Emilia Galotti*, act I, scene 4.

277

— Bad enough! The same old story! When you have finished building your house, you suddenly notice that you have learned something in the process that you absolutely needed to know before you *started* building. The eternal, tiresome "too late!" — The melancholy of everything *finished*! . . .

278

— Wanderer, who are you? I watch you go on your way, without scorn, without love, with impenetrable eyes — damp and downhearted, like a plumb line that returns unsatisfied from every depth back into the light (what was it looking for down there?), with a breast that does not sigh, with lips that hide their disgust, with a hand that only grips slowly: who are you? What have you done? Take a rest here, this spot is hospitable to everyone, — relax! And whoever you may be: what would you like now? What do you find relaxing? Just name it: I'll give you whatever I have! — "Relaxing? Relaxing? How inquisitive you are! What are you saying! But please, give me — —" What? What? Just say it! — "Another mask! A second mask!" . . .

279

People with deep sorrows reveal this fact about themselves when they are happy: they have a way of grasping hold of happiness, as if they wanted to crush or suffocate it, out of jealousy. Oh, they know only too well that it will run away from them!

280

"Too bad! What? Isn't he going — backwards?" — Yes! But you understand him badly if you complain about it. He is going backwards like someone who wants to take a great leap. — —

281

— "Will anyone believe me? But I insist on being believed: I have never been good at thinking about myself, and do so only on very rare occasions, only when forced, without any desire to pursue 'the matter,' ready to digress away from 'me,' never with any faith in the results, all due to an unconquerable distrust in the *possibility* of self-knowledge that has led me to the point where I sense a *contradictio in adjecto*[13] in even the concept of 'immediate knowledge' that is permitted by theoreticians. This whole state of affairs might be the most certain thing I *do* know about myself. I must have a kind of revulsion against *believing* anything definite about myself. Could there be a riddle here? Probably; but fortunately not one for *my* teeth. – Could this reveal what species I belong to? – But not to me: which is just how I want it to be. –"

282

"But what happened to you?" – "I don't know," he said hesitantly; "maybe the harpies flew over the table at me." – Every once in a while these days, a mild, moderate, restrained person will fly into a sudden fury, smash dishes, knock over tables, scream, throw fits, insult everyone – and finally go off, ashamed, furious at himself, – but where? And why? To starve far away? To choke on his memory? – The danger will always be considerable for someone with the desires of a high and discriminating soul, who rarely finds his table set and his food ready: today, however, the danger will be extraordinary. Thrown into a noisy, vulgar age and not wanting to eat out of a single one of its bowls, he can easily die of hunger and thirst, or, if he finally "digs in" anyway, he can be destroyed – by sudden nausea. – We have probably all sat at tables where we did not belong; and the most spiritual among us (who are also the most difficult to feed), are familiar with that dangerous dyspepsia that comes from a sudden insight into and disappointment over our food and dining companions, – the *after-dinner nausea*.

283

It shows both subtle and noble self-control when you reserve your praise (assuming you want to give praise at all) for things you *dis*agree with: – otherwise you would certainly be praising yourself, which offends good taste. Of course, this type of self-control offers people a handy opportunity and excuse for constantly *misunderstanding* you. In order to allow yourself this real luxury of taste and morality, you cannot live with fools of the spirit; you have to live among people whose misunderstandings and mistakes

[13] Contradiction in terms.

are subtle, and for that reason still amusing – or else you will have to pay dearly for it! – "He praises me: *that's why* he agrees with me" – this asinine inference ruins the better part of life for us hermits, because it brings asses into our neighborhood and friendship.

284

To live with immense and proud composure; always beyond –. To freely have or not have your affects, your pros and cons, to condescend to them for a few hours; to *seat* yourself on them like you would on a horse or often like you would on an ass: – since you need to know how to use your stupidity as well as you know how to use your fire. To keep your three hundred foregrounds, and your dark glasses too: because there are times when nobody can look into our eyes, or even less into our "grounds." And to choose for company that mischievous and cheerful vice, politeness. And to keep control over your four virtues: courage, insight, sympathy, solitude. Because solitude is a virtue for us, since it is a sublime inclination and impulse to cleanliness which shows that contact between people ("society") inevitably makes things unclean. Somewhere, sometime, every community makes people – "base."

285

The greatest events and thoughts – but the greatest thoughts are the greatest events – are the last to be comprehended: generations that are their contemporaries do not *experience* these sorts of events, – they live right past them. The same thing happens here as happens in the realm of stars. The light from the furthest stars is the last to come to people; and until it has arrived, people will *deny* that there are – stars out there. "How many centuries does it take for a spirit to be comprehended?" – this standard is also used to create the rank order and etiquette needed – by both spirit and star. –

286

"The vision is free here and the spirit elevated."[14] – But there is an inverse type of person who is also at a height and also has a free vision – but who looks *down*.

[14] Cf. Goethe's *Faust* II, line 11989f.

287

– What is noble? What does the word "noble" still mean to us today? How do noble people reveal who they are, how can they be recognized under this heavy, overcast sky of incipient mob rule that makes everything leaden and opaque? – There are no actions that prove who they are, – actions are always ambiguous, always unfathomable –; and there are no "works" either. Among artists and scholars these days, you will find plenty of people whose works reveal them to be driven by a deep desire for nobility. But this very need *for* nobility is fundamentally different from the needs *of* the noble soul itself, and almost serves as an eloquent and dangerous testimony to the absence of such needs. It is not works, it is *faith* that is decisive here, faith that establishes rank order (this old, religious formula now acquires a new and deeper meaning): some fundamental certainty that a noble soul has about itself, something that cannot be looked for, cannot be found, and perhaps cannot be lost either. – *The noble soul has reverence for itself.* –

288

There are people who cannot avoid the fact that they have spirit, however much they might turn and twist, holding up their hands to prevent their eyes from giving them away (– as if their hands did not betray them too! –): in the end, they are always shown to be hiding something, namely spirit. One of the most subtle ways of deceiving people (at least for as long as this is possible), and successfully pretending to be more stupid than you really are (a skill that is as handy as an umbrella, in day-to-day life), is *enthusiasm*: including what belongs to it – virtue, for instance. Because, as Galiani said, and he must have known –: *vertu est enthousiasme.*[15]

289

In a hermit's writings, you can always hear something of the echo of the desert, something of the whisper and the timid sideways glance of solitude. A new and more dangerous type of silence, of concealment, rings out in his strongest words, even in his cries. Anyone who has sat alone with

[15] "Virtue is enthusiasm" from Galiani's *Letter to Madame d'Epinay*, II, p. 276.

his soul in intimate dispute and dialogue, year in, and year out, day and night, anyone who has become a cave bear or treasure hunter or treasure guard and dragon in his cave (which might be a labyrinth but also a gold mine): his very concepts will come to acquire their own twilight color, the smell of depth just as much as of mildew, something uncommunicative and reluctant that blows a chill on everything going past. The hermit does not believe that a philosopher – given that a philosopher was always a hermit first – has ever expressed his actual and final opinions in books: don't people write books precisely to keep what they hide to themselves? In fact, he will doubt whether a philosopher could even *have* "final and actual" opinions, whether for a philosopher every cave does not have, *must* not have, an even deeper cave behind it – a more extensive, stranger, richer world above the surface, an abyss behind every ground, under every "groundwork."[16] Every philosophy is a foreground philosophy – that is a hermit's judgment: "There is something arbitrary in *his* stopping here, looking back, looking around, in his not digging any deeper *here*, and putting his spade away – there is also something suspicious about it." Every philosophy *conceals* a philosophy too: every opinion is also a hiding place, every word is also a mask.

290

Every profound thinker is more afraid of being understood than of being misunderstood. The latter might hurt his vanity; but the former hurts his heart and his sympathy which always says: "Oh, why do you want things to be as hard for *you* as they are for me?"

291

The human being is a diverse, hypocritical, artificial, and opaque animal, uncanny to other animals more because of his cunning and cleverness than his strength; the human being invented good conscience so that he could enjoy his soul as something *simple*, for once; and the whole of morality is a brave and lengthy falsification that makes it possible to look at the soul with anything like pleasure. Perhaps this point of view involves a much broader conception of "art" than people are used to.

[16] In German: *ein Abgrund hinter jedem Grunde, unter jeder "Begründung."*

292

A philosopher: this is a person who constantly experiences, sees, hears, suspects, hopes, and dreams extraordinary things; who is struck by his own thoughts as if from outside, from above and below, as if by *his* type of events and lightning bolts; who is perhaps a storm himself, pregnant with new lightning; a fatal person in whose vicinity things are always rumbling, growling, gaping, and acting in uncanny ways. A philosopher: oh, a being who is frequently running away from himself, frequently afraid of himself, – but too curious not to always come back to himself . . .

293

A man who says: "I like that, I'll take it for my own and protect it and defend it against everyone"; a man who can conduct business, carry out a resolution, be faithful to a thought, hold on to a woman, punish and defeat someone for being insolent; a man who has his anger and his sword, and whom the weak, the suffering, the distressed, and even the animals like to come to and, by nature, belong to; in short, a man who is naturally *master*, – if a man like this has pity, well then! *this* pity is worth something! But what good is the pity of the sufferer![17] Or particularly, the pity of those who preach it! Almost everywhere in Europe today, there is a morbid over-sensitivity and susceptibility to pain, as well as an excessive amount of complaining and an increased tenderness that wants to dress itself up as something higher, using religion as well as bits and pieces of philosophy, – there is a real cult of suffering. The *unmanliness* of what is christened "pity" in the circles of these enthusiasts is always, I think, the first thing that strikes your eye. – This latest type of bad taste needs to be forcefully and thoroughly exorcized; and ultimately, I would like people to put the good amulet of "*gai saber*" around their hearts and necks to fight it off, – "gay science," to make it germane to Germans.[18]

294

The Olympian vice. – In spite of that philosopher who, being a true Englishman, tried to give laughter a bad reputation among all thoughtful

---

[17] Nietzsche is again playing on the similarity between *Mitleiden* (pity) and *leiden* (to suffer).

[18] In German: *um es den Deutschen zu verdeutlichen* (literally: to clarify it to Germans).

people –, "laughter is a terrible infirmity of human nature, and one that every thinking mind will endeavor to overcome" (Hobbes) –, I would go so far as to allow myself a rank order of philosophers based on the rank of their laughter – right up to those who are capable of *golden* laughter. And given that even gods philosophize (a conclusion I have been drawn to many times –), I do not doubt that they know a new and super-human way of laughing – at the expense of everything serious! Gods like to make fun of things: it seems as if they cannot stop laughing, even during holy rites.

295

The genius of the heart, as it is possessed by that great hidden one, the tempter god[19] and born pied piper of consciences, whose voice knows how to descend into the underworld of every soul, whose every word and every glance conveys both consideration and a wrinkle of temptation, whose mastery includes an understanding of how to seem – not like what he is but rather like one *more* compulsion for his followers to keep pressing closer to him, to keep following him more inwardly and thoroughly: – the genius of the heart, that makes everything loud and complacent fall silent and learn to listen, that smoothes out rough souls and gives them the taste of a new desire, – to lie still, like a mirror that the deep sky can mirror itself upon –; the genius of the heart, that teaches the foolish and over-hasty hand to hesitate and reach out more delicately; that guesses the hidden and forgotten treasure, the drop of goodness and sweet spirituality under thick, dull ice, and is a divining rod for every speck of gold that has long been buried in a prison of mud and sand; the genius of the heart, that enriches everyone who has come into contact with it, not making them blessed or surprised, or leaving them feeling as if they have been gladdened or saddened by external goods; rather, they are made richer in themselves, newer than before, broken open, blown on, and sounded out by a thawing wind, perhaps less certain, more gentle, fragile, and broken, but full of hopes that do not have names yet, full of new wills and currents, full of new indignations and countercurrents . . . but what am I doing, my friends? Who am I talking about? Have I forgotten myself so much that I haven't even told you his name? Unless you have already guessed on your

---

[19] In German: *Versucher-Gott*. This could also mean the "experimenting god."

own who this questionable spirit and god is, who wants to be *praised* in this way?

Like everyone who, from childhood, has constantly been underway and abroad, I have had many strange and not unthreatening spirits run across my path, but especially the one I have just been talking about, who has crossed my path again and again – in other words, nobody less than the god *Dionysus*, that great ambiguity and tempter god, to whom, as you know, I once offered my firstborn[20] in all secrecy and reverence. I seem to be the last one to have offered him a *sacrifice*: because I have not found anyone who understood what I was doing then. In the meantime, I have learned much, all too much more about the philosophy of this god, passed on, as I said, from mouth to mouth – I, the last disciple and initiate of the god Dionysus: and can I, at last, start to give you, my friends, a small taste of this philosophy, as far as I am permitted? In undertones, which would be best, since it concerns many things that are secret, new, foreign, strange, uncanny. Even the fact that Dionysus is a philosopher and that, consequently, even gods philosophize, seems to me like something new and *not* without its dangers, something that might arouse mistrust precisely among philosophers, – among you, my friends, it has less opposition, unless it comes too late and at the wrong time: I have been told that you do not like believing in God and gods these days. And perhaps in recounting my story, I will have to take frankness further than will always be agreeable to the strict habits of your ears? Certainly, the god in question went further in dialogues like this, much, much further, and was always many steps ahead of me . . . In fact, if it were permissible to follow human custom in ascribing beautiful, solemn names of splendor and virtue to him, I would have to offer many praises for his explorer's, discoverer's heart, for his daring and genuine honesty, his truthfulness and his love of wisdom. But a god like this will have no use at all for this honorable rubbish and splendor. "Keep this for yourself," he would say, "and for those like you and anyone else who needs it! I – have no reason for covering my nakedness!" – You can guess: this type of divinity and philosopher is, perhaps, lacking in shame? – He once said: "I love humans under certain circumstances" – meaning Ariadne, who was present –: "I think humans are pleasant, brave, inventive animals that have no equal on earth, they find their way around any labyrinth. I am very fond of

---

[20] A reference to Nietzsche's first published book, *Die Geburt der Tragödie* (*The Birth of Tragedy*) (1872).

them: I think about how I can help them advance and make them stronger, more evil and more profound than they are." – "Stronger, more evil, and more profound?" I asked, startled. – "Yes," he said again, "stronger, more evil, and more profound; and more beautiful" – and at that, the tempter god smiled his halcyon smile, as if he had just paid a charming compliment. You can see: this divinity lacks more than just shame –; but you can also see that there are good reasons for supposing that the gods could learn a thing or two from us humans. We humans are – more human[21] . . .

296

Oh, what are you anyway, my written and painted thoughts! It was not long ago that you were still so colorful, young and malicious, so full of thorns and secret spices that you made me sneeze and laugh – and now? You have already lost your novelty, and I am afraid that some of you are ready to turn into truths: they already look so immortal, so pathetically decent and upright, so boring! And was it ever any different? So, what subjects do we copy out and paint, we mandarins with Chinese brushes, we immortalizers of things that *let* themselves be written – what are the only things we *can* paint? Oh, only ever things that are about to wilt and lose their smell! Only ever storms that have exhausted themselves and are moving off, and feelings that are yellowed and late! Only ever birds that have flown and flown astray until they are tired and can be caught by hand, – by *our* hand! We only immortalize things that cannot live and fly for much longer, only tired and worn-out things! And I only have colors for your *afternoon*, my written and painted thoughts, perhaps many colors, many colorful affections and fifty yellows and browns and greens and reds: – but nobody will guess from this how you looked in your morning, you sudden sparks and wonders of my solitude, you, my old, beloved – – *wicked* thoughts!

* *
*

[21] In German: *menschlicher*. This could also mean "more humane."

FROM HIGH MOUNTAINS

Aftersong[1]

```
              *
          *       *
        *           *
      *     *     *     *
```

Oh noon of life! Oh summer garden site
For celebrating!
There's restless joy in standing watch and waiting!
I wait for friends, I'm ready day and night
Where are you, friends? Do come! The time is right!

For you, the glacier clothes its old gray hue
In rose attire,
The rivers seek you, running with desire,
The winds and clouds climb high into the blue,
As high as birds – to keep their watch for you.

My table waits for you with each delight: –
Such lonely ledges
Are home to few, save stars and chasms' edges.
My realm – its bounds reach past the range of sight,
My honey too – who dreams they'll taste the like? . . .

– Oh friends, you're *there*! But – what grave ill portends? –
Am *I* a stranger?
You pause; your wonder wounds far worse than anger!
I *am* no more? – In face, or stride or hands?
But *am* I not what I am for you, friends?

So was I once another? Self-unknown?
I've left my own source?
A strength too often set against its own force?
A wrestler beaten by himself alone,
And wounded by a victory of his own?

---

[1] Nietzsche follows a very strict rhyme and rhythmic scheme in this poem; the rhyme is ABBAA throughout, and the meter follows a classical ode form (both are preserved in this translation).

I've looked where sharpest winds blow frozen air?
I've made my home here,
On glaciers where no other soul dares roam near,
Forgot both man and god, both curse and prayer?
Became a ghost who walked with polar bears?

– Old friends! See here! Your faces have gone white,
With love – and pain too!
Just leave in peace: there's nothing to detain *you*:
Here in the distant ice-filled rocky height –
This realm belongs to hunters, born to fight!

I'm now a *wicked* huntsman! Look – my bow
Is stiff and stock straight!
The strong alone can pull back such a taut weight – –:
Take care! *My* arrow's speed is far from slow,
The danger's great – so flee to safety! go! . . .

You're turning back? – Oh heart, this blow hits hard,
But hope must stay fast:
Hold open doors as *new* friends make their way past!
Old friends must be left back! Old memories barred!
You once were young – now, youth has been restored!

We shared one hope – that was our common band, –
Now – who reads these signs
That love had once inscribed, such faded half-lines?
They look just like a parchment that the hand
is *loath* to touch, – they're just browned and tanned.

What are they called? – since friendship's at an end –
Just ghostly brothers!
Who rattle nightly on my heart and shutters,
Who look at me and say: "you *were* my friend" –
– Those wilted words once bore a rosebud scent!

Oh youthful longing; how you failed to see
Dashed expectations!
Those friends turned family, seeming close relations,
– How they grew *old*, and turned their heels to flee:
For only those who change keep ties with me.

179

Oh noon of life! Oh summer garden bright!
Oh youth returning!
There's restless joy in waiting, watching, yearning!
I wait for friends, I'm ready day and night
The *new* friends now! Do come! The time is right!

        *   *

          *

This song is gone, – the longing cries are through,
Their sweet sounds ended.
The work of a magician I'd befriended,
The friend of noon-time – but – no! don't ask who –
It was at noon, when one turned into two . . .

Now we can feast, with triumph in the air,
The fest of all fests:
Friend Zarathustra came, the guest of all guests!
The world can laugh, the gruesome curtain tear,
The wedding day of light and dark was here . . .

    *   *   *   *
      *   *
       *   *
        *

Glossary of names

Aeschylus (*c.* 525–456 B.C.)   Athenian dramatist
Alcibiades (*c.* 450–404 B.C.)   Athenian statesman and general
Ariadne   Greek mythological figure
Aristophanes (*c.* 445–388 B.C.)   Athenian author of comedies
Athena   Greek goddess of war and wisdom
Augustinus, Aurelius (345–430)   Roman philosopher

Bacon, Francis, viscount of Verulam (1561–1626)   English philosopher
Balzac, Honoré de (1799–1850)   French novelist
Bayle, Pierre (1647–1706)   French philosopher
Beethoven, Ludwig van (1770–1827)   German composer
Bentham, Jeremy (1748–1832)   English philosopher
Berkeley, George (1685–1753)   Irish philosopher
Beyle, Henri *see* Stendhal
Bizet, Georges (1838–75)   French composer
Borgia, Cesare (1476–1507)   Florentine nobleman
Boscovich, Ruggiero Giuseppe (1711–87)   Dalmatian mathematician
    and philosopher
Bruno, Giordano (1548–1600)   Italian philosopher
Byron, George Noel Gordon, Lord (1788–1824)   English poet, author
    of *Manfred*

Caesar, Gaius Julius (100–44 B.C.)   Roman statesman and general
Cagliostro, Alessandro, Count (Balsamo, Giuseppe) (1743–95)   Italian
    adventurer
Carlyle, Thomas (1795–1881)   Scottish philosopher and historian

Catilina, Lucius Sergius (*c.* 108–62 B.C.)   Roman nobleman
Cicero, Marcus Tullius (106–43 B.C.)   Roman philosopher and
    politician
Circe   Greek mythological figure
Comte, Auguste (1789–1857)   French philosopher
Copernicus, Nicholas (1473–1543)   Polish astronomer
Cromwell, Oliver (1599–1658)   English statesman

Dante Alighieri (1265–1321)   Italian poet, author of *La Divina
    Commedia*
Darwin, Charles Robert (1809–82)   English biologist
Delacroix, Ferdinand Victor Eugène (1798–1863)   French painter
Demosthenes (384–322 B.C.)   Greek orator and statesman
Descartes, René (1596–1650)   French philosopher
Diderot, Denis (1713–84)   French philosopher
Dionysus   Greek god
Dühring, Karl Eugen (1833–1921)   German philosopher, author of
    Der Werth des Lebens and *Wirklichkeitsphilosophie*

Empedocles (fifth century B.C.)   Presocratic philosopher and
    statesman
Epicurus (341–270 B.C.)   Greek philosopher

Fichte, Johann Gottlieb (1762–1814)   German philosopher, author of
    Speeches to the German Nation
Flaubert, Gustave (1821–80)   French novelist
Frederick II (the Great) (1712–86)   king of Prussia
Frederick II of Hohenstaufen (1194–1250)   German emperor
Frederick William I (1688–1740)   king of Prussia

Galiani, Ferdinando (1728–87)   Italian economist, author of *Lettres à
    Mme d'Epinay*
Goethe, Johann Wolfgang von (1749–1832)   German poet, novelist,
    and statesman, author of *Faust* and *Die Leiden des jungen Werther*
Gogol, Nikolaj Vassilevic (1809–52)   Russian novelist
Guyon, Jeanne Marie de (1648–1717)   French writer

Hafiz (Mohammed Schams od-Din) (*c.* 1327–90)   Persian poet
Hartmann, Eduard von (1842–1906)   German philosopher

Hegel, Georg Wilhelm Friedrich (1770–1831)   German philosopher
Heine, Heinrich (1797–1856)   German poet
Helvétius, Claude Adrien (1715–71)   French philosopher
Heraclitus (*c.* 540–475 B.C.)   Presocratic philosopher
Hercules   Greek mythological figure
Hobbes, Thomas (1588–1679)   English philosopher
Hölderlin, Friedrich (1770–1843)   German poet
Homer   Greek poet
Horace (Quintus Horatius Flaccus) (65–8 B.C.)   Roman poet, author
    of *Epistolae*
Hugo, Victor (1802–85)   French novelist
Hume, David (1711–76)   Scottish philosopher

Jean Paul (Richter, Johann Paul Friedrich) (1763–1825)   German
    novelist

Kant, Immanuel (1724–1804)   German philosopher, author of *Critique
    of Pure Reason, Critique of Practical Reason and Groundwork to the
    Metaphysic of Morals*
Kleist, Heinrich von (1777–1811)   German dramatist and
    novelist
Kotzebue, August Friedrich Ferdinand von (1761–1819)   German
    dramatist
Kundry   Germanic mythological figure

Lambert, Anne Thérèse de Marguenat de Courcelles, marquise de
    (1647–1733)   French writer
La Rochefoucauld, François de (1613–80)   French moralist
Leibniz, Gottfried Wilhelm (1646–1716)   German philosopher
Leonardo da Vinci (1452–1519)   Florentine painter
Leopardi, Giacomo (1789–1837)   Italian poet
Lessing, Gotthold Ephraim (1729–81)   German dramatist and critic,
    author of *Emilia Galotti*
Locke, John (1632–1704)   English philosopher
Luther, Martin (1483–1546)   German theologian, leader of the
    Protestant Reformation

Machiavelli, Niccolò (1469–1527)   Italian politician, theorist, and
    statesman, author of *The Prince*

Marschner, Heinrich (1795–1861)   German composer of operas, among them *Hans Heiling* and *Vampyr*

Mendelssohn-Bartholdy, Felix (1808–47)   German composer

Mephistopheles   devil in Goethe's *Faust*

Michelet, Jules (1798–1874)   French historian

Mill, John Stuart (1806–73)   English philosopher

Minotaur   Greek mythological figure

Molière (Poqulin, Jean-Baptiste) (1622–73)   French dramatist, author of *Tartuffe* and *Le malade imaginaire*

Montaigne, Michel Eyquem de (1531–92)   French essayist and philosopher

Mozart, Wolfgang Amadeus (1756–91)   Austrian composer

Münchhausen, Karl Friedrich Hieronymus, Freiherr von (1720–97)   German nobleman

Musset, Alfred de (1810–57)   French writer

Napoleon Bonaparte (1769–1821)   French emperor

Nausicaa   Greek mythological figure

Odysseus   Greek mythological figure

Oedipus   Greek mythological figure

Pascal, Blaise (1623–62)   French philosopher

Pericles (*c.* 500–429 B.C.)   Athenian statesman

Petronius Arbiter (d. A.D. 66)   Roman writer

Plato (*c.* 427–347 B.C.)   Greek philosopher, author of *The Laws*

Poe, Edgar Allen (1809–49)   American poet and writer

Proteus   Greek mythological figure

Raphael (Raffaelo Santi) (1483–1520)   Italian painter

Renan, Ernest (1823–92)   French historian and philosopher

Roland de la Platière, Jeanne Marie (1754–93)   French writer

Rousseau, Jean-Jacques (1712–78)   French philosopher

Sacchetti, Franco (*c.* 1335–1400)   Italian writer, author of *Trecento Novelle*

Sainte-Beuve, Charles-Augustin de (1804–69)   French writer

Saint-Evremond, Charles de Marguetel de Saint-Denis, seigneur de (1610–1703)   French writer

Sand, George (Dudevant, Armandine-Aurore-Lucie, baronne de)
(1804–76)   French writer
Sand, Karl Ludwig (1795–1820)   murderer of Kotzebue
Schelling, Friedrich Wilhelm Joseph (1775–1854)   German
philosopher, author of *Of the I as Principle of Philosophy*
Schiller, Friedrich (1759–1805)   German poet and writer
Schlosser, Johann Georg (1739–99)   brother-in-law of Goethe
Schopenhauer, Arthur (1788–1860)   German philosopher, author of
The World as Will and Idea and *The Two Fundamental Problems of
Ethics*
Schumann, Robert (1810–56)   German composer of the opera
Manfred
Shakespeare, William (1564–1616)   English poet and dramatist, author
of *Hamlet*
Shelley, Percy Bysshe (1792–1822)   English poet
Siegfried   Germanic mythological figure
Socrates (469–399 B.C.)   Athenian philosopher
Spencer, Herbert (1820–1903)   English philosopher
Spinoza, Baruch (1632–77)   Dutch philosopher, author of *Ethics*
Staël-Holstein, Anne-Louise-Germaine de (1766–1817)   French writer
Stendhal (Beyle, Henri) (1783–1842)   French novelist
Sybel, Heinrich von (1817–95)   German historian and politician

Tacitus, Publius Cornelius (*c.* 55–115)   Roman historian, author of
Historiae
Taine, Hippolyte (1828–93)   French historian and art historian
Tiberius Claudius Nero (42 B.C. – A.D 37)   Roman emperor
Treitschke, Heinrich Gotthard von (1834–96)   German historian

Voltaire (Arouet, François-Marie) (1694–1778)   French novelist

Wagner, Richard (1813–83)   German composer of operas, among them
*Tannhäuser, Die Meistersinger von Nürnberg, Tristan und Isolde, Der
Ring der Nibelungen* and *Parsifal*
Weber, Carl Maria von (1786–1826)   German composer of operas,
among them *Der Freischütz* and *Oberon*
Wotan   Scandinavian mythological figure

Zarathustra   Persian prophet and priest

Index

Index

Index

Cambridge texts in the history of philosophy

Titles published in the series thus far